The Amateur Historian's Guide to

Medieval and Tudor London

+ The Amateur Historian's Guide to +

1066–1600

Sarah Valente Kettler
&
Carole Trimble

Capital Books, Inc.
Sterling, Virginia

Capital Books, Inc.
P.O. Box 605
Herndon, Virginia 20172-0605

ISBN 1-892123-32-0 (alk. paper)

Printed in the United States of America on acid-free paper that meets the American National Standards Institute Z39-48 Standard.

First Edition

10 9 8 7 6 5 4 3 2 1

Design and composition by Melissa Ehn at
Wilsted & Taylor Publishing Services
Illustrations by Kevin Chadwick
Map by Alan Kettler

LIBRARY OF CONGRESS CATALOGING-IN-PUBLICATION DATA

Kettler, Sarah.

The amateur historian's guide to medieval & Tudor London 1066–1600 / Sarah Kettler and Carole Trimble.

p. cm.

ISBN 1-892123-32-0

1. Historic buildings—England—London—Guidebooks. 2. London (England)—History—16th century—Anecdotes. 3. London (England)—History—To 1500—Anecdotes. 4. Historic sites—England—London—Guidebooks. I. Trimble, Carole. II. Title.

DA679.K44 2001
942.105—dc21

00-060368

Sarah dedicates her work to David Trachtenberg:
without you, this simply wouldn't have happened.

Carole dedicates hers to her mother, Shirley Keiser:
thanks for everything.

+

CONTENTS

ACKNOWLEDGMENTS

Many, many thanks to so many people! To our families for their patience and support. To Charlotte Sterling for introducing us to our publisher, Kathleen Hughes of Capital Books—and to Kathleen for believing in this project from the get-go. To our enthusiastic and candid readers: Caitlin Barrett, Catherine Bucknam, Lisa Piper, Peggy Robinson and Chuck Taylor. To the fabulous management and staff at the Franklin Hotel, Knightsbridge, London . . . and to our trusty London driver (and erstwhile fact checker), John McCarthy. And most of all to one another: what a team we make!

INTRODUCTION

This book was born out of frustration. Being devoted amateur historians of medieval and Tudor history, we embarked on our first trip to London together a few years ago with a great deal of excitement. Finally, we had discovered in each other a traveling companion equally obsessed with poking into every nook and cranny related to this period. We prepared carefully for the trip, researching the sites we wanted to visit and reviewing their history. But despite the fact that we were working with a multitude of guidebooks, when we actually began our exploration, we could not find many sites we knew existed and kept stumbling over others that were never to be found in any of the popular guidebooks. Discussing the situation over libations during a late afternoon pub break near the end of our trip, one of us said to the other that we should write our own book. A second beverage helped us decide that that was not a half-bad idea. This book is the result of that epiphany.

It has taken us a few years to get it done, but, finally, here is a guidebook that not only describes all the sites existing in London that date from the Medieval and Tudor Ages, but reviews the historical events that occurred at each as well. In addition, being the "serious" amateur historians we are, we could not resist tossing in anecdotes and sidebars about people and places that help bring this period of history alive for us.

We have tried to organize the information in the most logical way from a walking tour perspective, starting with all the sites located within the one square mile that was the walled City of London, then moving onto Westminster before venturing farther afield into Southwark and Chelsea. And while the chapters are organized thematically, they also generally fall into neighborhood groupings that make for easy walking tours. Whenever you see the word "City" capitalized, you will know we are referring to that one-square-mile area that played such a central role in the history of this period. First references to either people or places that are featured in sidebars or site references are highlighted.

To set the stage a little and help transport you back in time, here's a brief overview of what London was like from 1066 to 1600. The City itself was fully contained within the ancient Roman wall that surrounded one square mile, with access gained through one of seven gates. A population of 25,000 to 30,000 people was crammed into that space at the end of the 12th century. It had grown to about 40,000 to 50,000 people when the plague hit in 1348 and wiped out nearly one third of that population. Only scattered villages existed outside the City walls, with the exception of Westminster, which occupied a narrow strip of land near the River Thames. Covent Garden did not exist. London Bridge was a city unto itself, crowded with shops and houses that made passage difficult and dangerous. Most houses were wood framed, making fire a constant hazard, except for the great stone houses of the barons and clerics that lined the king's road, now known as the Strand. There were three rivers that fed into the Thames—the Fleet, now covered by Fleet Street; the Walbrook, which flowed through the center of the City; and the Ravensbourne. There were several deep-water ports, always crowded with ships, bustling with the trade that made London such an important and prosperous mercantile community. There were 126 churches, plus various priories and other religious houses. The Tower of London dominated the landscape, with the spire of St. Paul's Cathedral soaring above the City. The streets were small and narrow. Houses lined each side and their upper stories extended over the streets, making the passages dark and gloomy. Open sewers ran through these dark passages. Pigs and other animals meandered freely through the

City. London was a bustling, booming town, confident of its importance to the kingdom and determined to safeguard the ancient rights and privileges that set it apart from other towns in England and nurtured its independence.

Now, enjoy your trip back in time to medieval and Tudor London. Let us know how you like it.

TIME LINE

1066 The Norman Conquest is decided at the Battle of Hastings; London surrenders to William the Conqueror at Berkhamstead.

1078 Construction begins on the White Tower (Tower of London).

1079 William the Conqueror grants London its first charter.

1087 William Rufus (William II) is crowned at Westminster Abbey.

1097–1099 Westminster Palace is built.

1100 Henry I is crowned at Westminster Abbey.

1135 Stephen is crowned at Westminster Abbey; the monarchy is also claimed by Henry I's daughter, the Empress Matilda; civil war begins in 1139 and ensues for the next 14 years.

1154 Henry Fitzempress is crowned Henry II at Westminster Abbey.

1161 Pope Alexander III issues a Bull canonizing Edward the Confessor as saint.

1163 The first translation of Edward's body to a new shrine in Westminster Abbey is conducted by Archbishop of Canterbury Thomas à Becket.

1176–1209 The first non-wooden London Bridge is constructed.

1189 Richard Coeur (a.k.a. "Richard the Lionheart") is crowned Richard I at Westminster Abbey; the coronation is attended by Jewish merchants, triggering violent riots throughout London.

1191 The London Commune is formed under the authority of Prince John.

1193–1212 Henry Fitzailwin serves as the first Lord Mayor of London.

1199 John is crowned at Westminster Abbey.

1216 Henry III is crowned at Westminster Abbey.

1263–1265 Barons, led by Simon de Montfort, Earl of Leicester, and supported by the citizens of London, rebel against Henry III.

1269 The Chapel and Shrine of St. Edward the Confessor constructed by Henry III at Westminster Abbey is completed, and the second translation of the saint is carried out.

1272 Edward I is crowned at Westminster Abbey.

1307 Edward II is crowned at Westminster Abbey.

1327 Edward III is crowned at Westminster Abbey.

1348 The *Black Death* strikes London—one third of the population dies; a major plague pit for City victims is built on the Charterhouse site.

1371 Charterhouse is founded.

1377 Richard II is crowned at Westminster Abbey.

1381 The Peasants' Revolt takes place.

1391–1419 Dick Whittington serves four terms as Lord Mayor.

1399 Henry Bolingbroke deposes his cousin Richard II and is crowned Henry IV at Westminster Abbey.

1413 Henry V is crowned at Westminster Abbey.

1422 Construction is completed on the present Guildhall; Henry VI is crowned at Westminster Abbey.

1461 Edward of York deposes Henry VI and is crowned Edward IV at Westminster Abbey.

1470 The House of Lancaster wins back the crown for Henry VI; Edward IV flees in exile.

1471 Edward IV returns from exile and deposes Henry VI for the second time; Henry VI is subsequently murdered in the Tower of London.

1476 William Caxton assembles England's first printing press on the grounds of Westminster Abbey.

1483 Edward V inherits the throne of England upon his father's death but is never crowned; he and his brother, Prince Richard, are sent to the Tower under the protection of their uncle Richard, Duke of Gloucester. The Duke of Gloucester claims the crown as Richard III. This was the last sighting of the "Princes in the Tower."

1485 Henry Tudor deposes Richard III and is crowned Henry VII at Westminster; his marriage to Elizabeth of York unites the feuding houses of Lancaster and York and ends the Wars of the Roses.

1500 The earliest known painting of London, depicting The Tower, London Bridge and the City is created.

1509 Henry VIII is crowned at Westminster Abbey.

1529 Cardinal Wolsey falls from favor; Henry VIII obtains York Palace (henceforth Whitehall Palace), as well as Hampton Court.

1533 Henry VIII marries Anne Boleyn; English canon court declares Henry's marriage to Katherine of Aragon "null and absolutely void."

1535–1539 Dissolution of the Monasteries, including Westminster Abbey. Extensive Church-held lands are now available in London for residential development.

1547 Edward VI is crowned at Westminster Abbey.

1550 Southwark is incorporated into the City of London.

1553 Lady Jane Grey is declared Queen of England and reigns for nine days, before the crown is rightfully claimed by her cousin Princess Mary Tudor. Mary is crowned at Westminster Abbey.

1558 Elizabeth I is crowned at Westminster Abbey.

1559 The earliest known map of London and its environs is created.

1561 The great spire of St. Paul's Cathedral is struck by lightning and destroyed.

1568 Grisham establishes the Royal Exchange.

1580 Royal edict prohibits building outside the City gates.

1585 William Shakespeare is assumed to have arrived in London.

1598 "The Theatre" in Shoreditch is dismantled and moved to Bankside; it is renamed "The Globe."

1603 Elizabeth I dies at Richmond Palace.

MAP SITE DIRECTORY

4 The Tower

1. The Tower of London
2. All Hallows by the Tower
3. Tower Hill

5 Of Merchants & Men

4. Billingsgate
5. Fishmongers' Hall
6. Leadenhall Market
7. The Royal Exchange
8. The Jewry
9. The Guildhall

6 Of Monks & Markets

10. Christ Church & the Greyfriars
11. St. Bartholomew the Great
12. St. Bartholomew's Fair
13. Smithfield
14. Clerkenwell Priory & St. John's Gate
15. Charterhouse
16. St. Etheldreda's Chapel

7 Reaching for the Heavens

17. St. Andrew Undershaft
18. St. Bride's
19. St. Dunstan-in-the-West
20. St. Giles Cripplegate
21. St. Helen's Bishopsgate
22. St. Katherine Cree
23. St. Mary le Bow
24. St. Magnus Martyr
25. St. Olaves Hart Street
26. St. Margaret Pattens
27. St. Michael Paternoster Royal
28. St. Sepulchre-Without-Newgate (Church of the Holy Sepulchre)
29. St. Paul's Cathedral

8 Legal London

30. Gray's Inn
31. Staple Inn
32. Lincoln's Inn
33. Middle Temple Inn
34. Temple Church
35. Newgate Prison

9 Of Knights & Nobles

36. College of Arms
37. Baynard's Castle
38. Covent Garden
39. The Savoy
40. Charing Cross

(Continued on page xxii)

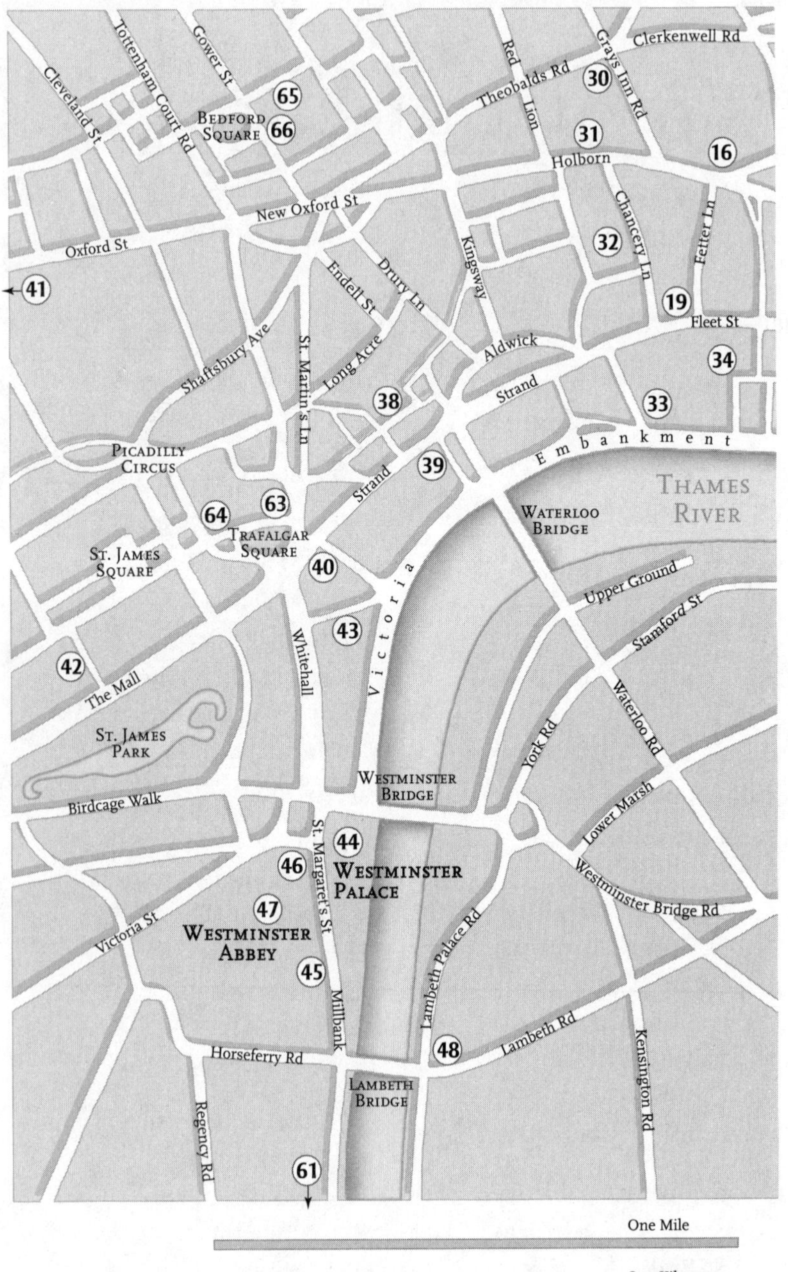

Clerkenwell Rd
Grays Inn Rd
Red Lion
Theobalds Rd
Gower St
Tottenham Court Rd
Cleveland St
Bedford Square
Holborn
Chancery Ln
Fetter Ln
New Oxford St
Oxford St
Kingsway
Endell St
Drury Ln
Fleet St
Aldwick
Shaftsbury Ave
St. Martin's Ln
Long Acre
Strand
Embankment
Picadilly Circus
Thames River
Waterloo Bridge
Trafalgar Square
St. James Square
Victoria
Upper Ground
Stamford St
Whitehall
The Mall
Waterloo Rd
York Rd
St. James Park
Westminster Bridge
Lower Marsh
Birdcage Walk
St. Margaret's St
Westminster Palace
Westminster Bridge Rd
Victoria St
Westminster Abbey
Lambeth Palace Rd
Millbank
Lambeth Rd
Kensington Rd
Horseferry Rd
Lambeth Bridge
Regency Rd
65
66
30
31
16
32
19
41
34
38
33
39
63
64
40
43
42
44
46
47
45
48
61
One Mile
One Kilometer

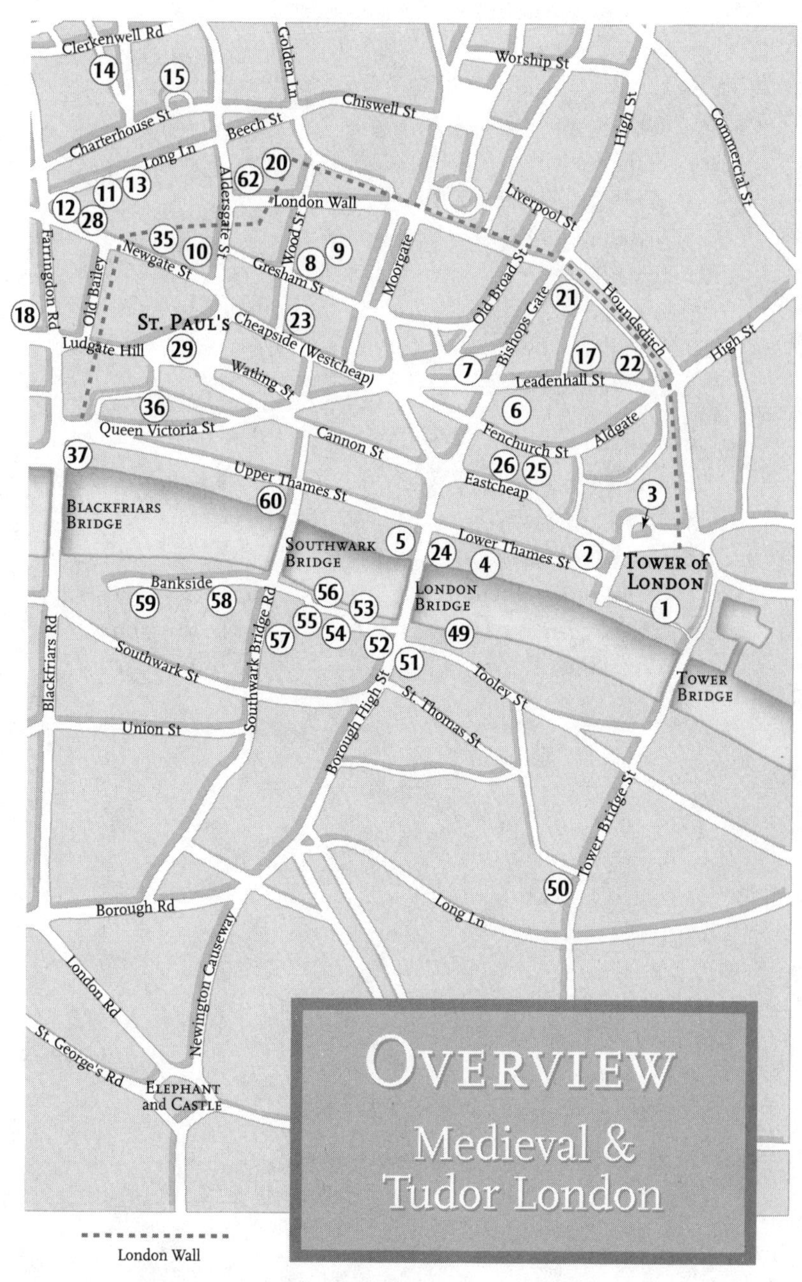

This map shows the general location of London's medieval and Tudor sites. It is for orientation purposes only. You will need a modern, detailed map in order to navigate your way to specific destinations.

(Continued from page xix)

10 Regal London

41. Tyburn
42. St. James Palace
43. Whitehall Palace
44. Westminster Palace
45. Jewel Tower
46. St. Margaret's Church
47. Westminster Abbey
48. Lambeth Palace

11 Shakespeare's Southwark

49. London Bridge
50. Bermondsey
51. London Dungeon
52. Southwark Cathedral
53. The *Golden Hind* Replica
54. Winchester Palace
55. Clink Prison Museum
56. Anchor Tavern
57. The Rose Theater Site
58. Shakespeare's Globe
59. Cardinal's Wharf
60. Queenhithe Stairs

12 Thomas More's Chelsea

61. Chelsea

13 Medieval & Tudor London on Display

62. The Museum of London
63. The National Portrait Gallery
64. The National Gallery
65. The British Museum
66. The British Library

The Amateur Historian's Guide to
Medieval and Tudor London

✠

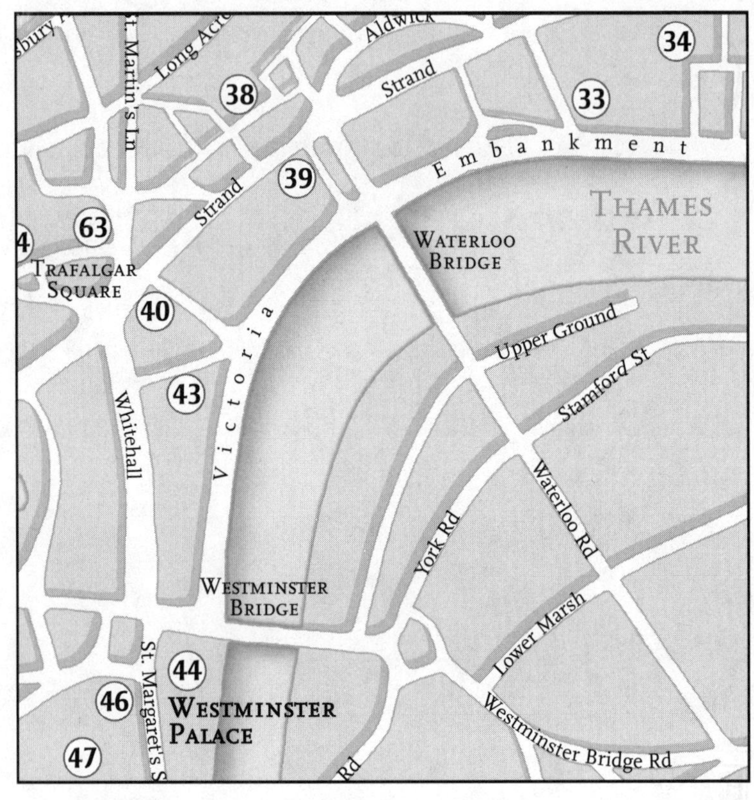
Long Acre
Aldwick
Strand
St. Martin's Ln
Embankment
Strand
Thames River
Waterloo Bridge
Trafalgar Square
Victoria
Upper Ground
Stamford St
Whitehall
Waterloo Rd
York Rd
Westminster Bridge
Lower Marsh
St. Margaret's St
Westminster Palace
Westminster Bridge Rd
Rd
34
38
33
39
63
40
43
44
46
47

CONTENTS

I

Getting There & Getting Organized

Over the course of writing this book, we have—as you can well imagine!—visited London numerous times. Through trial and error, and with the sage advice of friends and acquaintances in England, we have come up with several tips that make a visit to this great city all the more enjoyable. We share our insights with you here, and hope you'll find them as helpful as we have.

BEFORE YOU LEAVE HOME
(assuming home is not London)

We have found that in addition to obtaining your passport and purchasing your airfare, there are certain "advance preparations" that make a busy week in London run more smoothly.

Our guide covers a lot of territory, and the less time you spend getting organized in London, the more time you'll have to enjoy medieval and Tudor sites.

~ Make your hotel reservations

We travel to London frequently on business and have found the hotel that best suits our needs. If you are a regular visitor to London, chances are you have also found a "home base." If not, there are plenty of travel guides that specialize in hotel recommendations—that is not our purpose here. Consult a London hotel guide, ask your friends and family, but whatever you do, make certain that you have locked in your hotel accommodations well in advance. London has become a tremendously popular destination in recent years, and the more popular hotel choices are often filled months ahead of time. The other advantage to advance hotel reservations is that most hotels offer concierge services that will help you with our next two suggestions, *before you even check in!*

~ If you have a "must" on your restaurant list, book it now

Most people want a bit of flexibility in their travel plans, and we're no exception. We like the excitement of walking a neighborhood and poking into a restaurant that grabs our attention. However, if there is a restaurant that has come highly recommended, one that you will be bitterly disappointed not to experience, then pick up the phone and book a table ahead of time. As with hotels, many of the popular restaurants fill their premium dining hours (7:30–10 p.m.) weeks or even months in advance. Chances are your hotel will be glad to make these reservations for you.

~ Plan (and purchase) at least one performance ahead of time

Again, you don't want to pre-schedule every minute of your "down time"; there is a lot going on in London, and some of the most exciting options won't be known to you until you arrive. Still, if your trip will feel somehow "lacking" without a performance of the Royal Shakespeare Company, or an evening at the "hottest" West End show, by all means don't wait. Reserve now. You can do this from home via the Internet by going to *www.whatsonstage.com,* by calling the box office directly or by preying upon the congenial attitude of your hotel concierge.

~ Bring an extra passport photo

We'll explain why in our section *Upon Your Arrival in London.*

~ Pack wisely

First and foremost, don't forget to bring this book!!! Thank you. Now that we have that checked off your list, there are certain items from home that we have found make this particular trip more enjoyable:

- *A lightweight pair of binoculars*, because so many of the gargoyles, statuary and painted ceilings are hard to view with a naked eye.
- *Slightly up-scale leisure clothes* are the appropriate attire for touring churches, Westminster Abbey, Southwark Cathedral and the House of Parliament. There's not a dress code, per se, but you will feel more comfortable and will be treated with more respect if you dress with respect.
- *Walking shoes.* It goes without saying that these should be comfortable both for standing and for walking. Take the time to seek out comfortable shoes that don't look like they've run too many laps on the treadmill, and *break them in ahead of time.*
- *Reconsider that backpack.* We know it's convenient, but due to security concerns many places require that you check it in the coatroom. If you must bring one on your daily rounds, enclose a smaller bag within so that you can keep your wallet, camera, map and small essentials with you.

- *Local currency.* Although we don't recommend you bring all your cash in the local currency, you will want to have a day's worth of money in your wallet—that can be as much as £100, depending on your "day one" plans. Remember, this includes transportation from the airport, tips for transportation and hotel staff, at least one ride on the Underground and the purchase of your Visitor's Travelcard. Automatic Teller Machines (ATMs) abound in London, and nearly every place takes credit cards—in fact, the exchange rate often works in your favor when you pay with plastic! If you are planning to bring traveler's checks, we highly recommend bringing them in pounds sterling rather than in the currency of your homeland. Although *bureaus de change* and most banks will take traveler's checks in non-local currency, many shops and restaurants do not.

UPON YOUR ARRIVAL IN LONDON

You've checked into your hotel, unpacked your bags and you're ready and raring to go. Hold on a second, please! Chances are, you're jet-lagged. You may be a bit grumpy. Your feet are swollen from flying and you're not sure when that burst of energy is going to fade into a pathetic sigh of exhaustion. Much as we sympathize with your urge to head straight to the Tower of London, we are here to tell you: **don't go there.** Unless you are seriously strapped for time, or have not crossed time zones, or have somehow managed a decent night's sleep on the plane *(ha!)*, reserve the day of your arrival for these mindless activities that will, nonetheless, orient you for the days ahead. Believe us. This is the plan that works.

1. *Head to Victoria Station, passport in hand.* To the seriously sleep-deprived this will seem like cruel and unusual punishment, but this necessary evil will save you time and money in the long run. Hopefully, you have planned ahead and purchased several passport-quality photographs before you

left home, when you were bright-eyed and bushy-tailed *(that's a hint!)*. You will need these. If you do not have the requisite 2×2 photo, drag your red-eyed self into one of the instant-photo booths and have your picture taken *(don't worry—no one but you will closely examine this photo)*. Now, photo in hand, wend your way to the ***London Tourist Board (LTB)*** office in the station's forecourt, where you will purchase a weekly Travelcard. Available for tourists only (hence the need to present your passport), this handy "flash pass" allows you to travel through a custom-selected choice of Underground and bus zones at a substantially discounted fare. Best of all, you won't have to wait at any transportation ticket machine (unless you plan to flee town by train) for the duration of your stay.

While standing in line to get your pass, stock up on the free literature that abounds in racks along the wall—you're certain to find some choice activities to augment your trip. You can also purchase such novel London mementos as "Mind the Gap" tee shirts and Underground mouse pads, if you're really itching to start spending money. And don't leave this arcade without purchasing the official British Tourist Authority Map of London—we have found this indispensable!

2. *Combination Admission Packages—Yes or No?* Another purchase you may make at the London Tourist Board Office is a combination ticket to several historic sites. The ostensible benefit of this is a slightly reduced entrance fee *(we've yet to be able to figure out the exact discount)* and the purported ease of slipping past long queues of tourists to a "preferred" entrance. The downside is that invariably—at least for us—there are some restrictions that are annoying, such as the inclusion of at least one site on the ticket that you probably don't intend to visit, but for which you're actually paying admission. You have to decide this one for yourself. We have always been mavericks and prefer the autonomy of "pay-as-you-go."

3. *London Coaches Ltd.* Thought we were above this, did you? We're not . . . and neither are you! As you exit the Victoria Station forecourt, you will see row upon row of tourist buses, and a lively throng of sales agents touting the benefits of their particular tour. You want the London Coaches Ltd. (they run the famous double-decker red buses), which meets opposite the Victoria Underground station. Purchase the ticket for the 90-minute panoramic tour, which has the nifty added benefit of allowing you to "hop off/hop on" at any site that strikes your fancy. Now, from the open upper platform, with the wind wafting through your hair *(Rain? What rain?)*, you'll cruise past most of the sites highlighted in our book, while a trained "blue badge" guide calls out the not-to-be-missed details. Seeing the sites of London en masse will help orient you, and can actually make planning your own personal itinerary easier. This way, you will feel like you've at least *started* your tour of medieval and Tudor London, without putting forth too much effort. Should some site strike your fancy at the very moment when you're feeling particularly frisky, go ahead and alight. In fact, if the crowds appear particularly light at ***Madame Tussaud's,*** this would be a fine time to partake in a not-too-intellectual cook's tour of British history. Trust us. We would not steer you wrong.

SOURCES AND RESOURCES

Maybe it's just us, but we are addicted to accumulating as much literature as is possible to cram into backpacks and suitcases. In fact, we've been known to purchase additional suitcases hours before our return flight, just to store the plethora of fliers, pamphlets, postcards, brochures and, of course, books snarfed up on our excursions. We seem to operate under the assumption that "if it's printed, we have to own it." Of course, we are not necessarily encouraging you to succumb to this same weakness. However, there are some excellent sources of information (much of it free!) that will make your visit to London all the more pleasurable, and we do encourage you to check them out "while you're in the neighborhood." From information on theatrical performances, walking tours, open-air concerts and dining, to serious tomes on medieval and Tudor history, here are our top recommendations.

LONDON TOURIST BOARD

Victoria Station Forecourt, SW1
(020) 7932-2020
Open 8:00 a.m.–7:00 p.m. daily

THE CITY OF LONDON INFORMATION CENTER

St. Paul's Churchyard, EC4
(020) 7332-1456
Open 9:30 a.m.–5:00 p.m. Monday–Saturday

SOUTHWARK HERITAGE ASSOCIATION

Cathedral Street, EC1
(020) 7407-5911
Open 10:00 a.m.–6:00 p.m. Monday–Saturday, noon–4:00 p.m. random Sundays

TIME-OUT MAGAZINE

On sale at practically every newsstand, tobacconist, chemist and bookseller in London, *Time-Out Magazine* is your indispensable guide to "this week" in London: shopping, dining, exhibitions, performances, cinema schedules, television and radio listings, and much, much more to help you enjoy those hours when one more medieval site just might send you screaming out the door. *A word of caution for parents: this magazine covers "everything" that's on in London, some in graphic pictorial detail. You might want to think twice before handing the publication over to your younger children.*

THE MUSEUM BOOKSTORES

We haven't found one we don't absolutely love. Most of them have at least some books related to our period, and most of them will ship them back home for you *(relieving you, perhaps, of the need for that last-minute suitcase purchase)*. Among the best for books of medieval and Tudor interest are the Tower of London gift shops *(natch)*, the Guildhall Bookshop, the Museum of London Gift Shop, the bookstore at the British Museum and the bookshop at the National Portrait Gallery. For unique gifts and souvenirs *(that don't look like they were purchased in a museum gift shop)*, the Victoria & Albert is a must.

THE LONDON LIBRARY

14 St. James Square, SW1

(020) 7930-7705

Open 9:30 a.m.–5:30 p.m. Monday–Saturday,
until 7:30 p.m. Thursday

Not to be confused with the British Museum Reading Room or the Guildhall Library—both of which are fascinating resources if you want to check facts or simply immerse yourself in history—the London Library is a members-only organization with a huge array of books, the majority of which are specifically London-oriented. Annual membership is £100, but shorter, less expensive memberships are available for visiting academics, writers and literary Anglophiles.

WALKING TOURS

We would wager that no other city in the world offers as many walking tours, nor as many well-organized, informative and entertaining ones, at that! There are so very many to choose from, we have limited our recommendations to those we have experienced firsthand that offer tours specifically geared to our period of interest. They are as follows.

THE ORIGINAL LONDON WALKS

22 Kingdon Road, NW6

(020) 7624-3978

There's no need to book in advance, although you will want to write or call ahead for the varying winter and spring tours. There are almost 60 to choose from, many led by trained "off-duty" actors. These terms are highly entertaining, with a wide choice of topics that focus on—or at least touch upon—our period of history. The after-dark Ghosts of London tour that departs from St. Paul's had us looking nervously over our shoulder for evenings to come!

CITISIGHTS OF LONDON

213 Brooke Road, EC5

(0181) 806-4325

As above, there is no need to book in advance, although you will need to obtain a current schedule of tours. Well-trained authors, archeologists and historians lead informative "off the beaten path" walks on topics such as Roman London, Medieval Times and Shakespeare. Right up our alley, so to speak.

TRAGICAL HISTORY TOURS, LTD.

Sunnymeade
1 Bromley Lane
Chiselhurst, Kent
(0181) 467-3318

We have not personally experienced these tours, but they come highly recommended by several friends who have. You must reserve space ahead of time. These are not walks, per se, but five coach-and-walking tours, all with a focus on the grimmer, spookier aspects of British history. Several of the tours are actually day trips out of London *(which, by the way, just happens to be the subject of our next* ***Amateur Historian's Guide****!).*

HOW TO USE THIS BOOK

We have arranged the chapters of this book thematically; if you have a *specialized* area of interest within the broad medieval and Tudor time frame—the monarchy, the legal system, drama—we believe you will be able to readily spot that interest and concentrate your efforts accordingly. Coincidentally (or not, when you closely examine the way early London physically took shape), most of the sites in any given chapter are also in the same general neighborhood. There are some exceptions, of course. However, by and large, you should be able to select a theme, tool around the neighborhood, and soak in most of the relevant details in a little over half a day. We feel that you can easily cover the entire contents of this book in five to seven days, depending on whether *everyone* in your party shares the same level of passion you do, and depending, too, on how much time you choose to devote to London's many other delights!

MONEY MATTERS

London is a fabulous city, no doubt about it. It can also be fabulously expensive. For instance, half a day at the Tower of London for a family of four, with snacks and simple souvenirs, can easily run you £75. We have tried to give you the most recent accounting of entrance fees at the primary sites; however, fees do change, so take our advice and bring a small "slush fund." Even attractions that are technically "free of charge," such as the City churches, strongly "suggest" that you make a donation to help them defray their costs of operation. Where we cite "donation suggested," we have found that £2 per person is within the accepted range. You will also want to know that even the simplest handouts at any given site are not "free of charge"—you will pay between 20P and several pounds for on-site guidebooks. Hopefully, you will find the information in this book instructive enough that such discretionary purchases are kept to a minimum! One final tip: some fee listings for London sites include a category called "Concessions." These are discount prices for special groups of people—senior citizens, students and disabled persons. Generally, the discounts apply only for Brits, but if you are a senior citizen or student from another country and have identification to prove it, we suggest you whip it out and see what the admissions clerk says. Who knows—you might be able to save yourself a pound or two.

SARAH AND CAROLE'S GREATEST HITS

So, you only have a few days to indulge your hunger for medieval and Tudor history. So many attractions, so little time! Would you like our opinion on how to prioritize your visit? Of course you would. Here's our list of *not to be missed* treasures, divvied up over the course of several days.

~ One day in London? Off the beaten track!

If you only have one day to spare, make it count by discovering the remarkable but less-well-known attractions of London. We really do not think you can do justice to the Tower and Westminster in under half a day each, so avoid the crowds and take home pictures your friends and neighbors are less likely to have in their photo albums! Here's what we suggest you see.

- *St. Bartholomew the Great*
- *The Temple Church* (if open)
- *The Guildhall* or
- *Southwark Cathedral/Winchester Palace/The Globe Theater*

~ Two to three days?
The crème de la crème . . .

- *The Tower of London.* Allow at least four hours to enjoy fully—we've been known to spend six hours here and leave grudgingly!
- *Westminster Abbey.* Again, allow at least four hours, so you can be sure to include St. Margaret's Church and the Jewel Tower.
- *The Museum of London.* You will want to see the entire museum and peruse the shops—three hours should do it.
- *Any or all of the "one-day" attractions*

~ The luxury of five days or more?
London is yours!

You can easily complete all the tours in this book in a week, depending on the amount of time you want to devote to the more complex attractions, such as museums, the Tower, etc.

~ Ready for exercise?

Walk the Wall. It gets your legs moving, your blood pumping, and your mind stretching!

~ It's raining, it's pouring?

It's London. Ignore it. *(Although this isn't necessarily the time to catch an open-air performance at the Globe.)*

CONTENTS

2

Laying the Foundation

o really appreciate the London of medieval and Tudor times, it's helpful to have a sense of how the city grew. What events in London's pre-medieval past contributed to the city where Plantagenet and Tudor monarchs, Norman monks and City merchants, and generation after generation of common folk each carved an identifiable and unassailable niche? For a very basic understanding of the myriad factors that shaped the London we know and love, time-travel with us to some of the defining moments in London's earliest history.

ROMAN LONDON

The outline of the City of London, now as in medieval times, owes much to the 3,000-acre Roman settlement that was *Londinium.* Indeed, the boundaries of medieval and Roman London are virtually the same.

Roman interest in Britain began with the rule of Julius Caesar, who first invaded the island in 50 BCE.* Although there had been farming communities of tribal peoples throughout the London area for nearly 3,000 years, no settlers had ever cultivated the advantages of the strategic riverside site in a permanent, profitable manner. Caesar's army landed in Kent and advanced as far as Southwark on the River Thames, but found little there of note. The pioneer passion waned, and Julius and Company headed home. However, by the time Emperor Claudius arrived in 43 CE, the small mercantile community that had developed around the fledgling Thames port was viable enough to pique Roman interest. Although they may have originally entered at Westminster via a series of tiny islands, waiting for low tide in order to ford the river soon proved tedious for these go-get-'em types. The Romans were quick to construct a bridge across the Thames, near the site of the current ***London Bridge,*** and set about manning a supply depot on the shores. It was here, along the northern banks of that first Roman bridge, that the earliest roots of the City of London were set down.

If the Romans thought that the conquest of the insular Britons would be a fait accompli, they were in for a rude awakening. Years of continued and fierce opposition from the local clans culminated in catastrophe when in 60 CE the Iceni tribe, led by the East Anglican warrior queen ***Boudicca,*** burned the Roman settlement of Londinium to the ground.

It took nearly a decade for Londinium to recover from its devastation. But the settlement had far too much potential for Rome to allow it to lie idle for long. By 70 CE a massive recon-

*For years, the accepted method of historical dating has been to use "BC" ("before Christ," or those years prior to the birth of Jesus, arbitrarily designated as year 1) and "AD" (Anno Domini: the years following Jesus' birth). Many religions, however, do not recognize the birth of Christ, and some cultures use other methods of historical dating. In recent years, an increasing number of authors and historians have adopted the more inclusive "Common Era" dating system. We have chosen to follow course. When you see "BCE" (Before Common Era), know that we are referring to the years familiarly known as "BC." Similarly, "CE" refers to the period of time traditionally known as "AD."

struction took place; renovation and renewal were set about with great enthusiasm, and extraordinary measures were taken to fortify the outpost. No vengeful woman—or man, for that matter—would embarrass the Roman legions again. Their first step was to build a well-garrisoned fort in the northwest corner of the settlement by Cripplegate, at the top of what is now Wood Street. Covering nearly 12 acres, this fort could accommodate 1,000 troops in a suitably somber, threatening military atmosphere. By 200 CE, the Romans had surrounded their turf with a massive wall that would define the boundaries of the City for the next 1,000 years. By the start of the 3rd century, the Romans had clearly consolidated their rule, and it wasn't long before Britain found itself immersed in laws, language and a lifestyle that was completely Roman.

With Londinium properly fortified, the Romans began to capitalize on the settlement's most valuable asset: the River Thames. Modern studies indicate that at the peak of the Roman era the Thames may have been as much as four times its current width. With its inland port and highly accessible waterways, the Thames made Londinium the natural hub for lucrative trade with the Continent. This had long been Rome's master plan for the city; the historian Tacitus, whose father-in-law Agricola was governor of Britain from 77 to 83 CE, wrote that London "did not rank as a Roman colony, but was an important center for business and merchandise." From the river north, commerce flourished and Londinium grew dense with shops, offices and homes. By the 3rd century, London was a thriving commercial capital with over 50,000 residents. It was also the seat of the procurator and governor and one of Rome's more important outposts.

As the fortunes of the Roman empire began to flounder in the early 4th century, so did the prosperity of Londinium. In 410, the Emperor Honorius ordered all troops to return to Rome in order to arm the mother city against invasion. Left to their own defenses, the citizens of Londinium soon fell prey to hostile advances by the Saxons. London had entered the Dark Ages, and eventually—if only temporarily—faded from the pages of history.

~ Exploring Roman London

Today London sits atop the Roman city, and each attempt to create a modern legacy in steel and glass seems to reveal the City's ancient heritage, resting a mere 20 feet below street level.

Roman Londinium consisted of two large tracts of high ground, divided down the center by a long-vanished stream, the Walbrook. Near Cannon Street Tube Station, you'll find that the road to ***St. Paul's*** makes a pronounced dip—the only remaining evidence of that central Roman water source. The first Roman settlement was built on Cornhill, the eastern side of the Walbrook; it would be some time before the sprawl reached the western bank at Ludgate Hill, where St. Paul's now stands.

Surprisingly, there is much to see of London's rich Roman heritage, should you feel so inclined. At the head of the massive two-mile-long Roman wall, a major section of the first ***Roman Fort*** can be clearly viewed from an observation deck at the ***Museum of London.*** During the building of Cannon Street Station, evidence of the Governor's Palace (c. 80–100 CE) was discovered. Although nothing remains to be seen, it was a tremendous building with an expansive courtyard and large ornamental pool. Remnants of the colossal basilica and forum (an open courtyard roughly four times the size of Trafalgar Square) were excavated in 1887 during the building of ***Leadenhall Market*** at Cornhill. This was the largest basilica west of the Alps and an indication of the importance of London in the grand Roman scheme.

Within the past decade, construction activity adjacent to the ***Guildhall*** has unearthed substantial portions of the ***Roman amphitheater.*** The remains of numerous humans, as well as those of a bear and a bull, are testament to the sordid past this site shared with amphitheaters throughout the Roman Empire: one might easily argue that public killing was the favorite spectator sport of the times. It is hoped that at least a portion of these fascinating ruins will eventually be on view to the public; tentative plans call for the new £40 million art gallery to encompass a portion of the site as part of its permanent display.

Several of the many public baths—a Roman initiative to "civilize the British"—have been discovered near the old city gates. In addition, a portion of a private home on Lower Thames Street, which featured its own exclusive bath, has been uncovered. Unfortunately, the only "Roman" bath on display in London is ersatz—apparently an Elizabethan "Romanesque" fancy. You'll find it just off Surrey Street along ***the Strand.*** Major portions of the primary Roman bathhouse are nestled amid the foundations of modern office buildings in the vicinity of St. Paul's. The only portion of the complex on view to the public is at the bottom of the terraced garden at Huggin Hill.

When a favor from heaven was needed, the Romans liked to have all bases covered. Evidence of Londinium's eclectic spiritual life was found in 1954 with the discovery of the Temple of Mithras (240 CE), some 18 feet below the foundation of Bucklersbury House. The Christian-style temple (dedicated to a pagan deity!) was relocated to the forecourt of the building, which can be found on Queen Victoria Street (at Cannon Street and Walbrook). The statuary heads of Mithras, Minerva and Serapis, Bacchus and Cautopates, once integral to the temples of the times, are now on public display in the Museum of London.

Did you know?

In the 4th century, the Emperor Gratain renamed Londinium "Augusta"—a Roman honorific meaning "superlative"—so high was the esteem in which Rome held this trade center.

Ah, but there's more! The miliary (milestone) of Roman London, from which the distance of all Roman roads in Britain was once measured, is believed to be the London Stone. It is now incorporated in a glass-covered cubbyhole in the wall at the modern Bank of China, No. 111 Cannon Street, just opposite the tube station.

If you're more drawn to art than archeology *(and one can*

only express gasps of delight over old stones for so long), there are assorted Roman treasures that will excite you. Mosaics were an important part of Rome's artistic legacy and, with permission, you may see two beautiful examples in the ***Bank of England.*** A third, discovered in Leadenhall Street, is on display in the ***British Museum.*** It portrays the god of wine, Bacchus, seated upon a panther in brilliant tiles of yellow and amber.

The warrior queen Boudicca, who valiantly fought to drive out the Roman army, is commemorated by an imposing statue at the northern end of Westminster Bridge. Her fiery rampage left behind a city of ash, still witnessed in the layer of burnt clay that lies below street level in the vicinity of Lombard Street. Although not of our favorite period in history, Boudicca remains one of our favorite historical figures, and we *always* pause to pay homage when we emerge from the Westminster Tube. Her foe, the Roman Procurator Classicianus, is depicted in the bronze plaque alongside the Roman Wall at Wakefield Gardens, just off ***Tower Hill.*** His original tombstone is housed at the British Museum.

Both the British Museum and the Museum of London have interesting collections from London's Roman past, well worth a look if your interests are not strictly limited to the medieval period. In addition to those mentioned above, the Museum of London also houses an original bronze bust of Hadrian, various tools and household implements, a Roman girl's leather bikini and timbers from a barge found off Blackfriar's Bridge, whose ragstone cargo was intended for use in the construction of the Roman wall. The museum's dioramas bring to life a Roman family kitchen and dining area, complete with authentic tableware. Smaller but compelling exhibits may be found at ***St. Bride's Church,*** Fleet Street, where portions of a Roman home and the skeleton of a Roman woman are on display. ***All Hallows by the Tower*** incorporates Roman tiles in its lovely stone doorway, and its crypt displays a smattering of Roman relics.

We will be discussing Roman London again when we lead you on a tour of the ***London Wall,*** in Chapter 3.

BOUDICCA (D. 61 CE)

This warrior queen was the wife of Prasutagus, king of the Iceni, an indigenous British tribe from the Norfolk and Suffolk areas. Upon his death in 60 CE, Prasutagus's family was grossly mistreated by the Romans. Boudicca was beaten and her daughters raped. With the aid of neighboring tribes, Boudicca staged an uprising, raging through the countryside en route to London, and slaying an estimated 70,000 Roman citizens and their supporters. The governor of Britain, Suetonius Paulinus, launched a counterattack and defeated the rebels in battle in the British midlands. Rather than surrender to Rome, Boudicca committed suicide by poison.

THE SAXON CENTURIES

Londinium was not abandoned overnight. According to the *Anglo-Saxon Chronicles,* the remains of the Roman army from Kent took refuge within the city walls following a nasty battle with Saxons in 457. However, by the year 500, London seems to have been largely deserted. In fact, history gives the town no mention whatsoever for many years to come.

Unlike the Romans, the Saxons were country folk. Cities as complex as Londinium held little allure for them, despite the riches such a town could offer. Archeology implies that those who did seek out the settlement tended to cling to the outskirts of the wall, where open spaces suitable for grazing and crops could still be cultivated. Their primary settlement followed the approximate course of what is now known as the Strand. The villages of Ealing, Barking and Staines were ancient farmsteads whose names remind us of their Saxon roots.

References to London start to appear again in the annals of history with the emergence of Christianity in the British Isles. With the dawn of Christianity, London began to wake from its long slumber. Although faint traces of Christianity can be found among the early relics of Roman London, Britain had remained primarily a pagan country throughout Roman rule and into the Dark Ages. In 597, Pope Gregory sent the future St. Augustine and a retinue of papal emissaries to undertake the Catholic conversion of the "heathen" island. The mission proved surprisingly easy. To Augustine's great advantage, Ethelbert, King of Kent, had married a devout Catholic princess from France. Ethelbert was the first English monarch to embrace the new faith, and whatever his reason for adopting Catholicism, he did so with a convert's zeal. At his invitation, the Gregorians *(who are now making a bundle selling compact disc recordings of their sonorous chants)* set up headquarters at the old Roman church in Canterbury. A similar Vatican outpost was established in London, under the leadership of the city's first bishop, Mellitus. In 606, with the support of the new monarch, Sebert, Mellitus erected London's first cathedral, dedicated to St. Paul. In the end, it was easy come–easy go for the Catholics. Christian influence in London was surprisingly short-lived. Upon the death of Sebert, London reverted to paganism. The only other intensely Christian town, Canterbury, would henceforth serve as the seat of British Christianity.

This brief flurry of religious activity was enough to resuscitate the City of London. Although the area within the walls remained largely desolate—only St. Paul's Cathedral and a royal palace in the vicinity of Aldersgate gave the town any real stature—London slowly began to rebuild its reputation as a major center of international trade and influence. Strong enough to repel repeated Danish aggression in the 9th and 10th centuries, London—now known as Ludenwic—grew to become a major player in the world's commercial arena. (By the way, the Saxon suffix "wic" means trading center.) Before long, the City would amass the fiscal strength and political influence to create its own civic infrastructure, separate from that of the fragmented monarchy. This quasi independence would serve the City well for centuries to come, as we shall see in our exploration of the tumultuous Middle and Tudor Ages.

By the end of the 7th century, Christianity was on more sure footing in London. Among its most stalwart followers was Erkenwald, fourth Bishop of London and one of the few Saxons with lasting influence on the city. Between 675 and 693, Erkenwald established two important abbeys—one at Chester and the other on the outskirts of London at Barking. Erkenwald was a clever businessman as well as a charismatic man of the cloth. He established the right to charge a toll on every load of wood that passed into the City through what is now known as *(what else?)* ***Bishopsgate.*** After his death, Erkenwald was canonized, and his tomb in old St. Paul's remained a popular pilgrim destination throughout the Middle Ages.

~ Exploring Saxon London

If there is little in London today that reveals its Saxon heritage, the effect of more than 500 years of Saxon rule cannot be easily dismissed. It was during this period that the boundaries of most of London's central boroughs and parishes were established and a new street pattern was designed to replace the old Roman grid. Indeed, as you embark upon your tour of London, the byways you'll stroll far more closely represent the Saxon village of Ludenwic than that of Roman Londinium.

Aside from a handful of place-names, the actual artifacts of the Saxon era in London are scarce. Mitres (bishop's hats) adorn the corners of contemporary buildings along Bishopsgate and Wormwood Streets, a nod to Erkenwald's log tolls, and the crypt of All Hallows by the Tower is borne by a Saxon arch *(a welcome break after the countless Norman arches you'll be admiring, believe us!).* The medieval church of ***St. Ethelburga*** is dedicated to the memory of Erkenwald's sister; alas, it contains no vestiges of the Saxon era.

◇◇

NORMAN ARCHES!

Many times throughout this book, we will refer to "Norman arches" as the visual clue that you are, indeed, in the right place at the right time. What exactly is Norman architecture, and how does one distinguish it? Glad you asked . . . we think. Norman architecture (1066–1154) was heavily influenced by the Italian Romanesque style of design: sparsely decorated masonry, punctuated by the telltale rounded arch (as opposed to the pointed Gothic arch that would become so popular during the 13th through 15th centuries). You will see this in the most ancient buildings on your tour of London: ***The Tower, Westminster Abbey, St. Bartholomew's, Southwark Cathedral*** and the ***Temple Church,*** to name a few.

◇◇◇

ETHELBURGA

Sister to St. Erkenwald, Ethelburga was an influential religious force and a saint in her own right. Her abbey at Barking, established by her bishop brother, oversaw the activities of the ancient church All Hallows by the Tower. This would become one of the most important medieval houses of worship and remains one of London's oldest buildings.

◇◇◇

DAYS OF THE DANES

By the late 8th century, London had withstood repeated attacks from the Danes and had eventually succumbed to 35 years of Danish rule. The yoke was not lifted until London was reclaimed in 886 by the Saxon king Alfred of Wessex. Alfred "the Great" had turned his attention toward the Viking threat. He built a mighty fleet and rebuilt the crumbled City walls. Together with the "Sudewerke" (Southwark) on the opposite side of London Bridge, these formed the backbone of the mighty defense system comprised of fortified "burghs." Alfred appointed his son, Ethelred, governor of London and set him about the task of resettlement. The two market areas that comprise today's ***"Cheapside"***—East Cheap ("cheap" derives from the Saxon word *chepe,* meaning "market") for the common folk and West Cheap for royalty—owed their layout to Ethelred. Meanwhile, within the City walls, commerce and trade revived. Crafts such as weaving, metalworking and bone carving enjoyed a heyday, and by the 10th century merchants from every major continental land had established a permanent base of operation in London. It was during this era that the waterfront docks of ***Queenhithe**** and ***Billingsgate*** were constructed to accommodate the great increase in marine traffic. Also dating back to this time is the civic role of the *alderman,* a reflection of the city's respect for merchant wealth—and clout!

*The name "Queenhithe" would not apply until much later.

◇◇◇

ALFRED THE GREAT (849–899)

Of all the Anglo-Saxon rulers, none is better known or more respected than Alfred of Wessex. Alfred ascended to the Wessex throne in 871 at the age of 22. The early years of his reign were spent warding off repeated Danish invasions. Having fought several prolonged battles with the Danes as a young prince and soldier, Alfred began his monarchy by paying the Danes to leave his kingdom in peace and quiet *(danegeld: similar to the protection money paid to the Mafioso)*. This strategy worked until 873 when the Danes again attacked Wessex. The pattern of attack/payoff was repeated over the course of several years until, at last, in 878, Alfred succeeded in enforcing a period of prolonged peace. The 12 years that followed would be Alfred's most creative and fulfilling. He embarked upon an ambitious program of military reform and cultural enrichment. Thoughtful, well traveled, highly educated and driven equally by Christian ideas and a passion for his kingdom, Alfred left Wessex—and, to a large degree, most of his island home—far better than he had inherited it. By the standards of the time, he was exceptional . . . and history has treated him as nothing less.

◇◇◇

Alas, the Saxon salad days were numbered. By the end of the 10th century, the Danes had returned. With a mightier force than ever, they took the island of Britain by storm. At the advent of 1015, all of England, save London, had succumbed to Danish power. With its sophisticated civic administration, its mercantile wealth and the impressive strength of its armed forces, London was able to hold out until 1016, when the City negotiated its own separate peace with the great Danish statesman Cnut—a strategy the burghers of London would employ with several future monarchs, including William the Conqueror and King John. Ultimately, the Londoners accepted Cnut as king, but on terms they had made certain would be of benefit to London!

Apparently, the Danish invaders had spread their attention and resources too thin, creating an empire they could not, ultimately, sustain. With the death of Cnut, his successors—two hapless sons by two concurrent consorts!—were unable to enforce their claim to the British crown. With the death of second-son Harthacnut in 1042, the crown returned to the head of a "true Englishman," the man who would go down in history as

St. Edward the Confessor . . . the king who would leave the door open for the Norman Conquest.

~ Exploring Danish London

Although the Danish rule spanned 64 years, the lasting influence on London was minimal. Today, a mere handful of churches and streets bear names that reflect the Danish era: ***St. Magnus Martyr, St. Clement Danes, St. Olaves*** and Tooley Street.

CONFESSOR TO CONQUEROR

And now it *really* gets confusing! Well, here we go: in 1042, the throne of England passed to Edward, surviving son of Ethelred II ("the Unready"), who was the grandson, on his mother's side, of Richard, the first Duke of Normandy. So pious a man was King Edward that he was nicknamed "the Confessor," and the extremes to which he carried his piety would come to affect the nation in two significant ways. First, Edward's zealous religious beliefs led him to make a voluntary vow of chastity, leaving England without an heir to the throne and setting the stage for the Norman Conquest. Second, Edward was obsessed with the ambition to distinguish his kingdom by erecting the most lavish church in all Christendom. This drive, coupled with his rancor over being denied the financial support of the City of London, led Edward to flee the confines of the City walls in his search for a suitable site for his cathedral. His choice was typically eccentric: a swamp at the mouth of the Tyburn River, known as Thorney Island (modern-day Westminster).

At the time, Thorney could only be reached by a shallow-draught boat or a series of man-placed stepping stones. The citizens of London (especially those consigned to building the cathedral) must have thought Edward quite mad. Undeterred, he allocated one tenth of his entire royal treasury to the building of this "west minster," or western abbey. Abandoning his royal palace within the City walls, Edward went on to create a splendid royal residence alongside the cathedral site . . . the better to supervise firsthand the construction of his glorious tribute to St. Peter.

So near and yet so far. From this point on, Westminster would become the second London city, the center of royal justice and administration. The ancient port city downstream would retain the prosperity and clout of an independent merchant community—leverage that served it well in the past and would do so again. The London you see today evolved from the tensions and divided powers of these two very different "cities." Westminster would forever be associated with the monarchy and the seat of political power, while the City would grow increasingly, solidly mercantile, entrepreneurial and resistant to the pressures of both Crown and Church.

As for the self-righteous Edward, his peers and later historians may not have thought much of his rule, but the Vatican liked his style. He was canonized in 1161 and would become the favorite saint of another controversial monarch, Henry III. When Henry began rebuilding Westminster Abbey in 1245, it was only fitting that the focal point of his splendid remodeling was St. Edward the Confessor's gilded tomb.

We assume you know what happens next . . . no heir for Edward, a bastard uncle in Normandy who *swears* he's been promised the crown, lots of fighting with assorted Harolds, and a successful invasion on the shores of Kent that would forever change the face of England. William, Duke of Normandy, affectionately known as William "the Bastard," was crowned king of England at Westminster Abbey on December 25, 1066. And the rest, as they say, is . . . !

So, there you have it—a bird's-eye view of London's history from 43 to 1066. Lucky for you, there is no quiz at the end of this chapter. Instead, brush off your favorite pair of walking shoes, be sure to take along a great map, your camera and a small pair of binoculars, for we're about to embark upon one of the most informative and adventurous walking tours ever—**the London Wall Walk!**

CONTENTS

The London City Wall

WALKING THE WALL

rom the **Tower of London,** *start at the south end of the Tower Hill underpass.* OR, *from the* **Museum of London,** *start at the introduction panel in the gardens on the east end of the museum, then head to Aldersgate to start your tour.*

Before you embark upon a serious exploration of the historic square mile known as the City, we suggest you spend an hour or so walking the line of the ancient ***London Wall.*** Not only will this provide you with a sense of the boundaries of medieval London, but it will also reveal fragments of the City's history that would otherwise be missed on a "greatest hits" tour.

We also recommend that you invest in the publication *The London Wall Walk,* published by the Museum of London. It is inexpensive and available at the museum, the Guildhall Bookstore and certain London Information Centers and bookstores that specialize in London interests. Although the guide was published in 1985 and is somewhat out of date, it provides a handy outline of the walk, interspersed with relevant information about each of the 21 sites, many of which display actual sections of the wall. All excavated sites have received significant modern restoration, albeit as historically accurate as possible.*

Whether you use the official publication or set off on your own, you'll note that there are two ways to proceed—clockwise from the Museum of London heading west toward the Tower, or counterclockwise from the Tower east to the museum. Since we assume that you (like us!) must begin each trip to London with a visit to the White Tower, we suggest that you start from the Tower of London and follow the path of construction. Keep in mind that the modern road known as the ***London Wall Road*** is the City's main east-west thoroughfare. You will be walking through some high-traffic areas and during weekdays the sidewalks are thronged with office workers, particularly at lunch hour. You might find this walk most enjoyable after business hours or on a weekend morning. In any case, take along your best walking shoes and a dependable map and *have fun!* This is one of our very favorite London pastimes.

☞ Did you know?

The line of the defensive ditch that protected the London Wall is mirrored in the modern street known as "Houndsditch."

From the Tower Hill Tube you will be heading north in a counterclockwise loop that will conclude in the general vicinity of the Museum of London. Know that the westernmost and southern sections of the wall have yet to be unearthed. The list of sites, together with a comprehensive map (*we used* The Penguin London Mapguide *when writing this chapter*), will help orient you. Here's what you can expect to see on your walk.

1. *The Tower of London.* The medieval postern gate, visible along the Tower moat, may be viewed from the south end

*During the 1970s, the City did its best to map out the route of the wall, numbering pivotal sites, providing directional signs and erecting a written explanation at each point of excavation. Unfortunately, these efforts have fared far less well than the ancient wall itself *(so much for progress!)*. On our recent trips, we found many of the signs missing, site numbers changed and helpful legends *unhelpfully* removed. However, we have always found local passersby ready to assist on the few times we found ourselves truly offtrack!

of the Tower Hill underpass. There also is a remnant of the wall inside the Tower grounds, comprising part of the crumbling remains of the Wardrobe Tower, which was built on top of the wall.

2. *Tower Hill.* A 110-foot-long portion of the wall can be seen "up close" in the garden to the east of the Tower Hill underpass.
3. *Cooper's Row.* There is a 35-foot section of the wall in the courtyard of the bank building. The lower 14½-foot span is Roman, and marked by a red sandstone plinth. The patching you'll notice in the Roman fabric is generally attributed to Alfred the Great. The upper 5½ feet are medieval. Notice the arrow holes for archers.
4. *Emperor House.* Look for a 32-foot Roman wall fragment by the outside entrance near the rear of the building.
5. *Aldgate.* A description of the City gate can be found on the wall of Sir John Cass School, at the junction of Aldgate and Jewry Street.
6. *Duke's Place.* No, it's not a jazz club! It's just a small street with a pedestrian underpass where you'll find a preserved section of the wall.
7. *Bevis Marks.* There's a narrative on the wall of 10–16 Bevis Marks.
8. *Bishopsgate.* The line of the wall may be traced along Bishopsgate Street; a plaque on the northeast corner of Bishopsgate and Camomile marks the site of the gate.
9. *St. Botolph.* The line of the wall continues in Bishopsgate Churchyard, formed by the back of the shops on Wormwood Street.
10. *All Hallows.* This church was actually built flush with the wall, which lies 13 feet below ground level at this point.
11. *Moorgate.* A narrative plaque and site locator are on the northeast corner of Moorgate and London Wall Road.
12. *St. Alphege.* This impressive section of the northern wall was unearthed during World War II bombing that all but

destroyed St. Alphege. This church, too, had been built hard against the wall, and its ruins amid the flowering gardens make for a poignant stop on your walk.

13. *Cripplegate.* There is a descriptive panel at the corner of Wood Street and St. Alphege.
14. *City Wall and Towers.* Pieces of both may be seen in the churchyard of St. Giles.
15. *St. Giles Cripplegate.* A well-preserved tower is in the north end of the gardens at the east end of the Museum of London.
16. *Barber-Surgeon's Hall.* The lower levels of a second tower may also be found in the gardens at the east side of the museum, abutting the hall.
17. *City Wall and Tower, Redux.* Portions of the west side of the Roman fort, as well as a late-era tower on the west side of the wall, may also be found in the museum's east gardens.
18. *Roman Fort West Gate.* A major section of the gate's tower has been preserved in the basement of Bastion House, near the Museum of London (part of the modern Barbican complex). It is frequently open to the public for a closer view. The tower had a guardroom and access to the sentry walk along top of the wall.
19. *Roman Fort and City Wall.* There are fragments to be seen on the north end of Noble Street.
20. *Roman Fort and City Wall, Redux.* More is to be seen on the south end of Noble Street.
21. *Aldersgate.* A narrative panel is hung on the rails at the east side of Aldersgate.

ABOUT THE WALL

When your mission is to build an empire, you can't afford to make the same mistake twice. The London Wall was built under the Roman emperor Severus, sometime around 190 CE in order to defend Londinium against a second uprising by England's rural tribes (the memory of Queen Boudicca's fiery Icenian revolt burned bright in the minds of the Roman legions). Built of approximately one million Kentish ragstone bricks, interspersed with brick courses for added strength, the wall ran three miles long and enclosed an area of approximately 330 acres.

Construction of the wall began on the east of the (yet-to-be-built) Tower of London and ran north to Aldgate. Here it jogged northwest to Cripplegate, then turned south/southwest to Aldersgate and Newgate before veering down Ludgate Hill to the Thames. Initially, the threat of invasion by way of the river was not considered imminent and the riverfront was not walled for many years. In any case, the Thames wall was short-lived, eroded relatively quickly by the river tides. Eventually the River Thames itself became the final section of the defensive belt that secured London.

Massive as the wall was—about 15 to 20 feet high and 8 feet thick—the Romans perceived that it alone was not enough to protect their outpost from siege. In 296, under Emperor Constantius Chlorus, 21 bastions, or towers, were added to the wall. The best example of these massive towers can be seen near St. Giles Cripplegate and the Museum of London, although this particular tower was rebuilt during the Middle Ages.

☞ Did you know?

The medieval gatehouses were not the only portions of the City Wall to offer unusual accommodations. The ancient bastions were frequent homes to anchorites and hermits. Their commitment to self-denial was well served by the sparse, cramped quarters. The 13th-century hermitage St. James in the Wall turned the tower at St. Giles into a veritable ascetics' condo. By the way, the crypt of the hermitage chapel is currently preserved in Mark Lane.

Indeed, renovation to the wall was nearly ongoing. Even during the relatively dormant Saxon period, the wall remained in decent repair and in 1066 was still daunting enough to cause the Conqueror to think twice about a protracted siege.

Throughout the Plantagenet reign the basic construction was improved upon and the height periodically increased, partially to compensate for the rising ground levels. By building atop the Roman wall, medieval masons created, in effect, a second wall, built upon ancient foundations but varying in width and incorporating the early development of the Tower of London at its southeastern edge. Defense of this sort did not come cheap. Tolls charged at each gate, as well as rents from leasing out the gatehouses and towers, helped defray the costs. Was it worth it? Well, after Alfred the Great's reclaiming invasion of 886, the London Wall never again surrendered to force.

Originally, seven double gates set into the wall controlled access and egress to the City. From the Tower, these were Aldgate, Bishopsgate, Cripplegate, Aldersgate, Newgate, Ludgate and Dowgate. Eventually, Billingsgate became part of the Thames wall. Moorgate would be added much later.

Each night after the bells had tolled the medieval curfew, the City gates would be closed. Guards posted at each gate did more than bolster security; they served to foil those seeking to evade entry tolls. Over the years, each gate would develop its own interesting role in London's history, doubling from time to time as residences for upstanding citizens, workshops, warehouses and even prisons.

~ Aldersgate

This gate was possibly named after King Alfred's lieutenant Earlred. Throughout medieval times, Aldersgate provided access to the popular ***Smithfield Market***, as well as to ***St. Bartholomew's Priory*** and ***Charterhouse***, two important religious destinations. During the Tudor era, Aldersgate became home to one of the leading print shops in London. The *Folio Bible* (1549) and Foxe's *Book of Martyrs* (1563) were among the major works published here. We link Aldersgate with the end of the Tudor era, for it was through this gate that James Stuart first entered London to claim the crown left him by his cousin Elizabeth.

~ Aldgate

One of Londinium's busiest portals, this was the original Roman entry for the road that linked London and Colchester. During medieval times it gained prestige for its access to ***Holy Trinity Priory***, just beyond its gate. For 14 years, the gatehouse was home to Geoffrey Chaucer, a proverbial garret where he penned *Troylius and Criseyde.* Aldgate underwent frequent repairs and renovations; at one point it was largely restored with materials salvaged from the destroyed Jewish ghetto. The name is derived from the Saxon word *eldgat,* meaning "open to all." Mary Tudor first entered the City as the new queen of England via Aldgate.

~ Billingsgate

Once the opening in the short-lived river wall, it takes its name from the Saxon family *Belin.* Some of the richest Roman archeology has been found on the waterfront in this vicinity. During the Anglo-Saxon period, this was the quayside customshouse, collecting duty on a vast array of imports from the Continent.

~ Bishopsgate

This gate was named for the Bishop of London, who undertook the maintenance of the facility. In exchange, the bishop received one stick of wood from every cart entering the portal. With the heads of criminals displayed on spikes above the gatehouse, we suppose few drivers felt inclined to withhold the tariff.

~ Cripplegate

Originally the entrance to the Roman fort, Cripplegate remained in constant use into the Saxon and medieval eras. Two feasible roots of this name have been debated over time. The early English word for a low, cramped opening was *crippul,* and indeed, Cripplegate was the smallest of the wall portals, a postern intended only for foot traffic. On the other hand, it is also known that a welcoming committee of "cripples and lepers" milled about at this point, hoping to benefit from the mercy of softhearted travelers and pilgrims. The nearby church of St. Giles Cripplegate is dedicated to the patron saint of the physically handicapped. Connections with mercy aside, Cripplegate also served as a prison for common trespassers.

~ Ludgate

Named for the mythical King Lud, this gate was, prior to 1419, a prison reserved for debtors. Medieval statues of the hero and his two sons once adorned the gatehouse. They have been preserved and can be seen in the portal of ***St. Dunstan-in-the-West.***

~ Moorgate

Originally this was only a tiny footgate known as the Aldermanbury postern. In 1415 the "new" gate was constructed. Moorgate then provided easy access to the fens, or moors, where the City's youth could practice archery or the more "sinful" sports of football and hockey.

~ Newgate

The name lives on in infamy, having been lent to one of London's most notorious prisons. The original gatehouse did, indeed, serve as a jail from the reign of Henry II until Chaucer's day.

In 1760, an Act of Parliament abolished the City gates, and by the 1800s they had all been pulled down; the infernal traffic of London left no option. However, the gates still provide a visual image closely linked to the City, a "logo," if you will, that can be found on public buildings, signposts and the official literature of the district. Reproductions of the gates are on display at the Museum of London, a very fitting final stop on your tour of the London Wall.

◇◇◇

GEOFFREY CHAUCER (C. 1343–1400)

Religious writers aside, Geoffrey Chaucer was the first great poet to write in the English language, earning him the moniker "the father of English poetry." The son of a vintner, Chaucer was born in London and made his entry into the world of nobility by joining the household of the Countess of Ulster, who was married to Edward III's second son, Lionel, Duke of Clarence. One of Chaucer's many talents was marrying well. His wife, Philippa Rouet, was a lady-in-waiting to Queen Philippa of Hainault. Upon the death of the queen, Mrs. Chaucer joined the household of Constance, Duchess of Lancaster. Mrs. Chaucer's sister, Katherine Swynford, would become the Duke of Lancaster's (John of Gaunt's) mistress and eventual third wife. Family ties like these kept the Chaucers very well connected, and Geoffrey enjoyed a variety of lucrative and impressive posts, including controller of London customs and clerk of the works. He remained a Londoner all his life, never aspiring to the country estates of other gentlemen of his rank. A prolific writer, he is best known for his droll masterpiece, *The Canterbury Tales* (1387). And while this work may well be the bane of every high school student, there is simply no better "slice of life" insight into the world of 14th-century England.

◇◇◇

CONTENTS

4

The Tower

The Tower of London

or any true enthusiast of the Middle Ages and the Tudor era, the highlight of a trip to London is a visit to the Tower. This site, more than any other, most clearly serves as the anchor for this slice of London's history. A simple fort was built on the site as soon as William the Conqueror was crowned king of England in Westminster Abbey on Christmas Day after his October victory at the Battle of Hastings in 1066. Construction of the White Tower in approximately 1078 was meant to solidify the iron hand of Norman rule in England. And the demise of the Tower as a favored royal residence coincided with the end of the Tudor era. Elizabeth rarely stayed there. She hated it—for obvious reasons, one would think!

From the first moment you emerge from the Tube to see the Tower looming above, your imagination is fired and you are transported instantly back through the ages. You envision soldiers in chain mail pacing the walls and battlements, guarding against unknown dangers as well as the often truculent citizens of London. Once past the outer curtain wall, over the now dry moat and standing under the portcullis of the Byward Tower that guards the entrance to the Outer Ward, you imagine servants in homespun scurrying everywhere to meet the daily needs of the hundreds of retainers who lived at the castle when the monarch was in residence. And you visualize the nobles in their silks and satins engaged in whispered conversations as they plot both for and against their liege lord!

Because the history of the Tower is so complex and rich, this chapter is chock full of historical details, anecdotes and "slices of life" from the nearly 1,000 years in which the Tower has been a focal point of the London landscape. To fully appreciate the Tower and get the most out of your visit there, we suggest you read this chapter before you go. You can then use the *Quick Tour* section of the chapter to wend your way through the complex and identify the buildings you see before you. Of course, if you are really pressed for time and the Tower is a "must see" on your "to do" list, you can just follow the *Quick Tour.* That will at least provide you with the major highlights. We are confident that this quick dip into the Tower's history will whet your appetite for more and that you will be back for a longer visit—after you have had time to read the history.

Two other sites closely associated with the Tower's history, the church of All Hallows by the Tower and the Tower Hill execution grounds, also are covered in this chapter. A quick drop by both is well worth your time.

The Tower of London

EC3N (020-7709-0765)

Tower Hill Tube

OPEN

9:00 a.m.–7:00 p.m. Monday–Saturday, March 1–October 31
10:00 a.m.–7:00 p.m. Sunday, March 1–October 31
9:00 a.m.–6:00 p.m. Tuesday–Saturday, November 1–February 28
10:00 a.m.–6:00 p.m. Sunday and Monday, November 1–February 28
Closed December 24–26, January 1
Note: Last admission is 60 minutes before closing

ADMISSION

£11.00 Adults
£7.30 Children (5–15; children under 5 admitted free)

£8.30 Senior citizens, students and disabled persons
£33.00 Family ticket (up to 2 adults and 3 children)

TOURS

Free throughout the day; times are posted on signs past the entry point at the Middle Tower; specialized children's tours are available; self-guided audio tours are available for £2.00 with a refundable £10 deposit.

CONVENIENCES

There are bookstores, souvenir shops, snack bars and restaurants within and adjacent to the Tower.

If you can, you will want to plan to spend the better part of a day at the Tower. There is much to see. If you cannot, use the *Quick Tour* section of this chapter to whiz through the complex.

You also will want to wear very comfortable shoes, for there is much walking and stair climbing to do if you want to poke into every nook and cranny of the buildings where monarchs lived and ruled, royal captives were confined and sometimes killed.

>>>

THE TOWER TODAY

Formally known as ***Her Majesty's Palace and Fortress of the Tower of London,*** the Tower actually is a large complex of various buildings, courtyards and walls constructed over 900 years by various kings and queens for both aesthetic and defensive purposes. For nearly five centuries, it was the primary London residence of the reigning monarch. The events that occurred here are among the most famous—or, rather, infamous—and dramatic in history.

Today, the Tower is commanded by a constable who is appointed by the Crown, a custom that dates back to the reign of Stephen of Blois in the mid 12th century. The treachery of ***Geoffrey de Mandeville,*** the Tower constable who repeatedly flipped sides during the civil war between Stephen and his cousin, the Empress Matilda, prompted Stephen to end the practice of hereditary inheritance of this role. Stephen's successor, Matilda's son Henry II, never one to concede any more power or authority to one of his nobles than he absolutely had to, eagerly embraced Stephen's policy and made his own appointment.

Because the constable generally was an important man who was greatly trusted by the reigning monarch, his time could not be consumed wholly by guarding the Tower. The king generally had other tasks for him to perform as well. Therefore, the constable was assisted in his job by a lieutenant. Both were provided living quarters in the Tower.

This system for managing the Tower continues today. The Keys and Custody of the Tower are delivered to the constable in a formal ceremony by the Lord Chamberlain. The constable is given possession of the ***Queen's House*** in the ***Inner Ward;*** possession is then conveyed to the resident governor who actually lives there. Within the Tower walls is a thriving community of about 150 souls who guard, groom, repair, excavate and otherwise see to the proper care and maintenance of this most historic of palaces.

WHEN "CHRIST AND HIS SAINTS SLEPT"

When Henry I's only legitimate son, William, was killed in the disastrous sinking of the White Ship in 1120 just as it set out to cross the English Channel, sailing from Barfleur to England with a boatload of young nobles, Henry was left without a male heir to the throne. Determined that a legitimate heir of his blood inherit his kingdom, Henry promptly married a second time (his first wife, Edith/Matilda, died in 1118). However, this second marriage to Adeliza of Louvain produced no children—an odd quirk of fate given that Henry was renowned for his lecherousness (he fathered at least 20 bastards) and, after Henry's death in 1135, Adeliza went on to have children with her second husband.

In despair, Henry decided upon a desperate tactic. He recalled his daughter Matilda to England and forced his barons to swear an oath of homage to her as their future queen. This did not sit well with the barons. There never had been a woman ruler of England or Normandy and the barons were not at all sure they wanted to break with tradition. Even more importantly, they did not like Matilda herself.

Matilda had been married at age 8 to the Holy Roman Emperor and sent at age 9 to his court in Germany, where she was educated and trained to be an empress. She remained in Germany until 1125, when the emperor's death left her a widow without children at age 24. By all accounts, this education and experience had made her a haughty, arrogant, autocratic woman with no sense of humor and little ability to charm and manipulate the men over whom she was supposed to rule. Henry's English and Norman magnates were not happy at the thought that she was to be their queen and Henry knew it.

Therefore, after compelling in 1127 the first of several oaths of support he would force for Matilda, Henry then sought out a second husband for her, one who could support her claim militarily. He settled on Geoffrey, Count of Anjou—a disastrous choice. Matilda was horrified. Geoffrey was 10 years younger than she and not at all her social equal. She saw the marriage as a real comedown for her. But married they were, in 1128, and, as unhappy as the marriage was, they did manage to produce three children, Henry (b. 1133), Geoffrey (b. 1134) and William (b. 1136). Matilda, however, continued to style herself as "Empress," no doubt a sore point with her quarrelsome husband.

And, if the nobles disliked Matilda, they disliked Geoffrey even more. He was viewed as a lightweight who was also greedy and cruel. Therefore, when Henry died in December 1135, the barons were quick to cast aside their promises to support Matilda and rushed to pledge their loyalty to Stephen of Blois, the son of Henry's sister Adela and a grandson of William the Conqueror.

Stephen had been educated at Henry's court and had been a favorite of the king. While he too had been compelled to swear to support Matilda, Stephen was well acquainted with the true feelings of the barons regarding the prospect of Matilda as queen. Therefore, when Henry died, Stephen moved quickly to claim the throne for himself. Within three weeks of the king's death, Stephen had secured the support of the Church, most of the major barons of England and Normandy and the City of London.

Matilda and her few supporters were stunned at the speed with which Stephen had acted. Outmaneuvered and with little backing (even her ever-so-loyal husband Geoffrey refused to provide military support for a campaign in England), Matilda had no choice but to accept the fact that Stephen had stolen her crown.

That might have been the end of the story, except . . . Stephen was a terrible king. He was weak and vacillating. The many, many mistakes he made in dealing with his recalcitrant lords and bishops drove people into Matilda's camp and opened the door for her to wage a campaign to reclaim her throne. She landed at Arundel in 1139 to try to do exactly that.

Thus began a 14-year civil war that so ravaged England that contemporary chroniclers referred to it as a time when "Christ and his saints slept." Neither Matilda nor Stephen was ever able to gain enough strength to crush the other. And their personalities were such that each time one gained the upper hand, he or she would blunder seriously, offending key allies and inadvertently building support for the opposite camp. The stalemate did not end until 1153, when an ill and worn-down Stephen agreed to a treaty—forced upon both sides by the war-weary magnates—that permitted Stephen to remain king for his lifetime and then provided that Matilda's son Henry would succeed to the throne. Stephen died in 1154 and Henry was promptly crowned Henry II. Matilda never did wear the crown of England.

◇◇

QUICK TOUR

To quickly orient you to the Tower and give you a fast overview of the many medieval features of this fascinating place, we will take you on a rapid stroll through the complex. This is no substitute for a thorough exploration, but it will serve in a pinch if you are pressed for time.

Before you even enter the Tower proper, you get a major shot of medieval history. As you emerge from the subway that leads from the Tower tube stop to the Tower of London, you will find on your left the remains of a medieval tower postern. These are the only remains of a postern gate in London.

You enter the Tower by crossing the second of three causeways originally built by Edward I. You pass through the ***Middle Tower*** onto the third causeway, which spans the now dry moat. (The drawbridge was removed many years ago.) Now you are standing under the portcullis of the ***Byward Tower,*** which has guardrooms on either side that feature fine stone vaults and hooded fireplaces. Here is where the password for entry into the Tower at night is still demanded by sentries.

From the Byward Tower, you pass into the ***Outer Ward*** onto ***Water Lane,*** which leads past the ***Bell Tower,*** started during the reign of Richard the Lionheart and completed during the reign of King John. From there, looking up to your left, you will see ***Queen Elizabeth's Walk,*** the section of the inner wall that Elizabeth I paced for exercise when she was imprisoned in the Tower by her sister, Mary, in 1554.

Moving straight ahead down Water Lane, you come first to ***St. Thomas's Tower*** on your right, named for Archbishop Thomas à Becket, later canonized as St. Thomas of Canterbury, who was a constable of the Tower before he had his falling-out with Henry II and was executed. The tower was built by Edward I as part of his defensive expansion of the Tower complex and contained the monarch's private quarters. Today, this tower is the entryway to the restored ***Medieval Palace.*** Also within this building is ***Traitors' Gate,*** the water entrance that gained its name because of the number of state prisoners who passed through it, including Anne Boleyn and her daughter, Elizabeth.

Across from Traitor's Gate is the ***Bloody Tower,*** originally known as the ***Garden Tower,*** where legend has it that Richard III's hapless nephews, the "Princes in the Tower," were killed. Next to the Bloody Tower is ***Wakefield Tower,*** the only part to survive of the king's quarters constructed by Henry III. As you pass through the Bloody Tower into the Inner Ward, look up at the portcullis that guards this entrance.

On your right in the Inner Ward is a part of the curtain wall built by Henry III that created an ***Inmost Ward,*** nearly doubling in size the bailey of the ***White Tower*** that looms just ahead. Just past the wall are the foundations of ***Coldharbour Gate,*** which then was the only entrance to the Inmost Ward that lay between the White Tower and Henry's palace.

To the left is the ***Tower Green*** and the execution block marking the spot where seven people, including Anne Boleyn, lost their lives because of allegedly treasonous acts. Behind the block is the ***Chapel Royal of St. Peter ad Vincula,*** where Anne Boleyn is buried. On the opposite side of the Tower Green is the Queen's House that Henry VIII built for her and where she stayed before both her coronation and her execution.

Along the wall to the right (facing the Queen's House) is ***Beauchamp Tower,*** whose great room walls bear the graffiti left by many state prisoners, including Lord Guildford Dudley, husband of Lady Jane Grey. He was held here in 1554 before his execution on Tower Hill and supposedly carved "Jane" into the wall.

On the other side of the White Tower are a remnant of the

old Roman wall and the ruins of the Wardrobe Tower built by Henry III.

You have now completed a quick external survey of all the medieval features of the Tower.

THE YEOMAN WARDERS

Assuming that you have adequate time to thoroughly enjoy the Tower, we recommend that you start your visit by joining one of the tours conducted by the Yeoman Warders—more popularly known as "Beefeaters." The existence of the Yeoman as a guard force at the Tower dates back to at least the 14th century. They were formally established as Henry VII's bodyguard force in 1485. Yeoman Warders are selected from the ranks of warrant officers or color sergeants in the British Army, Royal Marines or Royal Air Force. They must also hold Long Service and Good Conduct Medals.

Today, the Yeoman combine their duties as guardsmen with their role as tour guides. Lucky for us that they do. They are very knowledgeable about the history of the Tower and can provide some fascinating tidbits about its more lurid past. Participating in one of their tours will help orient you to the medieval features of the palace that you will want to explore in more detail on your own later. It is also the only way that you can get into the Chapel Royal of St. Peter ad Vincula, where Anne Boleyn is buried.* The Yeoman Warders also will talk some about the more recent history of the Tower, about which, of course, we don't give a fig. But you can listen if you want and pick up more information about those features from other guidebooks or the shops at the Tower. We are focusing on the more ancient—and, to us, more fascinating—parts of the palace's history. *(We assure*

*The visit to the chapel is the last stop on the guided tour. It is customary to tip your Yeoman Warder guide as you exit the building. A pound per person is sufficient.

you that the Crown Jewels exhibit has little of interest to the amateur historian of medieval and Tudor England.) Specialized tours geared for children also are available.

THE WHITE TOWER

After your guided tour is done, you will want to make a beeline for the White Tower, the oldest part of the castle except for the sections of the Roman wall that can still be seen. Originally dubbed the "Tower of London," this keep lent its name to the rest of the complex as the walls and buildings of the palace were expanded. It became known as the "White Tower" after it was whitewashed inside and out by Henry III in 1240.

William the Conqueror ordered the construction of the Tower to guard against attack both from the Thames and from the citizens of London. They had not been exactly welcoming in their response to his defeat of the Saxon King Harold. Actually, he built three fortresses for these purposes—the Tower, ***Baynard's Castle*** and ***Montfichet's Castle.*** Only the Tower survived the intrigues and civil wars of the Middle Ages.

The site selected for the Tower, in what was then the southeast corner of the City of London, was one of great strategic value. Both the Romans and Alfred the Great had previously maintained fortifications here because the site commanded the eastern approaches to the City from both land and sea. From here, all river traffic could be easily monitored. In fact, the old Roman wall was incorporated into the Tower's defenses, forming the eastern and southern (riverfront) sides of the original curtain wall.

Originally, this fortress was a simple earth-and-timber castle. With the old Roman wall safeguarding the castle from a river attack, the Normans guarded against a land approach by digging a ditch and creating a bank surmounted by a palisade.

Construction of the stone tower was begun in about 1078 and was directed by Gundulf, a monk of Bek in Normandy who later became Bishop of Rochester. It was not completed until about 1097, eight years after the Conqueror died in Rouen. It is 90 feet high, with walls that vary in thickness from 15 feet at the base to 11 feet at the top.

Since its completion, the monarchy has done remarkably little remodeling. All later exterior additions or alterations were demolished in the late 19th century. Granted, most of the windows were altered in the 18th century—except for two pairs of the original Norman two-light windows on the top story above the entrance *(Christopher Wren at work!)*—and an additional floor was added in 1490, an unfortunate change that reduced the height and, therefore, the drama of the king's great chamber on the second floor.

However, the entrance today is in the same place and of the same type as that planned by Gundulf. Garderobes (latrines) set into the walls can still be seen. Look for two of them in the wall of the former king's chamber adjoining the chapel on the second floor and at the end of the king's great hall.

When you cross the threshold of the entrance to the White Tower, you are probably entering what was originally the constable's hall. The room next to it probably was his chamber. The cross wall would have been unbroken except for doorways at either end. Originally there was only one way up to the next level—the turret staircase in the northeast corner of the tower. This was a defensive measure. If enemies somehow managed to breach the outer defenses, gain access to the bailey, climb to the entrance doorway (the wooden staircase would have been burnt by the defenders), and overcome the defenders stationed at the doorway, they still would have had to fight their way across the hall, through the narrow doorways of the cross wall, and up a spiral staircase. The staircase that now takes you to the second floor was added later to give direct access to the private chapel in the tower, St. John's. A 40-foot well in the basement of the tower guaranteed that defenders would never be forced out because of thirst.

St. John's Chapel is the only chapel in Britain (and one of

the few Norman chapels throughout Europe) that looks *exactly* as it did when construction was first completed. It was built of the finest limestone, shipped over from Normandy. Some of the drama of this beautiful and serene space has been reduced by the placement of a display about medieval and Tudor record keeping in the center of the chapel. But, by blocking out the jarring distraction of the display cases, you can still get a sense of what it must have been like when monarchs such as Henry II and Eleanor of Aquitaine would have been in residence at the Tower and walked from the royal chambers next door to attend morning mass in their private chapel. And the record-keeping exhibit does have on display a copy of the *Domesday Book* commissioned by William the Conqueror to assess the financial value of his new possession.

☞ Did you know?

Unlike his daughter Elizabeth, Henry VIII loved the Tower, despite the uses he made of it. He made fast tracks there the day his father died, April 21, 1509, and the first official act of his reign was dated from there on April 23. He stayed at the Tower often throughout his long reign.

When you leave the chapel, you enter what probably was the private chambers of the reigning monarch. Today, this space is occupied by parts of an exhibit spread throughout the building that explains the construction and history of the Tower. Exhibit features in this room include a silent film depicting the construction and adaptation of the Tower through the centuries and a model of the Tower as it looked in 1547, with a slide presentation describing its history. Both the film and slide show are shown continuously.

Next door, in the former great hall of the keep, is a display of armor that includes two different sets of armor worn by Henry VIII, a lance that belonged to Charles Brandon, Duke of Suffolk, and various other pieces of warmongering accoutrements dating primarily from Tudor times.

One note of caution in visiting the White Tower: the route marked out for tourists traps you into at least walking through every exhibit and exiting through a crowded gift shop. This can be a little disappointing if you are not entranced with arms and armor and would prefer simply to dip into the exhibits of particular interest to you. However, the interior features of the White Tower itself are so terrific that it makes the whole experience worthwhile.

PRISONERS OF THE WHITE TOWER

The first prisoner confined to the Tower was Ranulf Flambard, Bishop of Durham, who was once Justiciar for William Rufus. Flambard was noted for his lack of scruples in extracting unwarranted sums of money from the citizenry and keeping a sizable portion of it for services rendered. As soon as Rufus died in August 1100, Henry I had the crook flung into the White Tower, where he languished in lavish confinement in the Banqueting Hall. This locale was key to the story's end, for it provided Flambard with the means to escape. After a lavish feast in "honor" of his guards in February 1101, the prisoner tiptoed past his dead-drunk watchmen, lowered a rope from the window, slipped down the rope and was away—a much different outcome than that experienced by many later "guests" of the Tower.

One of the more grisly episodes of the Tower's history (although there are many) involves St. John's Chapel. From September 1241 to March 1, 1244, Gruffydd ap Llewellyn, son of Llewellyn Fawr, the first prince of a united Wales, and Gruffydd's son Owain were held captive in the former King's Chambers in the White Tower. They were confined by Henry III after that monarch's intervention in a Welsh civil war of succession between Gruffydd and his brother, Davydd. On the night of March 1, Gruffydd and Owain attempted to escape the Tower by knotting sheets together and lowering them from the window of St. John's Chapel. Gruffydd, who by all accounts was a large, heavy man, descended first. The rope broke and Gruffydd fell to his death. Reportedly, his head was driven into his shoulders by the fall.

Other notable prisoners of the White Tower included the King of France John the Good and his son the Dauphin, who began their stay there in 1358. Charles, Duke of Orleans, also came first to the Tower after the Battle of Agincourt in 1415 to begin his 25 years of imprisonment in England. The duke's take on life in the Tower was summed up by the statement "I have many a time wished that I had been slain the *[sic]* when they took me." A better poet than a soldier, he wiled away his time in confinement penning verse. So impressive were the results of his labors that Henry VII had them bound into a lovely illuminated manuscript that he presented to his new bride, Elizabeth of York. *(Ah, the old romantic! You can bet your bottom dollar the tightwad didn't pay for them!)* One of the illustrations in this book depicts the duke in his Tower captivity. Although the drawing was done in about 1486, it is accurate in showing the complex of that time. Among its highlights is the now diminished Wardrobe Tower. The manuscript is in the safekeeping of the ***British Library.***

◇◇

THE FIRST EXPANSION

After initial construction was completed by William Rufus, the Tower remained essentially the same until the reign of Richard the Lionheart. Certainly during the civil war that raged for 14 years in the 12th century between Henry I's daughter Matilda and his nephew Stephen of Blois, the owners were too busy fighting each other and neither held the Tower long enough at any one time to undertake long-term construction projects. And the Tower's constable at the time, Geoffrey de Mandeville, was too distracted trying to remember which side he was on at any point in the war to want to review architectural plans. We don't know what Henry II's excuse was for failing to undertake either defensive or lifestyle improvements at the Tower in the early, relatively calm years of his reign. Perhaps he was preoccupied with consolidating power, warily watching Eleanor of Aquitaine, and chasing other women. Of course, later in his reign, he was too busy fighting his sons in order to retain his throne to consider architectural projects.

While Richard was off on Crusade in 1189, his chancellor, William Longchamp, Bishop of Ely, began expanding the Tower defenses. The project was completed during John's reign, which began in 1199. This was when both the Bell Tower, named for the belfry on the top, and the Wardrobe Tower, built on top of the Roman wall, were constructed. For at least 500 years, the curfew bell was rung from the Bell Tower. The current bell dates from 1651. The Wardrobe Tower served as the central office of finance and administration for the monarchy of Henry III. Henry also stored all the items of the royal regalia in this tower.

Also as part of the renovation carried out during the reigns of

Richard I and John, the bailey around the White Tower was almost doubled in size and the castle was fortified with a new curtain wall and ditch on the north and west sides of the bailey.

Notable prisoners of the Bell Tower (each of the Tower buildings hosted some!) included Sir Thomas More, who was imprisoned here in a vault, reportedly in miserable conditions, in 1534. He was executed on Tower Hill in 1535 by Henry VIII and then buried in the Chapel Royal of St. Peter ad Vincula. Another Bell Tower prisoner was John Fisher, Bishop of Rochester, who occupied the top floor while More had the bottom. Like More, Fisher was imprisoned and executed for his opposition to Henry VIII's break with Rome.

LUXURY LIVING

It wasn't until the reign of Henry III (1216–1272) that the focus of construction projects at the Tower shifted, at least at first, from defense to luxury living. The furnishings became more regal while master artists in gilt and decorative tile created spectacular works of art that can only be seen in tiny bits today. A new palace was constructed next to a new riverside wall. The bailey of the White Tower was transformed into an Inmost Ward that was bounded by Coldharbour Gate, Wakefield Tower, Lanthorn Tower and the Wardrobe Tower. Access to the Inmost Ward was gained only through Coldharbour Gate, a twin-towered gatehouse next to the White Tower whose foundations can be seen today. The wall of the Inmost Ward that ran between Coldharbour Gate and Wakefield Tower still exists. Henry established a royal menagerie within this space that housed, at various times, three leopards, a white bear, a lion and an elephant.

Wakefield Tower, built between 1220 and 1240 as Henry's personal keep, is the only part of the old palace that still exists. Originally, this tower was named Blundeville Tower after John de Blundeville, who was constable when construction was begun. Restored in 1967, it is the largest tower of the castle, except for the White Tower. In Henry's time, the bottom floor of Wakefield Tower guarded a watergate that allowed access into the palace. Henry's private watergate was on the opposite side of the tower and can be seen today from Water Lane. The upper chamber of Wakefield Tower was Henry's bedroom.

The original ***Lanthorn Tower*** was built at the same time as Wakefield Tower and probably was constructed as quarters for Queen Eleanor of Provence. The tower was destroyed by fire in 1774. The present building is a Victorian reconstruction, but it does contain an introduction to the Inmost Ward and information about the Medieval Palace. Also on display are some 13th-century artifacts, including Edward III's Great Seal.

Later in Henry III's reign, after his relations with his barons totally deteriorated *(a polite euphemism for civil war)*, Henry's attention shifted back to defense. Again, the area of the castle was doubled, for the first time moving some 50 feet east beyond the Roman wall to expand the Inner Ward on all three landward sides of the castle. This placed the White Tower in the center of the extended palace grounds. A new curtain wall, dotted regularly by guard towers, was built and a new moat was dug. In fact, Henry built

☞ Did you know?

On May 17, 1536, Anne Boleyn was taken to the Bell Tower, which had a terrific view of Tower Hill. From there, Anne was forced to watch the executions of the five men with whom she had been accused of committing adultery, Henry VIII's excuse for getting rid of this now unwanted wife. Adultery with the queen was then considered a treasonous act—it posed the threat of tainting the line of succession.

The first of the men to die that day was Viscount Rochford, Anne's brother, George. He was followed by Sir Francis Weston, a 25-year-old gentleman of the king's privy chamber; Sir Henry Norris, Henry's Groom of the Stole (a singularly important office that required Norris's presence whenever the king had to relieve his bladder and bowels); William Brereton, also a gentleman of the king's privy chamber; and Mark Smeaton, the court musician. Viscount Rochford was buried in the chapel of St. Peter's ad Vincula. The others were buried in the adjacent churchyard, Weston and Norris in one grave and Brereton and Smeaton in another.

Anne herself was beheaded two days later, on May 19, on Tower Green.

most of the 19 towers at the Tower of London, including ***Devereux Tower, Flint Tower, Bowyer Tower, Brick Tower, Martin Tower, Constable Tower, Broad Arrow Tower*** and ***Salt Tower.*** Those open to the public today, in addition to the ones already mentioned, are the Salt, Broad Arrow, Constable and Martin Towers. These towers are part of a "wall walk" that lets you pretend you are pulling guard duty along the battlements of the eastern curtain wall built by Henry III. The Brick Tower, which was rebuilt in the 19th century, today features bathrooms for women. (The facilities have several times won "Loo of the Year" awards. We can't speak for the men's facilities.)

The most famous prisoner of the Salt Tower was John Baliol, the one-time king of the Scots who yielded his crown to Edward I after he was defeated in battle. He lived in the tower from 1297 to 1299. In addition, the Salt Tower and the Martin Tower are noted for being cells for Catholic priests during the reign of Elizabeth I. The priests left their mark for history by carving their names and some inscriptions into the walls. This ancient graffiti, along with a well-preserved original hooded fireplace and garderobe, can still be seen in the Salt Tower.

An original fireplace and garderobe also exist in the Broad Arrow Tower, once home to Sir Simon Burley, tutor to the young Richard II. Burley was forced to take refuge in the Tower during the Peasants' Revolt of 1381. The first floor of this tower has been set up today much as it might have looked when Burley occupied it.

The Constable Tower, which was also rebuilt in the 19th century, today features maps and illustrations of the Tower of London in all its different configurations as various monarchs have remodeled over the past 900 years.

Martin Tower, which was first rebuilt in the 17th century, is now undergoing reconstruction again. This time, the tower is being recreated as the Jewel House that it once was.

The strongest of the towers built by Henry is now called Devereux Tower (not open to the public), which takes its name from Robert Devereux, Earl of Essex, who was held prisoner in it before he became the last person to be executed on the Tower Green in 1601. The strength of the tower is probably due to the fact that it is located in the northwest corner of the Inner Ward—it faced London. *(Oh, those pesky Londoners!)*

Of the other towers built by Henry, the Brick, Flint and upper story of the Bowyer towers were rebuilt in the 19th century. The Bowyer Tower still features an original vaulted chamber at ground level. Tradition holds that it was in the Bowyer Tower that George, Duke of Clarence, the brother of Edward IV, supposedly met his death in 1478 by drowning in a butt of malmsey (a barrel of wine) after he was convicted of treason.

◊◊

GEORGE, DUKE OF CLARENCE (1449–1478)

George, Duke of Clarence, the brother in the middle between Edward IV and Richard III, was tried at Westminster Palace for treason in 1478. A petulant, reckless and greedy man, George had rebelled against his brother numerous times and been forgiven. He finally crossed a line with Edward IV, who had his little brother arrested and committed to the Tower in June 1477.

The fact that Edward finally lost patience with Clarence has been attributed to many different causes. Two of the more intriguing theories are that the duke was posing a threat to the throne by circulating rumors that Edward was a bastard *(we're sure their mother, Cecily Neville, was thrilled with this)* and/or Clarence had evidence that Edward was plight-trothed (considered as good as marriage in those days) before he married Elizabeth Woodville. If true, this would have rendered Edward's marriage to her invalid and made bastards of their children, thus barring them from the succession to the throne. Such a prospect would have been certain to enrage the volatile and ambitious Elizabeth.

Either of these scenarios would have been enough to earn brother George a death sentence and Edward made sure he got it. But instead of a public execution, Edward showed mercy to his brother and ordered a private death in George's chambers in the Tower. The story is that the duke was drowned in a butt of malmsey, his favorite wine. Not a bad way to go.

◊◊

This expansion of the Inner Ward and curtain wall by Henry III incorporated into the Tower grounds the previously independent Chapel Royal of St. Peter ad Vincula. The church is believed to have been founded by Henry I, who wanted a public place to pray to demonstrate his piety to his subjects. He needed to, given the strong public suspicions about the death of his brother William Rufus. Henry III and his queen, Eleanor of Provence, apparently used the chapel for the same purpose, but probably with a good deal more sincerity. Henry had two large stalls put in so that he and Eleanor could worship in comfort. Regular church services are still conducted in the chapel, which serves as the parish church for the Tower community.

The church was damaged by fire in 1512 and was rebuilt by Henry VIII, who then used it as a burial ground for his discarded wives. Both Anne Boleyn and Catherine Howard are buried there. Alongside them in the chancel is Lady Jane Grey, "the Nine Days Queen" who was executed by her cousin Queen Mary for having the temerity to challenge Mary's right of succession after the death of Edward VI.

Other notables who are buried in the church were tumbled in hastily—and headlessly—under the nave or chancel without any ceremony or name markers. When the chapel was restored in 1876, bones were found in the chancel. Among the remains that could be identified were those of Anne Boleyn. She was then reburied under the marble pavement before the altar.

EXPANDING THE DEFENSES

Known as one of England's greatest soldier kings, Edward I (1272–1307) concentrated his construction efforts at the Tower on defense. This may also have had something to do with the fact that Edward never truly enjoyed a very comfortable relationship with the Londoners. They had sided with Simon de Montfort, Earl of Leicester, in the civil war the earl led against Edward's father, Henry III. And the Londoners had insufferably insulted his mother, Eleanor of Provence, once when she left the Tower by barge on her way to Windsor. From bridges over the Thames and from the banks, the Londoners pelted the queen with rotten food and garbage. Edward never forgave either offense and made London pay dreadfully for both (London's mayor was imprisoned in brutal conditions for many years and a heavy financial penalty was exacted from the City). Prudence, therefore, may have been his motivation for strengthening the defenses of the Tower against the surly citizens of London. Starting in 1275 and ending in 1285, Edward spent twice as much on construction at the Tower as Henry did during the whole of his nearly 60-year reign.

Edward started by digging a new moat, filling in his father's old one, and building a new curtain wall along the edge of the moat. Today, this curtain wall houses the apartments of the residents of the Tower. Then Edward built two rounded bastions, one each in the northwest and northeast corners of the Outer Ward, for archers to cover the moat as well as the high ground of Tower Hill. Both of these bastions were rebuilt in 1683 to accommodate gun emplacements. The current names of ***Legg's Mount*** and ***Brass Mount*** date from that time.

Edward also redesigned the landward entrance to the Tower. He created an elaborate approach that consisted of three causeways, all with drawbridges, and three towers with portcullises. *(Was this guy paranoid or what?)* With Edward's redesign, the Lion Gate on Tower Hill became the only land access to the Tower. This gate opened immediately onto a drawbridge at the end of a stone causeway that crossed the moat to the ***Lion Tower.*** The second causeway was a short one that turned from the Lion Tower to the drawbridge and gate passage of the ***Middle Tower.*** Beyond the Middle Tower, the main causeway continued over the moat to the third drawbridge in front of the Byward Tower, which served as the gatehouse of the Outer Ward. With the exception of the Lion Gate, the Lion Tower and its causeway, the configuration put in place by Edward remains the main entrance to the Tower today, though without the drawbridges. Only the foundations of the Lion Tower remain. They are marked by a semicircle of stones in the cobbles of the entrance path to the Tower. Below this path is the pit into which fell the weighted end of the drawbridge that linked the Lion Tower to the outer edge of the moat.

The Byward Tower still serves as the sentry post where the password must be given before access to the Tower is granted to night visitors. You can still see one of the two portcullises that Edward had installed. The guardrooms on either side of the tower feature fine stone vaults and hooded fireplaces. In the room above the gatehouse, there is a wall painting of the Crucifixion that dates from the reign of Richard II. Unfortunately, the painting is partially obscured by a Tudor fireplace and, even more unfortunately, this tower is not open to the public.

Edward also did some redesign of the river side of the Tower. He had the river pushed back to build a new curtain wall with new royal apartments alongside the Thames. This created a new Outer Ward between his new curtain wall and the one built by Henry that is now called Water Lane. The new apartments were constructed in St. Thomas's Tower. A small chapel in the tower is dedicated to Thomas à Becket, for whom the tower is named. The new king's chambers were linked with Wakefield Tower by a passage constructed over the new Outer Ward. This passage was rebuilt in the 19th century. Today, these chambers, together with Wakefield Tower, are referred to as the Medieval Palace.

☞ Did you know?

The Lion Tower got its name because it became home to the royal menagerie. For five centuries, exotic animals, always including some lions, were on display here. This probably did as much as all of Edward I's elaborate defenses to keep unwanted visitors away from the Tower. The Lion Tower was leveled in 1807. Some of the animals still housed there then were sent to the London Zoo.

When you enter this suite of rooms, you find yourself in what was once Edward's Great Chamber and bedroom. This room has not been reconstructed in order to illustrate how much the buildings of the Tower have been altered since the 13th century. Here, you can visit Edward's strongroom, based in a small turret overlooking the Thames, and view next door to it the remains of the king's garderobe. Also in this room is a model of how it might have looked in Edward's time.

Next door is the Great Hall that was reconstructed in 1993 and set up to look much as it might have in Edward's time, including the oratory reglazed with colored glass. Guides in period dress are stationed in this room to answer questions about what life was like in Edward's time.

You pass from the Great Hall through the covered bridge built by Edward to link his new royal chambers with his father's former bedroom in Wakefield Tower. Here, graceful, elongated windows flood the room with light while an immense fireplace provides warmth and additional light in winter. The room has been set up as it might have looked when Edward I used it as an audience chamber. The throne in the Presence Chamber is a copy of the Coronation Chair in Westminster Abbey.

The infamous legend associated with Wakefield Tower is that it was here that Henry VI was murdered while at prayer on May 21, 1471. A marble tablet in the oratory supposedly marks the spot where he was struck down. Every year on the anniversary of his death, white roses with purple ribbon from King's College at Cambridge and three white lilies with light blue ribbon from Eton College, both founded by Henry VI, are laid on the tablet at 6 p.m. The truth is that Henry was most likely kept in Lanthorn Tower where the king's quarters were then located since Wakefield Tower had long since been converted into a records storage facility.

After construction of St. Thomas's Tower, access to the Tower of London from the Thames was gained through a gate in that tower, then called St. Thomas's Gate. It was later renamed Traitors' Gate in acknowledgment of all the state prisoners who passed through it, including Anne Boleyn and, later, her daughter, Elizabeth. The timber framing the building above the gate is from the Tudor period.

St. Thomas's Gate leads directly to the Garden Tower, an appendage to Wakefield Tower. As you pass through this tower into the Inner Ward, look up and see the portcullis that kept unwanted visitors out in Edward's time. On the first floor, you can see the windlass that operates the portcullis. The top story of this tower was largely rebuilt by Edward III. From its luxurious features, including a good fireplace, a large window that once had a window seat and a richly tiled floor, it is obvious that the room was meant for important guests. That never changed. Even when the Tower's "guests" tended to be more those whose visits were not by their own choice, the room was still reserved for those of high rank. Among those who had the opportunity to enjoy the room's amenities was Archbishop of Canterbury Thomas Cranmer, who was a Tower guest in 1553 and 1554, courtesy of Queen Mary.

The Garden Tower was later renamed the Bloody Tower. Restored in 1975, it features a re-creation of the rooms in which Sir Walter Raleigh lived while he was detained as a guest of James I from 1603 until his execution in 1616. *(We know we promised to stop at 1600, but this hangover from the Elizabethan period deserves mention.)* The Bloody Tower may have gained its name from the legend that maintains it was where the "Princes in the Tower," 12-year-old King Edward V and his brother, Richard, the Duke of York, were killed by their evil uncle Richard III in 1483. The story *(although we are sure we don't have to tell you)* is that the brothers were smothered by henchmen of Richard. In actuality, the boys simply were never seen again after they entered the Tower, supposedly to prepare for Edward's coronation. No one really knows what happened to them. However, the skeletons of two children were found under stone steps that originally led to the south front entrance of the White Tower when workmen were demolishing the staircase in 1674. For the past few hundred years, these remains have commonly been assumed to be those of the two princes. However, they have never been identified positively. Despite this dubious detail, the remains were officially reburied in Westminster Abbey as those of the princes.

Interestingly, the princes' older sister, Elizabeth, whose marriage to Henry VII united the Houses of York and Lancaster and thereby ended the Wars of the Roses, also died in the Tower.

She died on her 38th birthday after giving premature birth to a daughter, Princess Catherine, who also died a few days later. Elizabeth laid in state in the Chapel of St. John before being transported in an elaborate procession for burial in Westminster Abbey. Clearly, the Tower was not a lucky place for the descendants of Edward IV.

In addition to the legend of the princes, two other stories of violent death are associated with the Bloody Tower. The eighth Earl of Northumberland committed suicide—he shot himself—while he was a prisoner there to avoid being convicted of committing treason against Elizabeth I in 1585. Then in the reign of James I *(we know, we know. He just keeps popping up too close to Elizabeth!)*, Sir Thomas Overbury was poisoned, also while he was a forced guest there. This little incident raised eyebrows all over England because the king was implicated.

Edward also enclosed the Inner Ward on the west side, placing the massive Beauchamp Tower halfway along his curtain wall. This tower, which extends 18 feet beyond the face of the wall, replaced the twin-towered gatehouse built by Henry III. In fact, the new tower incorporated the foundations of the earlier building. It is named for Thomas Beauchamp, Earl of Warwick, whom Richard II had imprisoned there from 1397 to 1399. Because of its large accommodations, this tower often was used for prisoners of high state. During Mary I's reign, these included John Dudley, Duke of Northumberland, and his five sons. This tower is rife with graffiti from prisoners, all preserved for your reading pleasure. In Elizabeth's time, Philip Howard, Earl of Arundel, died in the Beauchamp Tower.

COMPLETING THE DEFENSES

Edward III continued his grandfather's work in strengthening the defenses of the Tower. He completed the curtain wall along the river from the ***Well Tower*** to the St. Thomas's Tower. He also constructed the ***Cradle Tower,*** which became the private watergate for the king when the monarch's quarters were moved in or near the Lanthorn Tower. The Cradle Tower is open to the public and has a display that tells the story of one of the few successful escape attempts ever made from the Tower.

THE TOWER GREEN

Prior to the Wars of the Roses, the Tower Green was simply a lovely place to stroll in the castle's Inner Ward. It was Richard III who introduced a more sinister use of this tranquil space. It was to the Tower Green that Richard ordered the hapless William Hastings to bow and stretch his neck on June 13, 1483, after an ugly scene during a council meeting in the White Tower. Hastings was accused of treasonous acts and Richard summarily ordered his execution. This set a precedent for six more beheadings to take place on the Tower Green. Five were women, mostly of royal birth and rank, who were accorded the dignity of a private execution within the Tower walls. They were also the only women ever to be beheaded for treason. Men were still sent to Tower Hill, where Edward IV had introduced "both scaffold and gallows."

Anne Boleyn was the first woman to be executed on the Tower Green. She was beheaded in 1536 after being found guilty of adultery (then considered a treasonous act for a queen) in a trial conducted in Henry III's Great Hall in the Tower. The elderly Margaret Pole, Countess of Salisbury, the last of the Plantagenet House of York, followed her in 1571. She was 70 years old. Next was a twofer in 1542—Catherine Howard, Henry's fifth wife, and Lady Jane Rochford, who had been Catherine's accomplice in her adultery. And finally, in 1554 came Lady Jane Grey, "the Nine Days Queen." She was just 17.

The last person to be executed on the Tower Green was Robert Devereux, Earl of Essex, who died in 1601 after mortally offending Queen Elizabeth.

The site of all these executions is marked now with a block and a tablet commemorating those who died. Legend has it that no grass will grow on the Tower Green because of the blood spilled there.

THE QUEEN'S HOUSE

Across the Green from the execution block is the Queen's House (the name changes depending upon whether the reigning monarch is a man or woman). It was built originally by Henry VIII as a wedding present for Anne Boleyn. She stayed here before her coronation and again while she was a prisoner awaiting her execution. Ironically, her daughter, Elizabeth, also was lodged in the Queen's House during the time that Mary suspected Elizabeth of plotting against her in 1554. No wonder Elizabeth hated the place! The Queen's House also was Catherine Howard's prison.

Today, the Queen's House is occupied by the Resident Governor of the Tower.

◇◇◇

THE CORONATION PROCESSION

Henry III inaugurated the custom of the monarch departing from the Tower of London to lead a procession through the City of London prior to the coronation ceremony at Westminster Abbey. Later monarchs embellished the custom. By the time of Richard II, this was a grand and glorious affair, conducted on the day before the actual coronation, when the procession moved from the Tower to the Palace of Westminster. Pious Henry VI introduced the custom of creating Knights of the Bath the night before the procession. The young noblemen who were so honored underwent a ritual bathing and then stood vigil all night in the Chapel of St. John in the White Tower. After this ordeal, they again entered the royal presence, where their knightly spurs were fastened to their heels and their swords were girded on by the king himself. The last monarch to follow the tradition was Elizabeth I. James I and Charles I skipped the ceremony because of plague threats. Charles II staged the procession but skipped the preliminaries, even creating the Knights of the Bath elsewhere. The medieval custom ended with him.

◇◇◇

WILLIAM THE CONQUEROR
(1028–1087; REIGNED 1066–1087)

It all began with him. His somewhat cloudy claim to the throne of England—and the force with which he backed that claim—changed the course of English history and has had ripple effects down through the ages. The social order, religious structure and chivalric code that he imposed on Saxon England, and that was later carried into Wales, Ireland and Scotland, established a way of life that still echoes through the patterns of life today, influencing manners, culture and lifestyles.

The only son of Robert, Duke of Normandy, William began his illustrious career in a somewhat dubious manner. He was illegitimate and he was a minor, just 8 years old, when his father died while returning from Crusade. Before he left on what he knew was a risky venture, Robert had persuaded the Norman barons to recognize William as his heir. However—and Robert well knew it—in a time when might definitely took precedence over right, there was no guarantee that the barons would keep their word.

For whatever reason—probably because they saw profit in a minority rule—the barons of Normandy went along with the scheme and acknowledged William as duke after news of his father's death in Asia Minor was received. Chaos then reigned, as the barons took full advantage of the general weakness of a minority rule, until the mid-1040s when William could, at last, rule for himself.

As soon as he took over, William exerted iron control. He had learned hard lessons during his minority and now exerted a military and political expertise that took many by surprise. He quickly brought all of his own barons under control and then turned his sights on his neighbors. In "glorious" campaigns, he defeated the Count of Anjou and Maine and the Duke of Brittany and deeply embarrassed his overlord, King Henry I of France. He accomplished all this in less than 20 years. Bored and ambitious, William began looking around for new lands to conquer. He found one in England.

His distant cousin, and childhood friend, Edward "the Confessor" ruled England as a childless monarch. *(Edward was more saintly than kingly and had taken a vow of chastity. Surprisingly, his wife agreed to it. We'll let you draw your own conclusions.)* Edward had sought sanctuary a long time ago in Normandy when the tide was going against him in the ongoing power struggles besetting England. That was when he and William became friends. So, when Edward faced yet another threat to his throne—this time from his mighty father-in-law, Earl Godwin—Edward turned to William for help. William, of course, did not promise support without exacting a price . . . that Edward name him heir to the throne of England. Edward agreed—or at least so William claimed. But the tide of fortune in England changed yet again and by the time of his death in 1066, Edward was on good terms with his Godwin relatives and so named his brother-in-law Harold Godwinson heir.

Needless to say, William was enraged. He alleged, with characteristic fury, that Harold had sworn an oath to support William as Edward's successor. To William, Harold was a perjurer and a usurper *(or at least that was the political spin)*. With a surprising show of papal support, William began to strategize a full-scale invasion of England. The lure of English booty—and their leader's track record of success—provided the necessary "carrot" for recruiting that was needed to attract thousands of French and Norman men-at-arms to the cause.

William set sail on September 27, 1066; his landing at Pevensy was unopposed, Harold and the English troops being engaged in quelling a separate northern threat. It was not until October 14 that William and his Norman leagues were confronted by Harold and the English at Hastings. Despite the long, bloody battle, the strength of William's archers and cavalry, combined with the badly depleted, demoralized and exhausted English troops (they had just endured a forced march), assured a Norman victory. King Harold and his brothers were killed at the Battle of Hastings, leaving the English nobility with no clear leader . . . and no clear choice but surrender.

William King, greets William, Bishop and Godfrey, Portreeve, and all the burghers within London, French and English, friendlike. And I will that both be worthy of all the rights which ye both were worthy in King Edward's day. And I will that every child be his father's heir after his father's day. And I will not suffer that any man may offer you any wrong. God keep you.

—from the writ of William I in favor of the City of London, 1066

This was a surprisingly congenial statement for one who had just smashed, burned and pillaged his way from the fields of Hastings through the Kentish countryside, down the streets of Southwark, and across the River Thames! One could say, however, that William could afford to be cooperative. Or one could say that William could not afford *not* to be cooperative. He was well aware of the power, wealth and independent nature of the citizens of London. Certainly, representatives of the most powerful and wealthy merchants of the City must have trotted out in force, making a great show of offering William their support. And even more certainly, all parties well understood that this was an offer that came with long strings attached: London might have to submit to William's rule, but he would have to accept that the Londoners were accustomed to a large degree of autonomy and respect. If William allowed London to go its own way, all would be well—in fact, financially lucrative for the Conqueror. If he did not honor that tradition, well . . .

Thus, William rode into London virtually unopposed. He was crowned King of England with all due pomp and circumstance at his cousin Edward's newly completed Westminster Abbey, starting the coronation tradition still practiced in England today.

Despite this display of mutual support and respect, William never really trusted, or liked, the Londoners. When in England, he preferred to stay at the luxurious abbey at Barking, 10 miles from the City center. But William's time in England was minimal. He spent most of his reign expanding and defending his empire on the Continent. But his in-absentia presence was never out of the minds and sight of the newly conquered nation.

Despite his promise that "sons would be heirs to their fathers," William promptly set about confiscating both private and clerical lands, establishing

Norman baronies and bishoprics with Norman nobles and Norman churchmen to assure that his English strongholds were maintained at all costs. Even in London, his influence was felt and his message was loud and clear. Although he might have assured the populace that the foreboding White Tower, Baynard's Castle and Montfichet's Castle were there for the protection of the City, few were naive enough to miss the point: rebellions by the locals would be promptly and violently suppressed.

◇◇

✝ All Hallows by the Tower

Bayward Street, EC3 (020-7481-2928)
Tower Hill Tube

The church is located at the lower end of Seething Lane across from the bustling Lower Thames Street Highway.

OPEN
10:00 a.m.–5:00 p.m. Saturday and Sunday
9:00 a.m.–6:00 p.m. Monday–Friday

WORSHIP
Sung Eucharist: 11:00 a.m. Sunday
Holy Communion: 12:15 p.m. Monday
8:30 a.m. Tuesday
12:35 p.m. Wednesday
6:15 p.m. Thursday
1:10 p.m. Friday
Evening Prayer: 5:30 p.m. Monday–Friday

ADMISSION
Free, but there is a charge to enter the undercroft

CONVENIENCES
Good tours

OF NOTE
From the garden, the view across the City to the infamous Tower Hill execution site is particularly impressive.

Located in the Barking neighborhood, on the site of an ancient Roman villa, the parish church of All Hallows by the Tower (a.k.a. All Hallows, Barking) dates back to 675 CE. At that time, the church was controlled by the Saxon Abbey of Barking, headed by St. Ethelburga. The current parish church was founded by Richard I, but the legend that his "lion heart" was buried beneath the altar has long been debunked.

You'll find the church of All Hallows mentioned in much of the literature dealing with the Tower of London. For centuries, the church was the final resting place for the unfortunate souls who lost their lives on Tower Hill. It also bore grim witness to the demise of the medieval City. It was from the high steeple that Pepys watched with horror as the Great Fire consumed London, "the saddest sight of desolation ever I saw."

The ancient church was virtually destroyed in World War II. However, the present church does have several points of interest to medieval historians, beginning with the north entry wall, which bears one of the building's original Saxon arches. If you are not claustrophobic, there is a small but significant display of artifacts in the crypt. These include chunks of Roman pavement and tile, pottery fragments, ashes left in the wake of Queen Boudicca's fiery rampage and a model representing Roman Londinium. Of particular note is the stark crusading altar of Richard the Lionheart that was transported from Athlit, Palestine.

Americans will want to note that William Penn was baptized and John Quincy Adams was married here.

Tower Hill

Trinity Square, EC3
Tower Hill Tube

The last stop on this Tower tour is Tower Hill, the execution site for many of the prisoners first held in the Tower of London and then buried in All Hallows or later in the Chapel Royal of St. Peter ad Vincula. A chained area now marks the spot where, over a period of almost 400 years, 125 notable people—most sentenced to death for political acts deemed traitorous against the reigning monarch—marched up a scaffold to lay their heads on the block and wait for the executioner to deliver the axe blow that would separate head from body.

Ironically, it was the common people who set the precedent for Tower Hill's use as a major execution ground. Some of the first deaths to occur there took place in 1381 during the Peasants' Revolt. The common folk who had stormed the Tower of London and dragged Richard II's court advisors from the sanctuary of St. John's Chapel then carted these luminaries, including the Archbishop of Canterbury, to Tower Hill. There, they were summarily dispatched.

While most of the people executed on Tower Hill were of the nobility, there is some evidence that the merchant craftsmen of London also enjoyed the same privilege granted their betters—at least when it came to death by beheading rather than hanging, a rather dubious honor, one would expect. In 1384, a shoemaker was beheaded for inciting insurrection against the current Lord Mayor Sir Nicholas Brembre who had been knighted by Richard II for the role he played in putting down the Peasants' Revolt. Brembre himself was later executed in 1388—but by hanging at Tyburn—by Thomas, Duke of Gloucester, for the mayor's ongoing support of his king against whom Gloucester was then in rebellion.

The last person executed on Tower Hill was the 80-year-old Lord Lovat, who was beheaded in 1746. The block and axe used for his execution are now on display in the Bloody Tower.

Among the "Who's Who" of the Middle and Tudor Ages who lost their heads on Tower Hill are:

- *Sir Simon de Burley,* tutor to Richard II (1386)
- *Sir Roger Clifford,* a Lancastrian supporter who fell victim to Richard III's efforts to secure his crown (1484)
- *Lord Guildford Dudley,* husband of Lady Jane Grey (February 12, 1554)

- *Sir Thomas More and Bishop of Rochester John Fisher,* who opposed Henry VIII's break with Rome (1535)
- *Thomas Cromwell* (1540)
- *Duke of Somerset Edward Seymour,* Lord Protector of England during the minority of Edward VI (January 22, 1552)

CONTENTS

5

Of Merchants & Men

The Might of Mercantile London

The ancient Roman wall aside, nothing defined the medieval square mile of the City of London as much as its entrepreneurial personality. Strategically removed from the center of the regal power at Westminster, the City—long a thriving commercial hub—rapidly developed its own feisty fiscal and political independence.

Throughout the rest of the kingdom, the monarch may well have been held in awe; such was not always the case when the court resided in London. Indeed, the Crown was often uncomfortably dependent on the City's merchants for financial support during the frequent periods when the royal coffers were running low—and the merchants of the City were not above using the Crown's dependence to their distinct advantage. Under King John, the City was able to negotiate its status as a "commune," a legal corporation with more than a modicum of political self-sufficiency. In 1215, John confirmed the City's right to elect its own mayor (in fact, they'd been doing so for nearly 25 years, royal "permission" be damned!). Numerous rights of the City were reconfirmed as part of Magna Carta. And if Mayor

Dick Whittington was willing to destroy the promissory notes that helped finance Henry V's decisive battle at Agincourt, there were just as many times when the City officials were willing to "remind" the monarchy which side of its bread was buttered.

Clearly, the citizens of the City of London wielded considerable strength, and they would flex their muscles impressively throughout the medieval era. Their independent thinking and pervasive self-interest played out dramatically during Simon de Montfort's 13th-century parliamentary reform campaign, as well as during the Peasants' Revolt of 1381 and the Wars of the Roses, when the decidedly pro-Yorkist City refused, in 1471, to allow Kentish troops to pass through London in order to join the Lancastrian forces.

The magnificence of the Guildhall (c. 1192), the continued ascent throughout the 13th and 14th centuries of the trade guilds (which not only regulated specific business practices, but also eventually controlled who qualified as a London citizen and who did not!) and the formation of the "elevated" livery companies with their impressive finery are all testaments to the pride-of-place held by London's enterprising merchant class. As you wander the streets in this chapter, be on the lookout for telltale names, such as Ironmonger Lane, Bread Street, Fish Hill Street and Milk Street . . . reminders of the important role the merchant and his money played in medieval London.

◇◇

GUILDS AND LIVERY COMPANIES

The trade and craft guilds of the City of London evolved from the ancient *friths* of Saxon times. These mutual-aid societies served as a combined spiritual relief and social service network. As commerce expanded and became more sophisticated, the role of the guild grew, eventually including job training for apprentices, product pricing, quality control and standards for the work environment, so to speak.

The earliest known guild was that of the Weavers. It was formed in 1155 under the rule of Henry II. Witnessed by Thomas à Becket, the Weavers' charter provided for nationwide control over their craft. In exchange, the guild paid an annual fee to the Crown.

The guilds' power grew in tandem with their role in the City's social life. They erected grand halls in which to conduct their meetings and hosted elaborate banquets on state and religious occasions. If you visit in November, you may be able to partake in the Lord Mayor's Show, a fine example of the guilds' showy pageantry.

In 1271, 12 livery companies were established from the most prosperous and influential guilds. Entitled to wear the lavish uniforms or "livery" of their profession, these companies also took part in the elections of the sheriff and Lord Mayor. Privileges such as these stirred jealousy and the livery companies often were the target of protests from the "rank and file" of the day.

As they vied for power and prestige, the guilds became increasingly testy. In 1399, a major riot took place between the Fishmongers and the Goldsmiths. The dispute was arbitrated at the Guildhall by the Lord Mayor. Heavy fines were levied on those who were responsible for the violence.

Still, guilds and livery companies made considerable contributions to their professions and society. To this day, they continue philanthropic support of educational and professional causes.

Billingsgate

Lower Thames Street, EC3
Monument Tube

OPEN
Not open to the public

. . . as bad a tongue as any Oyster-wife at Billingsgate . . .
—Shakespeare, *King Lear*

If your meandering finds you in the vicinity of Lower Thames Street, look for the striking brass weathervane sporting a large, spiky fish. This is the former site of the Billingsgate Market, for over 900 years the central site for seafood in London. A rough-and-tumble hub of sights, smells and swearing (the foul-mouthed fishwives were renowned), the market dates to Roman rule, but moved to the Isle of Dogs in 1982. Still, vestiges of the old commercial center can be seen. Now, if you're the rare soul who can face raw sole at the crack of dawn, feel free to mosey on down to the "new" Billingsgate Market as the catch of the day floats in . . . around 5:15 a.m. A vacation stop most of your friends are sure to have missed!

☞ Did you know?

The "stews" of medieval London—as brothels were commonly known—derived their name from the public baths that were once prolific in the Billingsgate area. The communal baths consisted of immense wooden vats filled with steaming water, where men and women together would literally "stew" *au naturel*. This ancient version of the hot-tub party invited all sorts of illicit conduct and became the foundation for houses of ill repute.

While you're in the neighborhood . . .

Stroll past the corner of Lower Thames Street and St. Mary at Hill. On this corner, archeologists discovered a Roman bath, believed to have belonged to a private residence, c. 200 CE. Other artifacts on this site indicate that the house was very likely occupied until the late 5th century. You may also amble along the Thames to the Customs House; incoming vessels have been rendering duty here since 1275.

Fishmongers' Hall

London Bridge, EC4 (020-7626-3531)

Monument Tube

OPEN

Fishmongers' is not officially opened to the public, although if the managers are feeling lenient, they will welcome your visit.

From Billingsgate, we continue with our fishy theme to the headquarters of the seafood merchants, Fishmongers' Hall. One of the oldest of the 12 livery companies established in 1271,

Fishmongers' actually is much older. It probably predates the reign of Henry II. If you are lucky enough to be admitted, you'll be able to admire the dagger that Lord Mayor Walworth, a Fishmongers' member, used to fell the rebel Wat Tyler in 1381. You'll also find a painted wooden statue of the heroic Walworth, as well as an elaborately embroidered Tudor funeral cloth.

◇◇

THE LORD MAYOR

The Lord Mayor of London is Chief Citizen of the City of London, second only to the monarch. The post originated in 1189. The first Lord Mayor, Henry Fitzailwin, held the office for two decades. In 1215, King John granted a royal charter to the citizens of London, awarding them the right to choose their own mayor, subject to royal approval. The charter is still held in the Guildhall. Since then, the Lord Mayor has played a significant role in the City's unfolding history. During the Middle Ages, the Lord Mayor was present at the signing of Magna Carta (1215); played a key role in securing the support of Londoners for the barons' revolt against Henry III (1263–1265); slew Wat Tyler during the Peasants' Revolt (1381); and became the subject of legend and song, as did four-time 15th-century mayor Dick Whittington.

Since 1422, the Lord Mayor's Show has been a spectacular London pageant, held every November. An impressive ceremonial parade culminates with the elaborate Lord Mayor's Banquet, held for newly elected officials and other distinguished guests.

◇◇

Leadenhall Market

Whittington Avenue, off Gracechurch Street, EC3

Bank or Monument Tube

OPEN

7:00 a.m.–4:00 p.m. Monday–Friday

You are now in the heart of Roman London and at the pulse of the medieval mercantile district. Originally the site of the old

Roman forum and basilica, Leadenhall Market opened to the food trade in 1309 as a market for poultry and cheese. Under Mayor Dick Whittington, the City appropriated the building for civic use in 1411 and later retained the services of the architect John Croxton to convert the structure into a granary with the hope of carrying London through periods of bad harvest. Despite the Victorian arcades, the street pattern maintains its medieval design.

Tip!

Browse past the stands with their barrows abrim with tempting fare from the exotic to the wildly extravagant. This is a great place for a midday respite, with shops, bars and a vibrant noontime atmosphere. We also found the Waterstone's bookstore in Leadenhall to be one of the best bets for historians, amateur or otherwise. A broad range of fiction and nonfiction books on the Middle and Tudor Ages, a helpful and sympathetic staff, and a willingness to accommodate special orders and overseas shipping make this a "must" stop.

The Royal Exchange

Threadneedle Street, EC2 (020-7632-0444)
Bank Tube

OPEN

Unfortunately, increased security precautions at the Exchange have made access to the interior of this building impossible, unless you have direct connections to someone who can pull some strings on your behalf.

The present Royal Exchange is the third to be erected on this site. The first was built by Sir Thomas Gresham in 1565. It did not survive the Great Fire and has been rebuilt twice since then. Gresham, offended that a business center such as London required its merchants to conduct their business in the streets, "like common peddlers," built the Exchange at his own expense. It featured a vast central plaza, surrounded by galleries where merchants and tradesmen could conduct their business. Upon her first visit to the Exchange, Elizabeth I bestowed its "Royal" title.

The great plaza of Gresham can still be enjoyed—you will find it between Threadneedle and Cornhill Streets. From here, you can admire the outside of the building; look up and you'll see the stone statue of Gresham on the east facade of the bell tower and the gilded weathervane sporting the grasshopper motif from Gresham's crest. Inside—should you be lucky enough to obtain a pass—there is a handsome Turkish paving from the original Exchange and a statue of Elizabeth I, which dates from Victorian times.

While you're in the neighborhood . . .

Stroll along Cornhill, site of the Roman forum and basilica. You'll pass two Wren churches, St. Michael's and St. Peter's Cornhill. The second, entered by way of St. Peter Alley, stands guard before a medieval maze of minute passageways surrounding a serene courtyard.

MERCHANT WEALTH

The City of London was a thriving world trade center during the Middle Ages and prosperity of the merchant class was commonplace. Onetime alderman and sheriff Gybon Maufield of Billingsgate revealed through his account books that diversity was instrumental to the success of most merchants. Maufield conducted lucrative trade in a variety of goods, from gemstones to millstones, and was a profitable moneylender as well. (Geoffrey Chaucer was one of his clients.) Alas, poor Maufield still managed to live beyond his means. He died penniless in 1397 and his estates were seized by Richard II.

A lost treasure . . .

The Jewry

North on Old Jewry Street,
left on Greesham to St. Lawrence Jewry
Bank Tube

>>>

The troubled history of the Jews in London begins shortly after the Conquest and ends less than 225 years later during the reign of Edward I—a remarkably short time in an era that spans nearly six centuries. During the early Middle Ages, canon law forbade Christians to lend money on interest, and in desperate need of cash, the Norman kings encouraged the immigration of Jewish moneylenders from Rouen. Although the Crown restricted the Jews from owning inheritable land, the community was able to hold wealth in the form of valuables such as jewelry, silk, fur and books, which had been secured as collateral on loans made to London's privileged families.

It is important to note that although they suffered the most severe persecution, the Jews were not the only minority burdened with discrimination. Early London was clearly xenophobic: mobs turned frequently on immigrants, particularly any group perceived as a threat to livelihood. So it was, for instance, that German tradesmen could function in the City only through the Crown's protection, retreating to the walled enclave of Teuton House each evening. This nationalism, combined with the religious fervor of a city committed to "the one true faith" and steeped in the lore of the Crusades, made it inevitable that life for the Jews would be painful.

Until 1177, Jews throughout England were required to bring their dead to London for burial in the one designated Jewish cemetery at Cripplegate—an extraordinary hardship for a family in, say, Lincoln or York, whose religious law required burial within 24 hours of death. In 1181, Jews were forbidden to bear arms, and in 1222 an act was passed that required all Jews to wear a visible "badge of shame" on their outer tunic. This, it was assumed, would prevent Christians from "accidentally" mixing with Semites. Professions were restricted as well. Aside from moneylending, the only legal work available to Jews was medicine. It is worth observing that rabid anti-Semitism did not prevent the nobility from specifically seeking out the services of a *Jewish* physician, even when gentile doctors were on hand.

By 1130, the Jewish community had established itself on Jew Street, now known as ***Old Jewry.*** The neighborhood would experience ruthless upheaval in years to come. Setting out from either ***St. Olaves Church*** or ***St. Lawrence Jewry,*** you can walk the Old Jewry and perhaps glean a sense of the community that, on one hand, enjoyed vast royal privileges and, on the other, suffered horrid royal persecution. Although records of that time note that several impressive mansions graced the Jewry, in fact a mere 16 families enjoyed any sizable wealth as a result of lucrative moneylending. The majority of families lived in far more modest circumstances, many in abject poverty.

The London Jewry was leveled by fire and 30 Jewish families were killed in the bloody riots that followed the coronation of Richard I in 1189. This was a backlash from the Christian community over a delegation of Jews who dared to "defile" the consecrated halls of Westminster Abbey with their presence while paying homage to the king. Hundreds more died when the community was ransacked during Holy Week in 1264; those who were fortunate enough to survive were forced to convert at knifepoint. In 1286, the entire Jewish population was imprisoned on suspicion of coin clipping; by then their professional activities had been so curtailed that even the better-off families faced the constant threat of starvation.

In the summer of 1290, Edward I issued his long-feared decree: England's entire Jewish population of 16,000 was to depart the country. London's Jews left on October 9, three weeks prior to the national exodus. Their moveable property was taken by ship down the Thames to Dover, there to await passage to Flanders. Their real estate—houses, cemeteries, synagogues—was never legally theirs and reverted to the Crown.

It would be 400 years before the Jewish people would return, as a group, to London.

While you're in the neighborhood . . .

The church of St. Lawrence Jewry was built in 1196, and had the peculiar distinction of being a defiantly Christian presence in the heart of the Jewish ghetto. It is worth noting that Thomas à Becket was baptized here in 1118. Destroyed in 1666 and rebuilt by Wren, the church features a stained-glass window dedicated to Sir Thomas More, once a visiting lecturer at St. Lawrence.

◇◇

THE HANSEATIC LEAGUE

Below Dowgate at the site of the present-day Canon Street Station is the ***Steelyard***, stronghold of the Hanseatic League. Jam-packed with lodging, countinghouses and warehouses, this three-acre plot was a Germanic ghetto, granted to the Hanse by Henry III as an enclave where German traders could live under their own law and custom. The territory was walled with gates that were carefully locked at dusk each evening.

The League brought a boost in business, but it also provoked fierce resentment from Londoners who felt their own trade opportunities with Scandinavia had been severely curtailed. So strong were the anti-German sentiments that Edward VI revoked the Steelyard's privileges and the merchants were ultimately evicted by his sister, Elizabeth I.

◇◇

The Guildhall

Guildhall Yard, off Gresham Street, EC2 (020-7606-3030)
St. Paul's or Bank Tube

OPEN

10:00 a.m.–5:00 p.m. Monday–Friday

ADMISSION

Free of charge

Note: There are two caveats to visiting the Guildhall. First, this is not the easiest place in London to find for first-time visitors. Rest assured your perseverance will be rewarded: this is a treasure trove for medieval enthusiasts. Second, you *must* phone ahead or risk disappointment. The medieval crypt is not always open to the public and the Guildhall's Great Hall often closes—sometimes on very short notice—for private functions. Let none of this deter you! The Guildhall is one of our very favorite sites.

>>>

Pause for a moment and reflect on the fact that this site has served as the civic heart of London since the Roman amphitheater welcomed citizens to the first public hearings, nearly 2,000 years ago. There has been a guildhall on the grounds since 1192; the original "cottage" was much expanded during the 12th and 13th centuries. The medieval building that exists today was commissioned in 1411 through the beneficence of the guilds, whose members recognized the need to reflect the City's proud corporate status. Perhaps the magnificence of Yevele's recently completed ***Westminster Hall*** prompted the guilds to commission his protégé, John Croxton, to conceive a rival structure, for the resulting building was indeed quite bold. Although it has been handsomely restored on several occasions *(with the obvious exception of the jarring modern extension that serves as the new entrance)*, the Guildhall retains some of the most significant medieval construction in England.

Your visit should begin with a meander through the Great Hall. This 150-foot-long chamber was once the most splendid in London, designed to impress and intimidate. After all, for centuries this was the site of grand state affairs and the most serious criminal trials of the day. The 1546 heresy trial of Anne Askew and the framing of Henry Howard, Earl of Surrey, in 1545 were two of the most talked-about proceedings during the reign of Henry VIII. It was here, in 1553, that "the Nine Days Queen," Lady Jane Grey, was sentenced to death for treason, together with her husband, Lord Dudley; both were beheaded before the year was out. That same day, Archbishop Cranmer also had a "guilty" verdict levied against him in the Guildhall. Although Mary Tudor interceded to save his life, he would ultimately be burned at the stake in 1556 on grounds of heresy.

Although the roof and ceiling have been restored (albeit to replicate the arched stone roof the medieval building was *assumed* to have had), the walls are original to the ancient structure. They are resplendent with the standards of the 12 major livery companies and windows bearing the names of every Lord Mayor since 1189. To the rear of the Great Hall you will note the carved wooden statues of the giants Gog and Magog, silent guardians of the Guildhall since the 14th century. The only completely original window is in the south wall. Mayor Whittington's bequest provided for the Great Hall windows to be glazed with stained glass. These colorful windows were smashed by the righteous Cromwellians, who disdained such ornamentation as "idolatrous." Around the perimeter are statues of famous London dignitaries, although we could find none from our period of history. Today, many state ceremonies and banquets are still held in the hall, including the time-honored Lord Mayor's banquet, eagerly anticipated each November.

Proceed now (with an official escort, please) to the two vaulted crypts below the Great Hall. The primitive western crypt dates from the late 13th century. The eastern crypt, supported by six columns of blue Purbeck marble, dates from the 15th century. With its nave and center aisles, this is the most expansive crypt in all London. It is especially known for its painted ceiling and large end windows, which supply an unusual amount of natural light. You may want to have your guide point out to you the other segments of original medieval architecture throughout the Guildhall. Interspersed as they are with newer renovations, they are hard to decipher, even for the most "professional" of amateur historians!

While you're in the neighborhood . . .

Be sure to allow time to peruse the Guildhall Library (Aldermanbury Street, 9:30 a.m.–5:00 p.m., closed Sundays). Founded in 1423 by a bequest from Lord Mayor Dick Whittington, who also purchased the Great Hall's marble floors and stained-glass windows, it was London's first public library. Brutally ransacked in the 16th century, the library was gradually rebuilt. Today, it houses 140,000 volumes and 30,000 manuscripts. It is an unparalleled resource for anyone interested in the history of London. Do stop by the adjacent bookstore, where every amateur historian will find endless ways to increase his or her library—and blow the travel budget! In this building, you will also find the Clock Makers' Company Museum, where you may take a look at a haunting Mary, Queen of Scots, skull-shaped watch!

◆◆◆◆◆◆◆◆◆◆◆◆◆◆◆◆◆◆◆◆◆◆◆◆◆

☞ Did you know?

Just down the road from the Guildhall, you'll find the chapel of the Mercers' Company, which is believed to be the birthplace of Thomas à Becket. In 1189, a hospital was founded here in his memory. There is also a blue plaque commemorating his childhood residence in numbers 87–90 Cheapside.

◆◆◆◆◆◆◆◆◆◆◆◆◆◆◆◆◆◆◆◆◆◆◆◆◆

Also while you're in the neighborhood . . .

The newly opened Guildhall Art Gallery may be of interest to you. As mentioned in our chapter *Laying the Foundation*, much of the original Roman amphitheater was discovered during the excavation for this museum. Unfortunately, archeologists have not yet completed the necessary work to make these fascinating remains accessible to the public. However, the museum's undercroft is crafted out of the remains of a portion of the 13th-century Guildhall crypt—worth seeing if you are interested in how these too-often-underrated ancient spaces can be reclaimed for contemporary use.

◇◇

LADY JANE GREY (1537–1554)

Often overlooked in England's "Royal Lineup," young Jane Grey (actually, Lady Jane Dudley) was, in fact, the ruler of England, albeit for a painfully brief period of time. So short was her reign that it has earned her the historical nickname "the Nine Days Queen." One would bet they were nine days that Jane Grey gladly would have omitted from her calendar.

Cousin of King Edward VI and of the princesses Mary and Elizabeth Tudor, Jane was Henry VIII's grand-niece, descended from his sister Mary's second marriage to Charles Brandon, Duke of Suffolk. Henry himself recognized the link as an important one. Overlooking other eligible relatives (such as Mary Stuart of Scotland), Henry named Jane Grey fourth in line to the throne in the unlikely event that all three of his own children should die without issue . . . or be officially barred from claiming the crown of England. This formal sanction of Jane's position in the line of succession was the powerful chit used by various manipulative nobles, including poor Jane's ambitious relatives, upon King Edward's untimely death.

Political intrigue played a role quite early in Jane Grey's life. Before she turned 10 years old, she was placed in the household of Henry VIII's sixth wife, Queen Katherine Parr. Shortly after King Henry's death, Katherine made the poor choice of marrying Thomas Seymour, one of the era's more unsavory schemers. The Seymour family, Lady Jane in tow, took up residence in ***Cheyne Walk,*** not far from the center of court politics. Seymour's brother, the Duke of Somerset, was the Lord Protector and Seymour shamelessly used his connections to the throne to his own best advantage. He wasted no time in purchasing the wardship of Lady Jane from her father, who was not without his own greedy ambitions: apparently Papa Grey believed that Seymour intended to marry Jane to her cousin, the king. This was an unlikely scenario, as the Lord Protector had a daughter of his own slated for the monarch's hand. Whatever the political machinations, they came to naught. For unrelated reasons, Thomas Seymour was found guilty of treason and executed in 1549; Lady Jane was returned to the loving arms of the family that had literally "sold" her, some short years prior.

For the next several years, Jane—a gifted scholar and a reputed beauty—devoted herself to her studies. Her quest for formal education brought her under the influence of some of the finest Protestant minds of the time. This gained her the attention and regard of "royal watchers," at home and abroad, who feared that the sickly Edward would be replaced, upon his death, by his rabidly Catholic sister, Mary.

Meanwhile, the power that had once been wielded by Thomas Seymour was now being vaunted by John Dudley, Duke of Northumberland. An ambitious Protestant, bent upon his own rise in power and determined to prevent a Catholic monarchy, Northumberland hatched a plan with Jane's father (now Duke of Suffolk) to marry their children and press a Protestant claim to the throne upon young Edward's demise. On May 21, 1553, Jane Grey was married—apparently much against her will—to Guildford Dudley at the Dudleys' London residence. It is believed that the stress of this forced wedding, coupled with Jane's strong disregard for her father-in-law, provoked a serious emotional collapse that kept Jane bedridden for much of her 16th year. Meanwhile, the senior men in her life proceeded with a full-court press to convince the dying king to name his cousin heir to the throne, eliminating any formal recognition of his sisters' rights of succession. They succeeded with little time to spare.

Edward died on July 6, 1553. Although well aware of the scheming being done on her "behalf," Jane was overwrought by the news; wearing the crown of England was not an honor to which she aspired. She was well aware of the dangers that she could face when recognized by the vast number of her Catholic countrymen as the usurper of Mary Tudor's throne. Yet "wear the crown" she did, for nine brief days: Sunday, July 10 to Wednesday, July 19. Although never officially crowned, she was hailed as queen by the Council, signed several official documents, dined in state and—perhaps her most queenly act of all—flatly refused to have her husband, Guildford Dudley, named king. In what would be an ironic twist of fate, she reigned from the royal apartments at the Tower of London, just yards away from the chambers where she would spend her final months as prisoner of state.

For, indeed, Queen Jane's days were numbered. England—Protestant and Catholic, alike—was, by and large, a pro-Tudor nation. The strong tide of sentiment was with old King Henry's daughter Mary. On July 19, Princess Mary rode in triumph into the City of London and was heralded, far and wide, as the official Queen of England. Jane Grey obediently—perhaps even gratefully—relinquished title, crown and throne, and rather naively looked forward to a peaceful, if not blissful, married life.

It was not to be. Mary Tudor was not eager to mete out a harsh punishment for her cousin—but once again, Jane fell victim to her father's lust for power. The Duke of Suffolk wasted little time joining forces with the Protestant Wyatt Rebellion, aimed at driving Mary from the throne in favor of a Dudley monarch. Recognizing that Jane's mere existence would be a lightning rod for future plots of this sort, she ordered Jane and Guildford Dudley tried for treason.

The trial took place at London's Guildhall. Both parties were found guilty and on February 12, 1554, husband and wife were executed. Nineteen-year-old Guildford Dudley, despite his father's pretensions, was not eligible for a "noble" death and was executed as a commoner on Tower Hill. Minutes after her husband's headless body was carried past her window, 17-year-old Lady Jane was executed within the Tower's precincts, a "privilege" reserved for those of noble birth.

Jane and Guildford Dudley are buried in the Chapel Royal of St. Peter ad Vincula at the Tower of London. Unfortunately, their deaths were just the start of the ongoing religious-based executions that would earn Mary Tudor the moniker "Bloody Mary."

◊◊

CONTENTS

6

Of Monks & Markets

Spirited and Spiritual: The Other Side of Town

he mighty merchants of the City may have wielded their fair share of clout, but life in medieval London was by no means "all business"! An equally important influence in the life of early London were the many monastic and conventual communities, which provided the City with both a spiritual and an architectural touchstone.

Monastic orders began to arrive in London in the early 12th century. By the mid 13th century, they had become an important part of the City's life, providing not only spiritual succor but intellectual stimulus and medical relief as well. Four primary orders of monks resided in London by 1247: the Franciscan "Greyfriars," the Carmelite "Whitefriars," the Dominican "Blackfriars" (all of whom received their "nicknames" from the color of their habits) and the Augustinian, or "Austin," Friars. The Carthusians and Benedictines played significant roles, but had fewer London monasteries than the four larger mendicant brotherhoods.

Whether it was to provide an atmosphere of relief from the

central City's hustle and bustle, or whether it was the luxury of great expanses of less expensive real estate, most of London's monasteries lay just inside—or just outside—the ancient wall. For the same reason, the City's great open-air market at Smithfield and the festival grounds of St. Bartholomew's Fair were sited in these outlying areas. We've chosen, therefore, to group them together in this intriguing chapter—on feast days and at festivals, exploring the spiritual *(or the spirited!)* side of life, this is the neighborhood where London's nuns and monks rubbed shoulders with the average City citizen. Enjoy your tour!

Christ Church and the Greyfriars

King Edward Street at Little Britain, EC1

St. Paul's or Barbican Tube

OPEN

The ruins of the monastic chapel and the lovely gardens are open to the public during daylight hours. The churchyard is delightful, even in the rain!

ADMISSION

Free of charge

In its time, the monastery of the Greyfriars (c. 1239), with its magnificent church, was an awe-inspiring landmark for first-time visitors to London. Located just inside the City wall at Stinking Lane in Newgate, the church's aristocratic elegance belied its unsavory location next door to a butcher's slaughterhouse. No matter. At 300 feet long and 89 feet wide, with marvelous stained-glass windows, the church was one of the loveliest in all of London. Consecrated in 1306, Greyfriars marked the trend away from somber, brooding mendicant churches toward ecclesiastic architecture that was light, airy and celebratory. So impressive was the new design that it would have a profound effect on the development of the Perpendicular style of design.

All this magnificence was due, in large part, to the philanthropy of three 14th-century queens, each of whom developed a special affinity for the Franciscan order, in general, and London's Greyfriars Church, in particular. After Queen Eleanor of Provence, wife of Henry III, was buried in the chapel, her daughter-in-law, Queen Margaret (second wife of Edward I), took on the expansive remodeling of the church that would eventually rival St. Paul's. Her work continued through donations by Queens Isabella and Philippa. The lavish choir stalls, an attraction in and of themselves, were a gift in 1380 from the Countess of Norfolk. Greyfriars was further enriched when executers of Mayor Whittington's estate bestowed ample funds for a large library, 28 desks and numerous double settles. Integral to the attractions of the church were its many graves—the remains of not only Eleanor, Margaret and Isabella but also Queen Joan of Scotland (sister to Edward III) and an impressive number of leading aristocrats and merchants were laid to rest at Greyfriars.

Royal blessings would continue to favor this church for years to come. During the Dissolution of the Monasteries, Greyfriars escaped unscathed. The church—then renamed "Christ Church"—became a Church of England parish church under Henry VIII. The monastic enclave was one of the five City sites protected by an act of Henry's that provided for the conversion of church properties into welfare institutions. Later known as Christ Hospital, it was rededicated under Edward VI as an orphanage. Soon it was expanded to include a school for humanistic education, featuring resident masters of grammar, writing and music. Christ Hospital would eventually become one of London's favorite charities until it was lost to the Great Fire. Rebuilt by Wren, the structure was largely destroyed in the World War II air raids. Today, you will find the Wren tower and ruined masonry incorporated into a delightful garden. Imaginative outdoor sculpture alludes to the arches that once defined the church's interior. The on-site signage explains, in brief, the ancient beginnings of Greyfriars.

◇◇◇

THE DISSOLUTION OF THE MONASTERIES

When King Henry VIII broke with Rome in 1553 in order to take a second wife, he went on to proclaim himself Head of the Church of England. This was not a title blithely granted by a citizenry that had always taken its Roman Catholic identity quite seriously. Henry soon realized that a firm hand would be needed to enforce his self-appointed authority. Partly to exercise control and partly to divert the riches of the Church to his depleted coffers, Henry embarked in 1556 on a ruthless attack on all religious orders. Within four short years, over 800 British monasteries were closed, their stately buildings and fertile lands reverted to the Crown or given as tokens of appreciation to the king's "yes men."

The Dissolution of the Monasteries symbolizes the end of London's Middle Ages. An entire way of life was abolished, almost overnight. This was a multiple loss—physical, spiritual and social. Many of London's most striking medieval buildings were torn down and in their stead rose ostentatious mansions, more often than not built from recycled monastery stone. Of greater impact was the loss of social services provided by the monks. The monastic houses were refuges for society's outcasts—the sick, the poor, the elderly. Who would tend to these people now? There was a great cultural loss as well . . . no more worldly travelers seeking a night's comfortable lodging in exchange for news and lore gleaned from foreign lands . . . no more flourishing societies of scholars and writers drawn to monastic halls for informal debate.

In time, a slow, nonchalant rebuilding of social institutions and houses of worship would evolve. A case of "too little, too late," these newer foundations would never command the central role that the monasteries had served in London society.

◇◇◇

Ghost Alert!

There is a very good reason for scheduling your visit to Christ Church/Greyfriars during daylight hours. Not only will you find the gates to the lovely garden unlocked, but you will also avoid a frightening encounter with one of London's most notorious ghosts. It has long been alleged—despite her endowments to the church—that the tormented spirit of the wretched Isabella, "She-Wolf of France" and wife of the ill-fated Edward II, haunts the churchyard. Her clutching arms spring from the ground with a terrible rattling of chains. Consider yourself warned.

✝ St. Bartholomew the Great Priory and Hospital

Little Britain at West Smithfield, EC1 (020-7606-5171)
Barbican or Farringdon Tube

>>

OPEN

8:30 a.m.–4:30 p.m. Monday–Friday (closed Mondays in August)
10:30 a.m.–1:30 p.m. Saturday
2:00–6:00 p.m. Sunday (aside from services)
Bell Practice: 6:30 p.m. Thursday
Choral Service: 6:30 p.m. Sunday
You may also wish to join a guided Historic St. Bart's and Smithfield Tour, 2:00 p.m. on summer Fridays. Meet at the main gate of St. Bartholomew's Hospital. Fee: £4 adults, children free.

WORSHIP

9:00 a.m., 11:00 a.m. and 6:30 p.m. Sunday

ADMISSION

Donation suggested

The priory church of St. Bartholomew and the accompanying St. Bartholomew's Hospital are the surviving features of the four-building monastery founded here in 1123. As you enter the grounds, across a square directly opposite from the Smithfield Market, the hospital is straight ahead. The priory church is to your left, through the great 13th-century arch with its Tudor gatehouse above. This is a "*not to be missed*" site for any amateur historian, particularly if you are interested in the Norman period.

>>

The oldest surviving parish church in London* and the most complete example of Norman architecture is the church of St. Bartholomew the Great at Smithfield. At the time of its consecration, it was also the largest church in London—bear in mind that the nave once stretched from the present interior all the way to the gatehouse in Little Britain, and you'll have some notion of how "great" St. Bartholomew truly was.

*St. John's Chapel in the White Tower (Tower of London) actually predates St. Bart's, but it is not a complete church building and never functioned as a public house of worship.

St. Bartholomew was the result of malaria-induced dreams suffered by Henry I's onetime court jester, Rahere. So grateful was the clown for being saved from the disease's ravages *(as well as from assumed eternal damnation!)* that he established a monastery on ground donated by the king. Just for good measure, he joined the Augustinian order himself.

The original chapel—over 300 feet long—was largely demolished during the Reformation, but today's church still bears the vestiges of Norman roots. The choir, with its massive Norman arches, the ambulatory and the rebuilt 15th-century Lady Chapel are still intact. Here you will find London's only medieval baptismal font, as well as Rahere's elaborately painted tomb and effigy. Of further interest is an early-16th-century oriel window on the south side of the chapel, which allowed one Prior Bolton to watch mass without having to actually attend the service. See if you are able to find his *rebus** on the chancel panels. A harder-to-find tribute to Roger, Archbishop de Walran, Treasurer of England, Secretary to Edward III and Archbishop of Canterbury under Richard II, is located in the recess of the north ambulatory. You will also find handsome Tudor memorials, including that of the Elizabethan courtier Walter Mildmay, founder of Emmanuel College, Cambridge.

☞ Did you know?

After the Dissolution, the Lady Chapel at St. Bart's became a private residence. Two hundred years later, it served as the printing shop where young Benjamin Franklin was employed. In the north transept of the choir, the walls are still black from its days as a blacksmith's forge.

Rahere's fever-induced visions of Hades must have been vivid in the extreme. Never feeling that he had done quite enough to ensure salvation, he went on to found St. Bartholomew's Hospital, which has been in service ever since. When the leader of the Peasants' Revolt, Wat Tyler, was stabbed at Smithfield by Mayor Walworth, the kindly Augustinians carefully

*A visual play on words or a pun; in this case, the rebus depicts an arrow (bolt) piercing a cask (tun). The Fleet Street Tavern, The Bolt in Tun, takes its name from Prior Bolton's rebus.

bandaged his wounds, only to watch him be dragged off and beheaded *(an injury that eluded their medical expertise!)*. After the Dissolution, the hospital went secular and was saved from collapse by Henry VIII. The only statue of this king to be found in London can be seen above the Henry VIII gate, the main hospital entrance on West Smithfield Street. St. Bartholomew's Hospital was later run by Dr. Rodrigo Lopez, Elizabeth I's personal physician. He would be hanged at Tyburn in later years for allegedly attempting to poison his queen.

☞ Did you know?

Something about the Church of St. Bartholomew strike you as . . . *familiar?* Well, if you're a movie buff, chances are you're recalling one of the several interior scenes shot here in recent film history. Two of our favorites, *Shakespeare in Love* and *Four Weddings and a Funeral,* make lovely use of the romance and mystery of St. Bartholomew.

St. Bartholomew's Hospital has its own chapel on the grounds. It is known as St. Bartholomew the Lesser. This heavily restored building is best appreciated from the outside.

There are a variety of good guidebooks available at St. Bartholomew's, including a very clever children's guide and a brief biography on the life of Rahere.

Ghost Alert!

Ever the jester, the spirit of Rahere is a frequent visitor to both the priory church and the hospital of St. Bart's. He is often sighted on the stairway of the medical building, where he oddly appears to be floating several feet above the risers.

MEDIEVAL HOSPITALS

Over 850 years old, St. Bart's Hospital was one of London's two large and influential medieval hospitals. The other, St. Thomas's, dedicated to Thomas à Becket, was located at the foot of London Bridge in Southwark. Medieval hospitals may have been limited in their ability to abate or cure disease, but the scope of their services stretched well beyond health care. Hospitals truly provided *hospitality,* tending to the needs of travelers and pilgrims, as well as the country's poor, orphaned, homeless and outcast citizens. Doctors, as such, were not part of the picture. Medieval hospitals were run by monks and nuns. This was a logical extension of the belief that sickness and misfortune were the result of sin and could be cured through the intercession of a holy person.

AUGUSTINIANS

Known as the "black canons," the Augustinians enjoyed a more flexible rule than many religious orders. They were encouraged to work outside their cloister and served as parish priests for neighborhood churches, ran almshouses and administered care in hospitals. They enjoyed great popularity in the 12th century with Henry I's consort, Matilda, acting as their special benefactor. Some believe that it was the very spiritual Matilda who first guided her husband's jester, Rahere, toward the religious life.

The three great Augustinian priories of London's Middle Ages were St. Mary Overie (c. 1106, now Southwark Cathedral), Holy Trinity at Aldgate (c. 1108) and St. Bartholomew's. Holy Trinity was founded by Queen Matilda, who also founded a leper hospital at St. Giles.

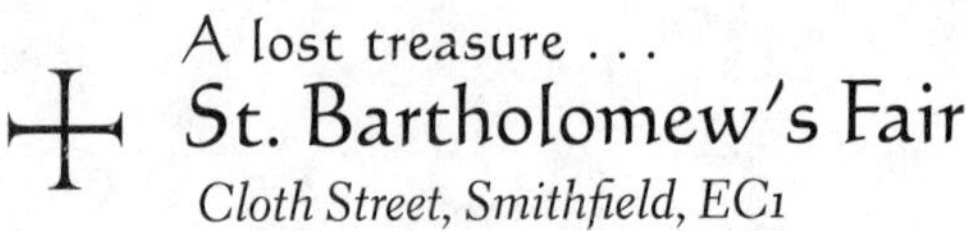

A lost treasure . . .

St. Bartholomew's Fair

Cloth Street, Smithfield, EC1

As you leave St. Bartholomew's Church, turn right and then right again. You are now in the vicinity of another of Rahere's contributions to Smithfield, the wildly popular St. Bartholomew's Fair. Unfortunately, you will have to rely on your imagination to conjure up the image of these "merrie" days; no vestiges of the festival site remain. Henry I granted the enterprising prior the charter to hold an annual fair on August 24, the feast of the monastery's patron saint, and to retain tolls collected from the event for the benefit of the hospital and priory. Lasting three full days, it was soon the biggest cloth fair in London, with merchants from throughout England and the Continent vying for clientele. One might say it was the forerunner of today's church bazaar, only tons more fun, for eventually the serious enterprise of the fabric trade gave way to a carnival of minstrels, fire-eaters, mimes and players. As you can well guess, St. Bartholomew's Fair was suppressed by the Puritans and ultimately disbanded in 1855.

◇◇◇

THE PEASANTS' REVOLT

When the mighty King Edward III died in 1377, he left a prodigious number of sons. Unfortunately, his eldest male child, known as the Black Prince, had predeceased the monarch by several years. Due to the complex laws of primogeniture, the Crown, which one would assume would pass to second-son Lionel of Clarence, was instead inherited by the Black Prince's eldest boy, 10-year-old Richard.

Seldom had the monarchy been in such a precarious position. Confidence in the throne was at low ebb. The imposition by parliament of a highly unpopular poll tax during that same year led to widespread unrest. The attempt to impose a second poll tax in 1381 turned underground rumblings into a proletarian revolt. Known to history as the Peasants' Revolt, it incited violence from Hampshire to Cheshire, but it was in London that the revolt came to a head in a climax that, ironically, was Richard II's proudest moment.

Led by an Essex priest, Jack Straw, and an ex-soldier, Wat Tyler, the rebels besieged the capital, hoping to confront the floundering government with their multiple complaints. The citizens of London apparently put up nominal resistance in the face of the angry mob, estimated by one observer as a horde of 60,000 (larger than the population of the City itself, which may have been one reason the rebels received cooperation). There was little love between the City and the Court at the time, and the City was further divided by its own internal battles, of both an economic and a cultural nature. Tradition holds that it was an alderman who let down the London Bridge drawbridge, allowing the rebels to surge across the Thames. A second City father stood passively by as the Essex brigade rushed through the open Aldgate. The rebellion swelled as London's own disgruntled riffraff joined the mob.

Rampant confusion and mayhem were the inevitable result. Seven Flemings were murdered in cold blood at ***Clerkenwell,*** where the church, hospital and palace of the Knights Hospitaliers were demolished. Thirty-five more Flemings and Lombards—singled out because of their foreign blood and roles as moneylenders—suffered a similar fate at St. Martin's Vintry. The fact that this was the center of the wine trade, and libations were flowing freely, may well have contributed to the senseless acts. The Fleet and other London prisons were emancipated and their inmates drafted for the cause. At the ***Temple,*** rooms were reduced to rubble and countless reams of civil records destroyed.

Just west of the City, along the road to Westminster stood the sumptuous riverside palace, ***Savoy,*** home of King Richard's powerful and controversial uncle, ***John of Gaunt.*** The Savoy was all too tempting a target for a crowd run amok. The duke himself was engaged in a Scottish mission, and hence avoided what almost certainly would have been his assassination. His valuable plate and extravagant furnishings were turned into a blazing bonfire; his jewels were trampled and consigned to the Thames. So despised was Gaunt that his attackers refused to profit from his treasure. One poor soul who did attempt to loot was tossed live onto the bonfire by his comrades. Thirty more rabble-rousers died when the Savoy wine cellar collapsed in a heap of burning rubble—a box of gunpowder carelessly heaped onto the blaze brought down the Great Hall and rendered the Savoy a shambles.

From the safety of the Tower, 14-year-old Richard II made a bold gesture: he sent word that he would meet the rebels in the open meadows of Mile End, just to the east of the City walls. Proud, courageous and convincing, he promised amnesty for all, as well as a charter of stunning reforms that would have abolished the distinction between serfs and freemen. Appeased, the Essex brigade began to head for home, but back in the City of London, fighting escalated. A separate band of malcontents stampeded the Tower, hauling Simon Sudbury, the unpopular Archbishop of Canterbury, and Sir Robert Halles, the Royal Treasurer, to the Tower Hill execution grounds. As the government had done to the criminal class time and again, the criminal class beheaded these scapegoats and placed their severed heads atop the spikes of London Bridge. A frightened young king sought overnight refuge in the royal wardrobe near ***Blackfriar's Monastery,*** and planned his response.

Upon the morrow, King Richard again faced a rebel mob, this group led by Wat Tyler. What exactly transpired between young Richard and Tyler on the grassy planes of Smithfield is not known for certain, but the situation was tense enough that London Lord Mayor William Walworth sprung to action, stabbing Tyler to death. Walworth's worthy dagger is proudly displayed at Fishmongers' Hall. In the ensuing mayhem, the youthful monarch rode into the fray and, standing tall in his stirrups, his reedy voice clear above the din, declared, "I will be your chief and captain!" Once again, the peasants were appeased—or perhaps they saw the writing on the wall, with their leader lying hacked to death on the ground. In any event, they allowed themselves to be led away to Clerkenwell, where they wisely dispersed.

Shocked out of its complacency, the beleaguered government regrouped. Richard's promises—whether sincere or false in intent—were overturned. The rebel leaders were aggressively hunted and hanged without trial. Jack Straw met his demise at Smithfield. John Ball was hung, drawn and quartered at St. Albans in the presence of the king. Mayor Walworth was elevated to knighthood.

And not another word about poll taxes was spoken during the reign of Richard II.

◇◇

Tip!

If the "common folk" are of particular interest to you, check the London Public Records Office, where you can see several fine examples of seals used by peasants in the Middle Ages to authenticate important documents. If you were not lucky enough to be a knight, only three motifs were available for you to use—flora, fauna and elaborate Christian crosses. By the 1300s, as a handful of peasants began to acquire rudimentary reading skills, mottos began to grow in popularity; some were religious, but a great many were bawdy. On periodic display is a 1225 document between the Earl of Chester and the people of Freiston and Butterwick, adorned with no fewer than 50 peasant seals.

◇◇◇

SMITHFIELD

Those fascinated with the more somber side of medieval and Tudor history will want to devote some time exploring the ancient market area of Smithfield *(although we strongly recommend a perfume-laced handkerchief or the requisite pocket-full-o'-posies . . . the smell around the Smithfield market is definitely one of the more memorable "aromas" you'll encounter on your trip!).*

It isn't merely 900 years of slaughtered cattle that taints Smithfield's history with blood. The bustle and trade of the livestock market were, at times, a mere backdrop for carnage of a more gruesome nature. Here, Scots patriot William Wallace was hanged, drawn and quartered: a plaque in his honor hangs on the exterior wall of St. Bartholomew's Hospital, not too far from the main hospital entrance. *(Does anyone else find it odd that a nation first inflicts a terrible traitor's death upon a man and then "honors" him with a plaque?)* Here, too, Wat Tyler was knifed to death by the Lord Mayor of London during the climax of the 1381 Peasants' Revolt. And it was here that countless Protestant martyrs were burned at the stake for heresy during the reign of Bloody Mary Tudor.

Meanwhile, jousting, tournaments, the annual St. Bartholomew's Fair and the friendly banter of the marketplace provided some of the merrier moments of entertainment on these "smooth fields." Today, Smithfield is Europe's largest meat market.

◇◇◇

✝ Clerkenwell Priory and St. John's Gate

St. John's Lane at St. John's Square, EC1 (020-7253-6644)
Farringdon Tube

OPEN
9:00 a.m.–5:00 p.m. Monday–Friday
10:00 a.m.–4:00 p.m. Saturday
(Museum hours)

TOURS
Guided tours 11:00 a.m. and 2:30 p.m. Tuesday, Friday and Saturday

ADMISSION
Donation suggested

Your next stop after leaving St. Bartholomew's is yet another priory with a rather different history: the priory of ***St. John's of Jerusalem,*** London headquarters for the Knights of St. John, also known as the *Hospitaliers.* To find the priory, proceed down Charterhouse Road, pass the meat market and turn right onto St. John's Street. This was once the ancient highway north and headquarters for the butchers' trade, where countless taverns and meat mongers stood cheek-to-jowl, a stimulating cacophony for the intrepid traveler. Bear left into St. John's Lane and just ahead you'll spot ***St. John's Gate.***

Built by Prior Dorcas in 1504, the gatehouse has served a wide range of purposes, including providing offices for Elizabeth I's Master of the Revels. Together with the 12th-century crypt from the priory church, this is the last vestige of the splendid monastery once dubbed "the glory of northwest London." We think the view is even more impressive from the other side. Turn left along Briset Lane, right onto Britton Lane and look closely for St. John's Passage, well hidden on your right. Follow this into St. John's Square and you're now at the heart of the former priory. Looking left, across Clerkenwell Road, you'll see the modern priory church with the gatehouse to its left.

Like the Temple Church, the original 12th-century church was modeled after the round Church of the Holy Sepulchre in Jerusalem. The peasant rebel Wat Tyler destroyed the original 12th-century circular church and much of the priory in 1381. It was quickly rebuilt and was the home of Henry Bolingbroke in the weeks preceding his coronation as Henry IV. Today, only the crypt remains, although the "footprint" of the entire ancient church is marked on the pavement outside. Assuming you have joined the requisite tour, you'll find the cool, dark crypt particularly inspiring. There are several exemplary memorials, including an alabaster effigy of Don Juan Ruiz de Vegara, the 16th-century Proctor of Castile, and the tomb of William Watson, the last English prior before the Dissolution.

☞ Did you know?

A number of the streets in the Clerkenwell vicinity bear names directly linked with the priory's medieval past. Aylesbury Street once stood within the priory's precincts, before becoming the property of the Earls of Aylesbury. Turnmill Street is named for the numerous watermills located on either bank of the Holborn that were once owned by St. John's. Vineyard Walk is linked to the ancient nunnery of St. Mary's Clerkenwell.

The name Clerkenwell refers to the many bountiful wells that blessed the community from London's earliest beginnings. This was the site chosen by the Guild of Parish City Clerks for the Easter season passion plays, and the moniker "Clerks' Well" lingered long after the theatricals became passé.

The ground floor of the gatehouse contains an interesting museum display on the history of the Hospitaliers. As with the crypt, the only access to the West Tower is by guided tour. Here, the Tudor-era stained-glass windows are of particular interest and the docents provide a thorough insight into the property's role in history.

THE KNIGHTS HOSPITALIERS

Commonly known as the Knights Hospitaliers, the Knights of St. John of Jerusalem were founded in the 11th century for the purpose of providing hospice and traveler's aid for pilgrims en route to the Holy Land. By the 12th century, their role had become more militaristic and the warrior monks went on to play an active role in the Crusades. Eventually, they would come to control Rhodes and Malta. The Norman knight John de Briset founded the London chapter of the organization on the site of Clerkenwell Priory in 1110. The Hospitaliers were suppressed during the Reformation, but were revived in the 19th century and are still active—although in a somewhat redefined role: the Hospitaliers provide valued volunteer ambulance services at major public events throughout the United Kingdom.

Charterhouse

Charterhouse Square, EC1 (020-7253-9503)
Barbican Tube

OPEN

2:15 p.m. Wednesday, April–July
To join the tour of the interior, meet inside the main archway on Charterhouse Square. You may also attend service in the chapel on Sundays at 9:45 a.m. Alternatively, apply in writing to *The Master* for a private tour of the facilities.

ADMISSION

Fee charged

Grim and grimmer. That's the story of Charterhouse, although not *entirely.* The property, once owned by St. Bartholomew's Hospital, was one of the largest plague pits (a mass grave for victims of the bubonic plague) in London, before Sir Walter de Manny founded his Carthusian monastery here in 1371 with the express purpose of offering prayers for victims of London's Black Death. Famous, if transient, residents included Sir Thomas More (long before he was beheaded) and Thomas Cromwell *(we know what happened to him!).*

Perhaps the most gruesome scenario involving Charterhouse transpired during the reign of Henry VIII, when the Carthusians made the brave, but unfortunate, decision not to recognize His Grace as the Supreme Head of the Church of England. In May 1535, the Prior of the Charterhouse, John

Houghton, and four of the monks, after refusing to swear to accept Henry's supremacy over the Church, were dragged by horses through the streets of London. They were hanged at Tyburn until they were half-choked, then cut down and revived with vinegar so they would be fully awake while the rest of the sentence was carried out—castration, disembowelment and decapitation. Their bodies were then cut into quarters, which were publicly displayed as a warning to others that they best adopt Henry's new religion, fast. Henry even went so far as to have one of Prior John's severed arms nailed to the Charterhouse gatehouse so the surviving monks would have a daily reminder of the cost of failing to comply with the new order of religious life.

Despite this savagery, the warnings did not work and still other Carthusian monks refused to acknowledge Henry's supremacy. So Henry upped the ante. This time, just one month later, four additional Charterhouse monks were chained upright to stakes, denied food and water and left to rot in their own filth until they starved to death—a very slow, agonizing death that appalled the citizens of London and did no good for Anne Boleyn's reputation. She was blamed for all the barbaric acts Henry ordered to establish the new religious order. Altogether, a total of 15 Charterhouse monks and lay brothers were executed over a period of three years before the slaughter stopped with the submission of the surviving monks in November 1537. Most of the monastic buildings were then torn down.

For a brief period, Charterhouse was used to stash Henry's tents. Eventually, it passed into the hands of John Dudley,

☞ Did you know?

As one can well imagine, great controversy followed on the heels of Henry VIII's radical Act of Supremacy and Act of Succession. His unpopular marriage to Anne Boleyn merely fueled the fire. A bold Franciscan friar risked a gruesome traitor's death when he predicted that if Henry did indeed marry Anne, dogs would lick his blood as they had done to Ahab's. And so it came to pass in 1547, as Henry's gargantuan corpse lay overnight en route to Windsor, that his coffin sprang open. Dawn brought the gory discovery of dogs licking his remains.

Duke of Northumberland, executed in 1553 for his attempt to place Lady Jane Grey on the throne, and later to Thomas Howard, Duke of Norfolk, executed in 1572 for complicity in a plot to place Mary Stuart on the throne. *(Do we detect a trend here?)* In fact, theory has it that the conspiracy that contributed to the loss of Mary Stuart's head, the Ridolfi plot, was hatched by Norfolk and his cohorts during a conference held within the Charterhouse walls.

Charterhouse was purchased in 1611 by Thomas Sutton, Master of the Ordnance under Queen Elizabeth I. His crest, the greyhound's head, can be seen on the pew ends in the chapel. Sutton endowed the handsome property as a center of learning. In time, Charterhouse became one of England's leading public schools. *(To the best of our knowledge, no graduate was ever executed.)* It now operates as Sutton Hospital, a retirement home for gentlemen pensioners. It is the only ecclesiastical foundation in London to retain its cloistered atmosphere.

THE PLAGUE IN MEDIEVAL LONDON

The Black Death of 1348–1349, which necessitated the plague pit at Charterhouse, was by far the most devastating epidemic to strike medieval London. One third of the City's population fell victim to the disease, including 27 of the monks at Westminster Abbey and all of the patients, save one, at St. James Hospital. However, the Black Death was certainly not the only plague to leave its mark on England's capital city. In 1394, Richard II's beloved Queen Anne of Bohemia was felled by the plague. Her husband was so distraught that he ordered the destruction of Sheen, Anne's favored residence, which she had helped design. The Sweating Death of 1485 caused a massive number of deaths—the mayor, his successor and six aldermen were among the City's casualties. Other epidemics struck London in 1499, 1513, 1531 and 1563, when an estimated 20 percent of London's population was felled.

SIR WALTER DE MANNY

He may not be one of the courtiers best known to amateur historians, but in his day Walter de Manny was exceptionally popular and influential. A relative of Queen Philippa of Hainault, de Manny arrived with her entourage in 1326 when she married King Edward III. A distinguished soldier and close friend of the Black Prince, de Manny was respected enough to act as guardian to the daughter of the Count of Hainault and was well enough regarded to be eulogized by both the king and John of Gaunt upon his death. De Manny's body and pieces of his tomb were discovered during post–World War II restoration work, enabling archeologists to better pinpoint the location of the medieval chapel and altar.

CARTHUSIAN MONKS

Carthusian monks were dedicated to a life of solitude and prayer, with a suitably ascetic diet to help inspire such saintly behavior. The order originated as St. Bruno's Contemplative Order, which was established in 804 near Grenoble in Chartreuse. The name was anglicized to Charterhouse upon the monks' arrival in London. A distinguishing feature of a Carthusian monastery is the huddle of individual cells, set into a garden wall. Each monk spent the better part of his life in solitary prayer and contemplation in these impossibly tight quarters. There have been 25 such cells identified on the grounds of Charterhouse.

St. Etheldreda's Chapel

14 Ely Place (020-7405-1061), EC1
Northeast side of Holborn Circus
Chancery Lane or Farringdon Tube

OPEN

8:30 a.m.–6:30 p.m. daily

WORSHIP

Mass: 8:00 a.m. and 1:00 p.m. daily
Choral: 11:00 a.m. Sunday

ADMISSION

Free of charge

This is Britain's oldest Roman Catholic church, dating from the 13th century. It withstood the Reformation (becoming, briefly, a Protestant house of worship), the Great Fire and the bombs of World War II. Built during the reign of Edward I, it was originally the private chapel for the residence of the Bishop of Ely.

After the Reformation, the entire property was acquired by the Elizabethan chancellor, Christopher Hatton. His descendants tore down the residence, but left the chapel intact. It would reach its low point as a neighborhood saloon before being restored as one of the area's most inspiring churches.

> ☞ Did you know?
> Henry VIII is said to have first been introduced to the future Archbishop of Canterbury Thomas Cranmer in the cloisters of St. Etheldreda's.

With its airy nave flooded with light from the magnificent stained-glass windows, St. Etheldreda's is especially glorious on a sunny morning or in the evening. Admire the carved wooden relics, then venture into the vaulted crypt (c. 1252) built atop ancient Roman pavement. The 12-foot-thick walls and blackened beams make this a particularly distinctive example of medieval architecture.

To find this gem, you must persevere. Proceed down Holborn or Charterhouse to Hatton Garden. Turn left at #8 and head down the very narrow Ely Court alley, past the tiny Ye Mitre Pub (c. 1546, *and yes, you may stop in for a pint!*). You will emerge into Ely Place.

A lost treasure . . .

Ely House

My Lords of Ely, when I was last in Holborn,
I saw good strawberries in your garden there;
I do beseech you, send for some . . .

—Shakespeare, *Richard III*

All that remains of Ely House is St. Etheldreda's Chapel, your last tour of monastic London. Set a few paces apart from the gaudy urban palaces that adorned the Strand, the Bishop of Ely's grand manor possessed a dignity all its own. Hospitality there stretched beyond the ecclesiastic to embrace such distinguished residents as Edward the Black Prince and John of Gaunt, who resided at Ely House after losing his Savoy Palace to the rebel fires of the Peasants' Revolt. Shakespeare sets Gaunt's famous "this sceptered isle" speech from *Richard II* at Ely House.

Fame did not come to Ely House through its inhabitants, however. Ely House was renowned for its gardens, lush with fragrant roses and strawberries. When forced to relinquish his manor to Elizabeth's chancellor, Christopher Hatton, the Bishop of Ely was able to negotiate the right to stroll amid the blossoms and to gather, for his own enjoyment, a total of 20 bushels of roses each year. The strawberries would be immortalized in Shakespeare's *Richard III*, where they are specifically requested by the Duke of Gloucester.

BLACKFRIAR MONKS

Although not a part of this tour, per se, the Blackfriar's neighborhood gets its name from the black-frocked Dominicans who settled in London in the 13th century. The ruins of their monastic enclave were unearthed during excavations in the 1980s. This is an area rich in history, although little remains to be seen. It was here, in 1382, that the Dominicans assembled to decree the writings of Wycliff as heretical. Shakespeare staged the divorce decree between Henry VIII and Katherine of Aragon at Blackfriar's Monastery. And, in 1596, James Burbage, Shakespeare's renowned associate, established London's first enclosed theater in what is now called ***Playhouse Yard.*** Since we've been discussing other monastic orders in this chapter, we thought you'd find this of interest.

CONTENTS

....7....

Reaching for the Heavens

Much Ado About Churches

If it seems like a medieval enthusiast could spend a week touring churches in London and see little else, well . . . it only seems that way. Had you actually arrived in London as a 12th-century tourist, however, the impression of a "town of steeples" would have been even more overbearing. At the time that William Fitz Stephen wrote his *Descriptio Londoniae,* in 1183, London was home to 13 monastic or conventual churches and more than 100 parish churches. This translates into one church for every three acres, or—based on the contemporary population of 30,000—a house of worship for every 300 residents.

Although a series of devastating fires (particularly the Great Fire of 1666) and the ransacking associated with the Reformation left most medieval churches in ruins, some of these ancient structures have survived, and they provide the amateur historian with fascinating insights into the life and times of medieval Christians. Some of these churches, such as All Hallows by the Tower and St. Etheldreda's (as well as the Abbey and Southwark

Cathedral), are so closely linked with a specific site or neighborhood that we've included them in the appropriate chapters. As for the others, this chapter will give you a glimpse of the institution that most intimately influenced the medieval mind and so closely shaped the political climate of the era.

Finally, we have chosen to list the churches alphabetically, rather than arrange them "walking tour" style. The map we have provided can help you plan a route, should an ecclesiastic stroll strike your fancy.

Tip!

The opening hours and worship times of the City churches change frequently. The City Churches Development Group publishes a frequently updated guide to opening times and services, available in the information section of most of the sites mentioned here. It is your best guide *(although by no means foolproof)* for planning visits to specific churches.

St. Andrew Undershaft

St. Mary Axe at Leadenhall Street, EC3 (020-7283-2231)
Aldgate Station Tube

OPEN
8:00 a.m.–5:00 p.m. Monday–Friday

WORSHIP
Used for Bible Study only

ACCESS
Request access from the staff at St. Helen's Bishopsgate

Dedicated to the patron saint of Scotland, St. Andrew dates back to 1147. A rather uninspiring structure, St. Andrew holds a special place for all of us amateur historians who earn our keep by the pen. Here lies parishioner John Stow, a simple tailor by trade, whose detailed account of the City in 1598 was, perhaps, the first *Amateur Historian's Guide to Medieval and Tudor London.* In an annual April memorial service, the Lord Mayor of London lays a new quill pen in the hand of the striking marble effigy and awards the prior quill, along with *Stow's Survey of London*, to the school child who has written the best London-based essay. Keeping Stow company are the remains of Hans Holbein the Younger.

Andrew Undershaft was one of four City churches to survive intact both the Great Fire and World War II. Unfortunately, our own era has not been so kind. Terrorist attacks in 1992 and 1993 severely undermined the ancient building, which has only recently been reopened for public use.

☞ Did you know?

"Undershaft" means "under the maypole." St. Andrew Undershaft was originally known as St. Andrew Cornhill. The current name dates from the 15th century, when every spring a festive maypole was erected on the church grounds. The "pagan, heathen" custom was banned in 1517 after the apprentice riots on Evil May Day.

St. Bride's

Bride's Lane off Fleet Street, EC4 (020-7353-1301)
Blackfriar's or Chancery Lane Tube, off Ludgate Circus

OPEN

8:30 a.m.–5:00 p.m. Monday–Friday
9:00 a.m.–4:30 p.m. Saturday
9:30 a.m.–12:30 p.m. and 5:30–7:30 p.m. Sunday

WORSHIP

8:30 a.m. Holy Communion in the crypt, Monday–Thursday
11:00 a.m. and 6:30 p.m. Sunday

ACCESS

St. Bride's is tucked in behind many tall, modern structures.
Be patient in your pursuit, and feel free to ask directions!

Disregard, if you will, that the "wedding cake" architecture is Wren's.* The atmosphere of St. Bride's is ancient and authentic. Indeed, parts of the crypt are *so* very ancient and authentic you may well feel the hair on the back of your neck rise!

Archeology reveals that our Roman, Saxon and Celtic ancestors worshiped on this site as early as the 6th century, and tradition holds that St. Bride's was the first church in London to practice the Christian faith. Its significance was not lost on the monarch. In 1205, the *Curia Regis,* principal court of the country, was held at St. Bride's. King John held a meeting of Parliament here in 1210, and King Edward III issued a writ confirming the Charter of the Guild of St. Bride in 1375. In the Middle Ages, St. Bride's was one of four City curfew churches, warning all within earshot to "drink up" and "scramble home," for both the taverns and the City gates would soon be locked tight. Of course, it is appropriate that this "Cathedral of Fleet Street" was the site of the City's first printing press, and that Wynkyn de Worde, successor to London's first printer, William Caxton, was buried before the high altar in 1535. Search out the £200,000 facsimile of Caxton's Bible, on display in the crypt; although modern, it is a sight to behold!

Although the 15th-century incarnation of St. Bride's was destroyed in the Great Fire, the ancient crypt has artifacts *(and we believe a few poltergeists)* from all its past eras, as well as a small museum that focuses on Fleet Street and the publishing business. All of the exposed stone in the building's lower level is clearly marked by era and approximate age, which we found particularly informative. Can you spot the touching memorial to Virginia Dare, the first white child born in America? Her parents were married at St. Bride's.

*A word about Christopher Wren: we know he is much admired. We know he was an architectural genius. We know that modern London would not look the same without his graceful touch. However, we also recognize that Mr. Wren was no lover of medieval design, and in his efforts to leave his imprint on the City, many of the historic jewels that survived the Great Fire were razed. Sorry, but we do get a tad sour about things like that.

Ghost Alert!

Our visceral reaction during our first visit to the crypt at St. Bride's was so intense that years later it still makes the pulse quicken and the skin crawl. 'Nough said.

St. Dunstan-in-the-West

Fleet Street, EC4 (020-7405-1929)
Monument Tube

>>

OPEN

9:30 a.m.–3:00 p.m. Tuesday and Friday
10:00 a.m.–4:00 p.m. Sunday

WORSHIP

Romanian Orthodox Liturgy: 11:00 a.m. Sunday
Holy Communion: 12:30 p.m. Tuesday
Vespers: 5:00 p.m. Saturday

>>

Okay, okay. So the church is not medieval, or even Tudor; there *has* been a St. Dunstan's on this site since 1185. The statue of Elizabeth I that graces the exterior dates from 1586, making it not only one of the few contemporary likenesses of the queen available on our tour *but also* the only outdoor statue of Elizabeth in London! The exterior bell tower statue was salvaged from Ludgate in Victorian times, along with three interior statues, assumed to represent the mythical King Lud and his sons. These are located in the vestry.

Now aren't you sorry you complained?

St. Giles Cripplegate

Fore Street, EC2 (020-7606-3630)
Barbican or Moorgate Tube

OPEN
9:15 a.m.–5:15 p.m. Monday–Friday
9:00 a.m.–1:00 p.m. Saturday

WORSHIP
8:00 a.m., 10:00 a.m. and 11:30 a.m. Sunday

TOURS
2:00–5:00 p.m. Tuesday

One of the oldest churches in the City, St. Giles was first established in 1090 as a lazar house by Henry I's Queen Edith/Matilda, a.k.a. "Good Queen Maude." Evidence of an even earlier Saxon-era chapel has been found on the site as well. The current church was built in 1340, although massive reconstruction in both 1545 and the post–World War II era has left only the ancient tower intact.

Like St. Bride's, St. Giles was one of four curfew churches whose tolling bells at 9 p.m. beckoned citizens home to the comforts of hearth and bed. Inside, you'll find several important tombs, including that of author John Foxe (d. 1587) and naval expert Sir John Frobisher (d. 1594). The poet John Milton is buried here, and it is interesting to know that Sir Thomas More's parents were married at St. Giles, as was the famous Elizabethan actor Edward Allen; he

Did you know?

Lazar houses served as a type of medieval "hospice" for those suffering from leprosy. The name derives from the biblical story of Lazarus, who was raised from the dead by the healing touch of Christ. Like most medieval illnesses, leprosy was considered punishment for sin. Those inflicted by the disease were cast apart from society, forced *(in the best-case scenarios)* into communal living with other lepers, and reduced to begging for sustenance. In addition to St. Giles, there were medieval lazar houses at St. James and in the vicinity of the current St. Katherine's Dock in Southwark.

married the stepdaughter of Shakespeare's friendly rival, Philip Henslowe. Allen also built and operated the Fortune Playhouse (1599) just steps away from the church.

Outside, there are some particularly noteworthy ruins from the Roman bastion and portions of the City Wall that border the churchyard. The modern lake on this site approximates the proportions of the medieval ditch.

St. Helen's Bishopsgate

Great St. Helen's Street, EC3 (020-7283-2231)
Liverpool Street Tube

OPEN

9:00 a.m.–5:00 p.m. Monday, Wednesday, Thursday and Friday
Closed Saturday

WORSHIP

12:35 p.m. and 1:15 p.m. Tuesday
10:15 a.m. and 7:00 p.m. Sunday

The largest surviving ancient church in London, St. Helen's boasts a rather unusual design, the result of the fact that this was once *two* houses of worship. The first was a 13th-century parish church, dedicated to the mother of Emperor Constantine. The second was the chapel of a Benedictine convent founded for the daughters and widows of London nobility. On the convent side of the church is a "*squint*," which once allowed the nuns to observe the parish masses. This small window on secular life was apparently not enough to sate the good sisters, who eventually had to be admonished to "abstain from kissing secular persons," a habit to which they had become "too prone."

However, the melding of St. Helen's cloistered and "public" spaces would eventually prove fortuitous. The fact that a parish church shared a roof with the convent prevented St. Helen's from being destroyed during the Reformation. Instead, the convent was disbanded, its lands sold to Thomas Cromwell's nephew, and St. Helen's Bishopsgate left to stand, unharmed.

Among the attractions of St. Helen's are its handsome brasses, including one of a woman in a heraldic mantel. There is also an exemplary collection of memorials, including those of Sir William Pickering (d. 1576), faithful soldier and scholar under four Tudor monarchs; Sir Thomas Gresham, founder of the Royal Exchange; and Sir John Crosby, merchant and one-time owner of ***Crosby Place*** in Bishopsgate. There is an outstanding monument to Sir Julius Caesar, Elizabeth I's Admiralty Judge, and an attractive window in memory of parish resident William Shakespeare.

St. Katherine Cree

86 Leadenhall Street at Creechurch Lane, EC3
(020-7283-5733)
Tower Hill or Aldgate Tube

OPEN
10:00 a.m.–6:00 p.m. Monday, Tuesday, Thursday and Friday
Closed weekends

WORSHIP
1:05 p.m. Thursday

One of the eight medieval churches to survive the Great Fire of 1666, St. Katherine's was, nevertheless, extensively rebuilt by Inigo Jones in 1628. The original church predated 1280, when it stood as St. Katherine's Christchurch on the grounds of Holy Trinity Priory. The only portion of the church that dates from medieval times is the lower portion of the tower—and this, in fact, was originally part of a different building!

However, if you are interested in ancient guilds and livery companies, step inside and admire the ceiling. The striking coats of arms painted there are replicas of those awarded in ancient times to specific trades. The ceiling paintings are extraordinary examples of medieval heraldic art.

> ☞ Did you know?
>
> The priory of Christchurch built St. Katherine's so that the local citizens would not disturb the monks at worship.

The chapel contains the tomb of Sir Nicholas Throckmorton (d. 1570), who was a key advisor to Elizabeth I. Tradition holds that the elder Holbein (d. 1543) was buried under the altar of the preceding church.

St. Magnus Martyr

Lower Thames Street, EC3 (020-7626-4481)
Monument Tube

OPEN

9:30 a.m.–4:00 p.m Tuesday–Friday
10:15 a.m.–2:00 p.m. Sunday

WORSHIP

11:00 a.m. Sunday

Throughout the Middle Ages, the St. Magnus green was an important gathering place where local citizens congregated, shouting down the official heralds as they read their proclamations and ogling criminals as they bore their public humiliation. The church was closely linked with Old London Bridge. In fact, the approach to the bridge used to pass right through the porch of the church building. As you enter the gates, you can still see the stones from

> ☞ Did you know?
>
> St. Magnus was the Earl of the Orkney Islands, just off the coast of Scotland. A respected Christian leader, Magnus was murdered by his cousin in 1110. A favorite Scottish legend tells of St. Magnus appearing from the clouds and charging through the streets of Bannockburn, heralding Robert the Bruce's victory over Edward I's army.

Old London Bridge, as well as remains from a Roman-era wharf. A wonderfully crafted scale model of the medieval bridge is on display as soon as you enter the church.

Miles Coverdale, author of the first English translation of the Bible, was vicar of St. Magnus from 1563 to 1565. Unfortunately for medievalists, the church you see today is the product of Wren.

St. Margaret Pattens

Rood Lane, East Cheap, EC3 (020-7623-6630)
Monument Tube

OPEN
8:00 a.m.–4:00 p.m. Monday–Friday

WORSHIP
1:15 p.m. Thursday

Rebuilt by Wren in 1687, St. Margaret Pattens still possesses a number of relics from the ancient past. Look for the 1067 inscription on the old stone porch. During the Middle Ages, pattens—a type of metal-spiked shoe cover that protected footwear from muddy roadways—were manufactured and sold in Rood Lane. The church is named for this trade and continues the association by displaying a number of pattens in the glass cabinets in the entryway. St. Margaret's baptismal register is over 450 years old, and a glorious silver communion cup, c. 1543, is probably the oldest of its kind in London today.

✝ St. Mary le Bow

Bow Lane, Cheapside, EC2 (020-7248-5139)
St. Paul's or Bank Tube

OPEN

6:30 a.m.–6:00 p.m. Monday–Thursday
6:30 a.m.–4:00 p.m. Friday
Closed weekends

WORSHIP

7:45 a.m. Tuesday; 1:05 p.m. Wednesday; 5:45 p.m. Thursday; 1:05 p.m. Friday

CONVENIENCES

The Place Below Restaurant (020-7329-0789)
Open 7:30 a.m.–2:30 p.m. Monday–Friday

Yes, it's another *Wren* church, but Mary le Bow and the churches that preceded it on this site did play a role in the history of London in the Middle Ages. The later Plantagenet kings and queens presided over numerous pageants and processions from the stone pavilion erected outside the church. In fact, Philippa, Edward III's consort, and many others were injured when the grandstand collapsed during the Black Prince's birthday processional. Wren's tower balcony was built to commemorate this 1330 tragedy.

> ☞ Did you know?
>
> In 1196, during the reign of King John, the citizens of London grew weary of the ever increasing tax burden. Their discontent was flamed by William Fitz Osbert, who promptly found himself on John's blacklist—definitely not a good place to be. Foreseeing his arrest, Fitz Osbert killed the local constable and fled to Mary le Bow to seek sanctuary. The church was set afire to flush Fitz Osbert out *(see, what we implied about dear John was true!)*. The rabble-rouser and nine accomplices were hanged at Smithfield.

The *"Bow Bells,"* too, have been long famous: they rang the nightly curfew for the City citizens and they're also referred to in the legend of Dick Whittington, summoning the young man back to London to assume the task of mayor. Indeed, it's traditionally asserted that the only *true* Londoner (or "cockney") is one born within earshot of the Bow Bells. Unfortunately, the original bells did not survive the Great Fire.

Of interest to you will be the church's Norman crypt, which dates back to 1090, the oldest Christian religious structure in London. The space has been beautifully transformed into a very contemporary *(and delicious!)* vegetarian restaurant—history with a side order of tofu, hold the sprouts!

St. Michael Paternoster Royal

College Hill off Upper Thames Street (020-7248-5202), EC4
Cannon Street Tube

OPEN
8:00 a.m.–5:30 p.m. Monday–Friday

WORSHIP
9:00 a.m. Monday–Friday

Of all the historic characters closely linked to the City of London's history, few have been as glorified as Dick Whittington. Four-time Lord Mayor of London, Whittington's true life and personality are often hard to separate from myth, despite the awe-inspiring bequests he made to the City upon his death and the plethora of worshipful stories told in his honor. However, we do know that St. Michael Paternoster Royal is very much "Dick Whittington's Church," and the connection is most interesting.

Although the parish dates from 1219, Whittington is credited with founding the church, for it was his endowment that enabled the church to be remodeled in the 1400s. Whittington looked upon the project as a small religious village, going so far as to endow an almshouse next door and a College of Priests just to the north. He claimed the adjacent lot for his own City residence.

Dick Whittington must have lived by the motto "Once is not enough." Not only was he Lord Mayor of London for four terms (1397, 1406, 1416 and 1419) but also he was buried at St. Michael's three separate times: upon his death in 1423, again after vandalism during the reign of Edward VI, and finally during the reign of Mary Tudor. Although his grave has been "missing" since the Great Fire, explorations have unearthed a mummified cat—perhaps the feline of the famous Whittington legend? A beautiful glass window on the west wall honors both the man and his furry friend.

St. Olaves Hart Street

Seething Lane and Fenchurch Street, EC3 (020-7488-4318)
Tower Hill Tube

OPEN

9:00 a.m.–5:00 p.m. Monday–Friday

WORSHIP

11:00 a.m. Sunday

The original St. Olave's was founded in the 11th century; the current church—the third on this site—dates back to 1450. Having survived both fire and bombs, this 15th-century church—often described as a country church in the heart of the City—has a charming churchyard and numerous Tudor memorials of note. There is one dedicated to Elizabeth I, who stood as godmother to Elizabeth Sidney during her 1585 baptism at St. Olave's, and another to Samuel and Elizabeth Pepys, who

☞ Did you know?

St. Olave's was one of six London churches dedicated to the canonized Norwegian King Olaf and one of the few reminders left of the City's Danish era.

worshiped here for many years. Perhaps the oddest "person" said to be buried at St. Olave's is Mother Goose. Church documents record her interment on September 14, 1586. A plaque on the outside gate commemorates the event.

St. Sepulchre-Without-Newgate (Church of the Holy Sepulchre)

Giltspur Street and Holborn Viaduct, EC1 (020-7248-3826)
St. Paul's Tube

OPEN
11:00 a.m.–3:00 p.m. Tuesday

WORSHIP
12:30 p.m. Holy Communion, Thursday

One of the most impressive landmarks in a neighborhood of important buildings, the 15th-century Church of the Holy Sepulchre has long been linked with the Old Bailey, opposite. For centuries, a dour churchman would take to the streets outside the church and ring the sorrowful handbell as a source of "inspiration" for prisoners on the eve of their execution. In the morning, the tower's tenor bell would toll their execution.

ANCIENT RUINS

~ All Hallows Staining

Mark Lane

All that remains of the 15th-century church is the stone battlement tower, which contrasts starkly with the modern offices that surround it. Don't despair! From the tower, you can enjoy Carole's favorite pastime, and descend into the vaulted 13th-century Norman crypt.

~ St. Alphege, London Wall

London Wall

Not so much a church, but rather an elaborately preserved 14th-century ruin that is often confused, because of its location, with the remains of the Roman wall.

~ St. Ethelburga

Bishopsgate

Founded in 1250 and rebuilt in 1390, St. Ethelburga is the smallest of the ancient City churches. A mere 51 by 30 feet, this is the perfect example of a typical medieval parish church, designed to accommodate a family, their household and, perhaps, a handful of neighbors. Tragically, terrorist bombs caused extensive damage in 1993 and, although parts of the church are visible from the street, doubt remains as to whether St. Ethelburga will ever be rebuilt.

A HOST OF LOST TREASURES

The churches listed at the front of this chapter have tangible links to the Middle and Tudor Ages that you can still retrace with a visit. There are also numerous churches throughout the City that are linked in name or spirit to medieval and Tudor London, even though they have been completely rebuilt in the aftermath of disaster and contain no vestige of their pre-fire past. Here is a rundown of fully rebuilt churches whose medieval predecessors you may have come across in your reading. Countless other ancient churches have long since vanished; their only trace remains in the written accounts of times past.

~ St. Andrew by the Wardrobe

Queen Victoria Street

Founded in the 13th century and rebuilt by Wren. The name refers to its location adjacent to the King's Great Wardrobe, where the monarch's state apparel was kept. Just beyond this church is a tiny public garden with a statue and plaque honoring William Shakespeare. Check it out!

~ St. Benet, Paul's Wharf

Upper Thames at Queen Street

Founded in the 11th century; rebuilt by Nathaniel Wright, 1677.

~ St. Botolph Without Bishopsgate

Bishopsgate

Believed to predate the Norman Conquest, the church was rebuilt by James Gold in 1725. It is associated with Tudor-era worthies, including Edward Alleyn, founder of Dulwich College, author Stephen Gosson and the playwright Ben Johnson, whose firstborn son, Nicholas, was buried in the church, victim of the plague.

~ Holy Trinity Priory

Leadenhall Street at Aldgate

Yet another foundation by the pious Queen Edith-Matilda, Holy Trinity Priory was established in 1108. Endowed with lands once held by the *Cnitchen Guild* (the most ancient of knightly organizations, dating from the reign of King Edgar), Holy Trinity was the biggest landowner in London, until its destruction during the Reformation. The remains were not discovered until excavation efforts after World War II. Holy Trinity, however, lived for years in one of London's best-loved fables. It seems the first Norman prior of Holy Trinity spared no expense on accoutrements. So lavish were his vestments and so plentiful his books that not a penny remained to provide food for the ecclesiastical staff *(we can relate!)*. When the women of the parish noted the pitiable state of the hungry canons, they each vowed to send a loaf of bread every Sunday—a tradition that continued for many years to come. St. Thomas à Becket's mother, Matilda, was one of the generous souls, and she carried her commitment one step further. Every year on his birthday, she would weigh young Thomas and send along a parcel of goods equal to the future saint's weight!

~ St. James Garlickhythe

Garlick Hill and Upper Thames Street

Founded in 1170, rebuilt in 1326 and again, by Wren, in 1676–1682. Burial site of six medieval Lord Mayors. An annual festival of the Vintners' Company, initiated over 500 years ago, terminates at this church. Participants carry nosegays, which in earlier times offset the pungent odor from garlic sold in this neighborhood.

~ St. Martin le Grand

London Wall at Aldersgate

A plaque on the wall marks the site of St. Martin le Grand, the most ancient of all London monasteries, Westminster excepted. St. Martin's was founded in 1056 by Ingelric as the College of Secular Canons; it was confirmed in a charter by William the Conqueror in 1068. Despite its location, smack in the heart of the City, St. Martin's remained independent of any civic authority, defiantly providing sanctuary to any criminal lucky enough to find his or her way to its doors . . . with an interesting exception: in 1480, thieves boldly robbed the convent of St. Martin's, then brazenly sought sanctuary in the chapel next door. Their pleas for leniency fell on deaf ears—three were promptly hung and the other two were pursued to death.

~ St. Martin Ludgate

Ludgate Hill

Records of this church go back as far as 1174, when the ancient church stood just inside the City wall at Ludgate, the first gate to honor curfew each evening. The church was associated with William Sevenoake, an abandoned child who was taken in by a tender family, apprenticed to a merchant and who went on to become Lord Mayor in 1418. Sevenoake returned the charity by founding numerous almshouses and a free school. ***Note:*** The west wall of this church is part of the medieval City Wall.

~ St. Mary Abchurch

Abchurch Lane

Founded 1198. Rebuilt by Wren in 1681–1687.

~ St. Mary Aldermanbury

Aldermanbury and Love Lane

If you're looking for this church, whose history stretches to Saxon times, you'll have to look to Westminster College in Fulton, Missouri, USA. Subsequent to its World War II demise, the church's remains were shipped abroad to be used in a memorial to Churchill. The gardens have been preserved and a plaque on the site gives a synopsis of the church's legacy.

~ St. Mary Aldermary

Queen Victoria Street

The name *alder* means "older," and with a history that dates to 1080, St. Mary is, indeed, one of the alder churches of the City. The church and its rector, Henry Gold, were embroiled in the scandal surrounding the Maid of Kent, a religious fanatic who predicted the demise of Henry VIII should he divorce Queen Katherine of Aragon. The hysterical woman was hung for treason in 1534, and her unfortunate supporter, Reverend Gold, joined her in death at Tyburn. The current building is Wren, 1682, but boasts a "medieval" interior plan.

~ St. Michael's Cornhill

Gracechurch Street and Cornhill

Established in 1055, this was the burial site of three generations of John Stow's ancestors. You may pay your respects in the tiny medieval churchyard to the south of the tower. This 1669 Wren church suffers from a heavy dose of Victorian embellishment.

~ St. Olave de Monkwell (Churchyard)

Silver Street

Directly opposite the church of St. Giles Cripplegate is the tiny churchyard of St. Olave, Silver Street. This was once the parish church of William Shakespeare, although how often he attended service is a matter of speculation. There is no evidence that the Bard was particularly devout. After 1602, Shakespeare was a resident of the Mountjoy household, across from St. Olave, and apparently he played matchmaker between the landlord's daughter and a neighborhood apprentice. Fittingly, their marriage took place in this church.

St. Olave was destroyed in the Great Fire and was *not* rebuilt by Wren . . . nor by anyone else.

~ St. Nicholas, Cole Abbey

Queen Victoria Street

Founded in the 12th century; rebuilt by Wren in 1671.

~ St. Peter's Cornhill

Gracechurch Street at Cornhill

The church claims a history that dates to the reign of King Lucius in 179 CE. Part of St. Peter's treasures include a very rare 4th-century translation of the Old and New Testaments, reproduced by a church scribe in 1290. The church is Wren, 1667.

~ St. Vedast

Foster Lane, Cheapside

13th-century foundation; rebuilt by Wren in 1695.

LONDON: A PILGRIM'S HEAVEN

When you consider the hardships presented by travel in the Middle Ages, it's striking to realize how many common people left their hometowns for far-flung destinations. Family visits, military duty and the search for a kinder master or more profitable work were among the incentives that might compel one to pack a few belongings and strike off along paths that were barely beaten and, more often than not, plagued by footpads and wolves.

By far, the most popular reason for medieval travel was the religious pilgrimage. Not only was the hope of special blessings—maybe even a miracle!—a powerful lure, but such journeys offered the pilgrim the chance to enjoy some of the most beautiful and sophisticated towns of the day, in the company and protection of fellow travelers. London, as one might suspect, was a very popular destination for pilgrims, from both the English shires and abroad. Not only was it an easy journey from the revered shrine of St. Thomas à Becket in Canterbury (for those on a spiritual junket), but also London offered two particularly revered shrines, each with its own advantage for the devout.

St. Erkenwald (d. 693), former Bishop of London, was renowned for his alleged intercession on behalf of penitent sinners; he was enshrined at St. Paul's Cathedral, an awe-inspiring center of faith. The equally impressive Westminster Abbey offered the shrine of St. Edward the Confessor (d. 1066), former king of England, to whom incurables attributed wondrous powers. These, together with smaller churches and their sacred relics culled from "minor" saints, provided the pilgrim with the hope of being cured of pain, avoiding damnation and securing God's everlasting mercy.

When the praying was over, the capital city offered a host of temptations to lure the less dedicated pilgrim back into the snares of sin and vice. Luckily, no tavern or den of iniquity was more than a stone's throw from one of London's many parish churches!

St. Paul's Cathedral

Ludgate Hill, EC4 (020-7236-4128)
St. Paul's or Mansion Tube

OPEN

Cathedral: 9:30 a.m.–3:45 p.m. Monday–Saturday
Galleries: 9:30 a.m.–4:15 p.m. Monday–Saturday
Crypt: 8:45 a.m.–4:15 p.m. Monday–Saturday
Closed for sightseeing on Sunday

WORSHIP

11:00 Sunday

ADMISSION

Fee charged

TOURS

11:00 a.m., 1:30 p.m. and 2:00 p.m. Monday–Saturday

True, the spectacular dome and soaring spires of Christopher Wren's masterpiece is exclusively "Restoration" in its glory—no physical evidence remains of the prior cathedrals' ancient roots. Yet we believe a visit to St. Paul's is an essential stop on any tour of medieval London. Besides, we know you're going to go there anyway—everyone does—and so you may as well be up to snuff on the *real* history here. The role the cathedral played in the religious, political and social life of the Middle and Tudor Ages may well be overshadowed by the present building's grandeur, but it should not be forgotten!

The spiritual nature of this City hilltop is believed to stretch back to Roman times, when it has been speculated that a temple to the goddess Diana graced this site. Its exclusive association with London's patron saint, Paul, dates to the reign of the Saxon king Ethelbert. Here, in 604 CE, London's first bishop, Mellitus, dedicated a primitive wooden church to Paul's honor. In what was to become an unfortunate pattern, the church burned to the ground about 70 years later.

The second church—the first real cathedral—on the site was built by London's fourth bishop, St. Erkenwald, in 675–685. Subsequently enshrined in St. Paul's, Erkenwald's tomb was, for many years, the site of many reported miracles and a popular destination for medieval pilgrims. Erkenwald's cathedral was torched by Viking invaders in 961, and the subsequent cathedral succumbed to flames in 1087. Work began on a fourth cathedral that same year, under the guidance of Bishop Maurice, and although it was in every sense an ecclesiastic trendsetter, it would henceforth be known as "Old St. Paul's."

Old St. Paul's was clearly one of the most important church buildings of its time. The largest medieval church in all of Europe (larger, even, than the present St. Paul's), it stretched about 600 feet long and boasted the tallest church spire ever built (conservatively estimated between 460 and 489 feet high). The spire was destroyed by lightning in 1561, drastically changing London's skyline. It would never be replaced, despite philanthropic donations from Queen Elizabeth and several leading citizens.

The end towers of Old St. Paul's were vast enough to double as prisons—John Wycliff was held and tried here for heresy in 1377—and the stunning rosette window on the east side of the cathedral inspired both fashion and prose in its day. It is no surprise, then, that such a magnificent structure would evolve, over the course of six centuries, as a pivotal landmark in London history.

The cathedral was the awe-inspiring center of an important cluster of religious buildings that included a chapter house, a parish church, the impressive bishop's residence, a boys' school and the separate Jesus Bell Tower. Although the complex was walled and gated, the grounds and cathedral of St. Paul's soon became the preferred gathering spot of the City, attracting citizens of every rank and ilk. It was here that impromptu debates, as well as the official "folkmoot"—town meeting—would provide the populace with the opportunity to harangue over the issues of the day. Lawyers would brief their clients, a master could hire a promising laborer, craftsmen would hawk their wares . . . and shady ladies hawk theirs, as well. Broadsides were issued from St. Paul's and many of the most important manuscripts of the time, including several of Shakespeare's plays, were emitted through the ad-hoc book trade that sprung up on the church grounds. Books were burned here, as well, including Tynsdale's unauthorized English translation of the Bible in 1527, and the controversial writings of Martin Luther. So lively, so boisterous, and at times so *un-religious* did St. Paul's become that in the mid 16th century a proclamation was issued that forbade the riding or leading of horses through the cathedral building. It was of little avail—the nave became a common thoroughfare, more closely resembling a shopping mall than a house of worship.

Monarchs were wise to the importance of St. Paul's and often selected the cathedral over Westminster Abbey when setting the stage for popular support. Upon his triumphant return from Agincourt, Henry V attended the official mass of thanksgiving at St. Paul's. Likewise, the defeat of the Spanish Armada brought Elizabeth I to the cathedral to offer "God's public thanks for that triumphant victory over the Spanish fleet called invincible." In 1569, the first public lottery was conducted outside St. Paul's—the proceeds helped to finance Her Majesty's armed forces.

Yet, despite its moments of glory, the cathedral was both overused and misused. It gradually fell into sore neglect. During the late Tudor and early Stuart eras, the disrepair was shocking. Inigo Jones would embark upon its restoration under Charles I, but the Great Fire of 1666 was to destroy all that remained of medieval St. Paul's . . . then, as now, the favorite church of Londoners.

CONTENTS

+ The Inns of Court + Gray's Inn + Staple Inn
+ Lincoln's Inn + Middle Temple Inn
+ Temple Church + Newgate Prison

8

Legal London

The Inns of Court

he Inns of Court deserve a nod of appreciation, not merely for preserving some of London's finest medieval architecture and for formally establishing the legal education process still in use today, but for continuing, in large part, the important role they've played in City life for nearly 700 years.

From the late 1300s until the early 19th century, the Inns of Court served as London's only "university," training young men for the bar, as well as expanding their knowledge of music, dance, drama and literature. No longer the nation's only source of legal studies, and now admitting women as well, the Inns still retain the exclusive right of supplying barristers eligible to argue in the English courts; all law students must have at least one year of training at the Inns of Court before they can be "called to the bar."

Physically, the Inns still function in ways similar to their ancient past. Each Inn provides lodging for its members and offers such amenities as rich libraries and chapels for contemplation. Unchanged since the 14th century, the Great Hall still provides a focal area for lectures, meetings, moot courts and social events.

Not all of the Inns of Court buildings are historic, and few are accessible to the general public. We have tried to capture the "*not to be missed*" medieval and Tudor highlights in this chapter.

Gray's Inn

Gray's Inn or High Holborn, WC1 (020-7458-7800)
Chancery Lane or Holborn Tube

OPEN

6:00 a.m.–midnight Monday–Friday, grounds only
The buildings of Gray's are not open to the public; however, the porter encouraged us to phone ahead and see if any special tours might be offered during future visits.

ADMISSION

Free of charge

TIP!

The dormitory-style cafeteria in Gray's Inn Hall offers simple, inexpensive lunches, and may be your one and only chance to see at least part of the ancient building.

Despite its remote location at the north end of Chancery Lane, Gray's is well worth a visit, if only to stroll through the stunning gardens, which are located inside Chancery Lane Square at Field Court. These are the only Inn gardens open to the public on a regular basis. They were designed by Sir Francis Bacon, Treasurer of the Inn in 1597 and a resident of Gray's for a full half century. There is a statue in his honor at the far corner of the garden, in front of Holker Library.

Originally the manor home of Sir Reginald Gray of Wilton, the property was once set amid the open fields and windmills outside the City walls. The manor eventually became a hotel for lawyers and a seat of legal training in the 14th century. Eminent members of Gray's include William Cecil, Secretary of State and Lord Treasurer under Elizabeth I, as well as Shakespeare's well-heeled patron, the Earl of Southampton. It was under his patronage that Shakespeare debuted *A Comedy of Errors* here in 1594.

Unfortunately, the oldest* and most beautiful building,

****Gray's Inn Chapel,** built in 1698, replaced the 14th-century house of worship.

Gray's Inn Hall, was severely damaged during World War II, but much of it has been faithfully restored. The only chance you may have to see even a portion of the interior of this building is to arrive at lunch hour, when the cafeteria opens to the public. Of particular note is the handsome carved screen, generally agreed to be London's finest example of Elizabethan carving. It merits further interest as an "Armada Screen," crafted from the planks of a captured Spanish galleon. If the opportunity presents itself, be sure to enjoy the assorted paintings of Elizabeth I and her elder statesmen.

While you're in the neighborhood . . .

Visit Old Mall, on Holborn Circus, between Furnival Street and Fetter Lane. This was the site of Barnard's Inn, an adjunct of Gray's Inn and residence for nearly 100 law students, per term, during the Middle Ages.

Staple Inn

Holborn, WC1 (020-7742-0106)
Chancery Lane Tube

OPEN

9:00 a.m.–5:00 p.m. Monday–Friday (Courtyard only)

ADMISSION

Free of charge

Set apart from the official Inns of Court, and a bit off Holborn's beaten path, Staple Inn can be found tucked behind a row of Elizabethan-style town houses. Do not be tempted to enter through the lavishly gilded wrought-iron gates; the route you seek is the more subtle stone entry, c. 1545, with its understated "Staple Inn" etched about the iron hitching posts on either side. This will lead you to the more historic portion of this ancient Inn of Court.

The Staple Inn was established in 1378 as a trade center for wool merchants; London's critical wool supply was inventoried, weighed and taxed here. By 1400, the property was leased by the Inns of Chancery for the purpose of training barristers. In 1529, it was incorporated as part of Gray's Inn to serve as the equivalent of America's "freshman dorms" *(one can only wonder what madcap antics went on at a medieval frat party!)*. The building you see directly in front of you was erected in 1581–1586. Although it was much restored after World War II, it remains the only authentic example of Elizabethan half-timbering in London. The surrounding shops, however, are more Victorian than Tudor in their sentiment.

☞ Did you know?

When you exit Staple Inn, look for the two striking plinths standing guard smack in the middle of Holborn, just opposite the tube station. One bears a silver dragon, the other a silver lion. The twin beasts are boundary markers for the City of London. You will see them at several other junctions throughout your visit to this historic "square mile."

Lincoln's Inn

Lincoln's Inn Fields and Chancery Lane, WC2
(020-7405-6360)
Holborn or Chancery Tube

OPEN

Grounds: 7:00 a.m.–7:00 p.m. Monday–Friday
Chapel: 12:30–2:00 p.m. Monday–Friday
Hall: By prior appointment. Write to *Treasurer of the Inn, Porter's Lodge, Chancery Lane.*

ADMISSION

Free of charge

Lincoln's Inn is the oldest (c. 1393), the best-preserved and, in many ways, the most interesting of the four Inns of Court. Nowhere in London is the medieval collegiate atmosphere so well captured. Historians generally accept that the Lincoln's Inn Society was originally established in the nearby vicinity by Henry Lacy, Earl of Lincoln, whose arms the Society has adopted. What we do know is that by 1412 the rapidly growing Society had moved into a separate mansion owned by the Bishop of Chichester. The Society's freehold was granted in 1580.

You may approach the enclave from Lincoln's Field. Before Inigo Jones lent an air of formality to the promenade, this was a Tudor/Stuart execution field. The 14 unlucky souls found guilty in the infamous ***Babington Plot*** were hung, drawn and quartered on this site in 1586, the last in London to suffer this gruesome traitor's death.

☞ Did you know?

Although women could not be buried at Lincoln's Inn Chapel until 1839, this did not prevent them from abandoning their unwanted children on the steps of the chapel for the Society to rear. More often than not, these youngsters were given the last name of "Lincoln."

However, we find the more interesting approach is from Chancery Lane. Proceed down Chancery until you pass the corner of Cursitor Street. Just across from numbers 40–43 Chancery Lane you'll pass through Lincoln's Inn's gatehouse. This modern-day replica of the ***Lambeth Palace*** gatehouse thoughtfully incorporates the original Lincoln's Inn oak doors. Above the Chancery Lane archway, you can spot the arms of Henry Lacy, Earl of Lincoln, as well as those of Henry VIII and Thomas Lovell.

Directly ahead is Old Hall, an authentic early Tudor residence. Although the hall dates from 1485–1492, tradition holds that Ben Jonson, Shakespeare's contemporary, laid some of the bricks for the "modern" addition during Elizabeth I's reign. Remarkably, the hall withstood the bombs of World War II. The stained-glass windows at the north end of the hall depict the coats of arms borne by distinguished members of Lincoln's Inn—see if you can spot Sir Thomas More's. Clearly *(and rightly so!)* Lincoln's Inn is proud of its association with More; on our last visit, there was an extensive display of More memorabilia, as well as a diorama on the *Black Book of Lincoln's Inn.* The "Book" is the oldest continuous record of any of the Inns of

Court, dating from 1423 through the present. Minutes of the Council, names of all who are called to the bar, and detailed memoranda make the Black Book a fascinating insight into both the legal and the daily life of Lincoln's Inn. If the law, per se, is not your "thing," you will be certain to appreciate the lovely linenfold paneling and the remarkable Old Hall roof. Notice that many of the hall's stones are numbered—in the 1920s, Old Hall was completely dismantled, the stones cataloged, and the building painstakingly refitted.

For those of you familiar with the "quads" of America's Ivy League colleges, look no further for their inspiration. A few of these buildings date from the Tudor era but have been heavily renovated. Search out the small room off Hale Court (just past building #21). Here you'll find some fascinating murals from the 16th century—one carved from ancient Roman cement, another painted on plaster—and a piece of the 1581 gatehouse. Back out on the quad, you'll discover that the ancient vaulted passage leads to a collection of homes built in the 1520s and 1530s. Their complex polygonal turrets are a unique example of intricate Tudor brickwork.

While you're in the neighborhood . . .

Wander over to nearby Carey Street, past the Bankruptcy Courts. You'll find a memorial to Sir Thomas More (1478–1535), member of Lincoln's Inn. Also on Carey Street, at the corner of Chancery Lane, is the Knights Templars Pub, a welcome reminder of the original landowners of much of the Inns of Court real estate.

◇◇

THE BABINGTON PLOT

Perhaps it is unfair that one of the most notorious conspiracies against Elizabeth I should forever bear the surname of Sir Anthony Babington. He was not, after all, the mastermind of the plot to murder Elizabeth and place her imprisoned cousin, Mary Stuart (Mary, Queen of Scots), on the throne of England. However, for many years Babington had been a major force behind England's pro-Catholic movement. A student of Lincoln's Inn, Babington was one of a close-knit group of pro-Mary sympathizers and seemed to delight in his role as a courier for illicit communications between the captive Scottish queen, her secret agent Thomas Morgan and her supporters abroad. From the early 1580s, Sir Anthony also actively aided Catholic missionaries; he helped organize a network of "safe houses" from which the continental Catholics could operate and assisted in their stealthy transport across his homeland. Clearly, he was not interested in keeping his religious proclivities—nor his anti-Elizabeth sentiments—a deep, dark secret.

In May 1586, Anthony Babington was approached by an ardent supporter of Mary Stuart, an ordained priest by the name of Ballard, with the tantalizing tale of a planned English Catholic uprising, which—on the vow of the Spanish ambassador and key French officials—would be aided by a foreign invasion. The plan was to murder Elizabeth, release Mary and crown her the rightful Queen of England. At first enthusiastic, Babington apparently caught a major case of cold feet and made the critical error of applying to Elizabeth's spy master, Sir Francis Walsingham, for a license to leave *(flee!)* the country. Walsingham's suspicions keenly aroused, he fostered a friendship between one of his key agents, Robert Poley, and the hapless Sir Anthony.

In an unguarded moment, Babington discussed with Poley the legal issues that would surround Elizabeth's murder. Poley, of course, reported every detail to Walsingham, who had already intercepted a letter from Thomas Morgan to Mary, urging the Scottish queen to send Babington a written endorsement of the proposed conspiracy. Walsingham forwarded Morgan's letter on to Mary, then intercepted her reply before forwarding it on to Babington. This back-and-forth of letters surrounding the plot to murder Elizabeth, release Mary, and restore a Catholic monarchy to England—and Walsingham's cunning role as the undetected, hostile mediator—would ultimately lead to Elizabeth's long-awaited decision to send Mary Stuart to the block, as well as to the trial and execution of the nest of "Babington Plot" conspirators.

Babington acted less than admirably upon his arrest. He placed full blame for the enterprise on Ballard. He begged and bribed for his release and ultimately bungled an escape attempt. Along with Ballard, Sir Anthony Babington was hung, drawn and quartered at Tyburn on September 20, 1586. Apparently his agony was so shocking that Elizabeth ordered the remaining conspirators to "merely" be hanged until dead.

◇◇

✠ Middle Temple Inn

Middle Temple Lane, EC4 (020-7427-4800)
Temple Tube (except Sundays) or Blackfriar's Tube

»»

OPEN

10:00 a.m.–12:00 p.m. and 3:00–4:00 p.m. Monday–Friday
Closed August
It is best to phone ahead to assure entry; hours can be erratic.

ADMISSION

Free of charge

»»

Let him that is a true-born gentleman,
from this breir pluck a white rose with me.
—Shakespeare, *Henry VI*

Of the four Inns of Court, many prefer the quiet, secluded atmosphere of Middle Temple. The entire setting evokes the flavor of ancient times, and the history of our favorite era abounds here.

If you are able to gain permission, begin by wandering through the lovely Middle Temple Gardens. Just beyond Fountain Court is where Shakespeare set the stage for the confrontation between the houses of York and Lancaster, symbolized by the plucking of white and red roses, which still flourish in the gardens each spring.

North of Fountain Court sits Middle Temple Hall. Completed in 1573, it is a striking example of Tudor architecture. We were the beneficiaries of a well-informed guide, who *(just for the asking!)* took us on a personal tour, which truly made Middle Temple Hall come alive for us. As you enter the building, see if there is someone willing to do the same for you. The staff seemed truly eager to be of assistance.

Middle Temple Hall is generally considered to be the finest Elizabethan hall in all England. It is massive—101 feet long and 41 feet wide, crowned by its signature double-hammerbeam roof, crafted of Windsor Forest oak. The stained-glass windows throughout the hall are stunning; luckily, forethought prompted those in charge of Middle Temple Hall to remove them to the country for safekeeping prior to World War II's air raids. The intricately detailed Elizabethan rood screen, which frames the minstrel's gallery, did not fare as well. It was smashed during strikes on London, only to be painstakingly reassembled.

Middle Hall was a gift from Edmund Plowden, a highly renowned Elizabethan law reporter and Treasurer of the Inn. Plowden envisioned an impressive, yet congenial, gathering place where students of the law could congregate, share a fine meal, listen to learned speakers and debate the finer legal issues of their time in a collegiate atmosphere. He began his work in 1562, and Middle Temple Hall was officially opened by Queen Elizabeth in 1574. One of the most lavish celebrations of her reign took place here—a two-day fete in honor of the heroic return of Sir Francis Drake from his 'round-the-world sail.

☞ Did you know?

The Middle and Inner Temples share land once held by, and later confiscated from, the Knights Templars. As you stroll the campus, certain clues will indicate whether you are in Middle or Inner Temple territory. The Middle Temple sports the Lamb and Flag logo, while the Inner Temple marks its property with Pegasus.

Be sure to take a close look at the two bencher's tables on exhibit. The larger of the two, at 289 feet, was a gift from Elizabeth I. It was made of wood from Windsor Forest trees and serves as the head table for all state and other formal occasions celebrated at Middle Temple Hall. The smaller table, nicknamed "The Cupboard," is where today's lawyers sign their names when enrolled as members of the Inn. It is not generally on view to the public, but it's worth asking for a glimpse. The story is that the table was constructed from the hatch covers of the ***Golden Hind,*** the vessel in which Middle Temple member Sir Francis Drake completed his famed sail. Ask to have the protective cover moved aside, the better to see the original wood. A virtual Tudor treasure trove, Middle Temple also displays the oldest-known English globe (c. 1572), the Earl of Leicester's jousting trophies and delicate glass etchings that bear the arms of persons instrumental to the history of Middle Temple: Henry II, who consecrated the famed Temple Church; Edward III, the first monarch to decree that English law be debated in the English language, rather than Latin or Norman French; Elizabeth I, who formally dedicated Middle Temple Hall; and, of course, favorite sons Sirs Drake and Raleigh. The Minstrel's Gallery is a mini-museum on the history of the hall, which includes some interesting artifacts, notably a 1584 book on witchcraft and several statutes written during the reign of Elizabeth.

Despite its calm, studious demeanor, Middle Temple was not exclusively devoted to scholarly pursuit. Upon occasion, Middle Temple Hall doubled as a theater. Shakespeare's own troupe staged its premier performance of *Twelfth Night* here on February 2, 1602. An enthusiastic Queen Elizabeth was on hand at opening night. This is the only known venue of a Shakespeare premier known to still exist, and an anniversary staging of the comedy is scheduled at Middle Temple for 2002.

While you're in the neighborhood . . .

The names of many Tudor luminaries grace the streets surrounding Middle Temple. The Arundel Street thoroughfare marks the property of Arundel House, home of the Earl of Arundel and the Duke of Norfolk *(not flatmates, we presume)*. Elizabeth I's favorite, Robert Devereaux, was honored twice. Devereaux Court is named for him, although the Earl of Essex kept house in Essex Street; this spectacular manor had its own Thames-side dock.

✝ Temple Church

King's Bench Walk at Inner Temple Lane, EC4
(020-7797-8250)
Temple or Blackfriar's Tube

OPEN

11:00 a.m.–4:00 p.m. Monday
11:00 a.m.–1:00 p.m. Wednesday
2:00–4:00 p.m. Thursday
11:00 a.m.–4:00 p.m. Friday (except 1:45–2:15 p.m.)
Closed Tuesdays, Saturdays and Sundays, after services

TIP!

Of all the sites in our book, the Temple Church has the most erratic changes to its posted opening hours. Do yourself a favor—call ahead to verify that you can gain admittance!

Whether your passion is medieval history or simply the architecture of that era, a visit to the Temple Church is one of London's most rewarding stops. Built in 1170–1185, this round church was inspired by Jerusalem's Church of the Holy Sepulchre. It miraculously survived the Great Fire, suffered terribly in the May 1941 Blitz, and is the oldest surviving circular church in England. The church was consecrated during the reign of Henry II and its western doorway is the best reflection of this Norman heritage. The oblong chancel was added to the circular structure in 1240 and is a fine example of Early English architecture. Together, the round church and the chancel offer a fascinating display of tombs and memorials.

☞ Did you know?

Quite frequently, the tombs of medieval knights were adorned—like those found in the Temple Church—with marble effigies depicting a warrior armed for battle. The reclining, knees-crossed position was long believed to symbolize a knight's participation in the Crusades. Now scholars believe that the crossed knees might represent a knight who intended to "take the cross," but who ultimately did not. The silent effigies aren't telling.

Of primary importance are the particularly moving effigies of nine fully armored crusading knights, dating from the 12th through the 14th centuries. These are some of the very oldest statues to be found in England. Badly damaged during the Blitz, they have since been repaired, using as much of the original material as possible and adding nothing new. Included in the group is the effigy of one of the most pivotal characters of the 13th century, William Marshall, Earl of Pembroke, who served as Marshal of England under King John and was appointed Regent during the minority of Henry III. Look, too, for Geoffrey de Mandeville, Earl of Essex, political weathercock and one of the most dangerous and despised figures in the civil war between Stephen and Matilda.

☞ Did you know?

The Temple Church is a Royal Peculiar, a house of worship that answers only to the monarch. London's other peculiar is Westminster Abbey. Now head for the nearest pub and order a pint of *Old Peculiar,* an unusual, but tasty, dark brew and a perfect tribute to all things peculiar and ancient!

As you enter the chancel, head toward the northwest corner of the choir. There you will find access to the ancient "penitential cell," with two narrow windows looking into the church. A holding bin for those who disobeyed Temple rule, this sorry chamber is less than five feet in length and is known to have been the death chamber for at least one errant knight.

Searching for monarchs? The north* window with the Holy Lamb and Flag also bears the figures of Henry I and Stephen. The south (or Pegasus) window has representations of Henrys II and III. In the south wall recess, a mysterious tomb has long puzzled Temple archivists. The coffin, opened in 1810, contained the bones of a small child at the foot of an adult skeleton. The child is now believed to be William Plantagenet, infant son of Henry III, who is known to have been buried in Temple Church in 1256. But who is the adult? The effigy shows a fully

*When attending service in the Temple Church, the Middle Temple members sit on the north side of the chancel, under the Lamb and Flag. Members of the Inner Temple are seated on the south side, protected by their symbol, Pegasus.

adorned bishop, whom many believe to be Heracliu of Jerusalem, the man who consecrated the origir more colorful story presumes him to be Sylvester d Bishop of Carlisle, who apparently fell from his hors joying a tad too much of the knights' hospitality.

The on-site guidebook is well worth the investmei lead you, with far greater detail, on an illuminating hunt—one you're not likely soon to forget.

◇◇

THE KNIGHTS TEMPLARS

If three ideals could sum up the medieval concept of glory, fe pete with the Church, Chivalry and Crusades. No organizati these ideals as fully as the Knights Templars. Founded in France i monastic warriors had as their mission the protection of pilgrims en Holy Land. They arrived in England in the early 12th century and, w endorsement from King Stephen, began to actively recruit knights der. By the year 1250, their extensive monastic enclave covered most south of Fleet Street, property they held until their suppression in 13

The fall of such a powerful, revered and wealthy society is one of bizarre tales in English history. The position of the Templars was initi ened in 1291 with the fall of Acre, the final Palestinian outpost of Chr Ever alert to opportunities for increasing his own power and wealth, Kir of France wasted no time in capitalizing upon the Templars' misfortu first attempted to unite the Templars with their brother organizati Knights Hospitaliers, with visions of becoming the leader of the combi ders, thus reaping double clout and resources. The proposal was resoun jected by the Templars' chief, Jacques de Molay. Not one to take "no" for swer, Philip designed a dastardly plot aimed at ruining the Templars onc for all. His evil plan succeeded. Philip had all of the Templars arrested an tured, exacting shocking—and probably false—confessions of sodomy, phemy and devil worship. With the cooperation of Philip's compatriots, P Clement V and England's Edward II, the effect on the Templars was devas ing. In London, the English master of the Temple, William de la Nore, die prisoner in the Tower of London, while other members of the order were merc lessly tortured as their French comrades had been. By 1312, the Templars wer officially suppressed and their lands given to the Hospitaliers.

Despite the deadly actions of the monarchy, the loyalty of the citizenry toward the Templars did not simply die away. Before long, rumors were spreading in both England and France that a curse had been cast upon all whose hands

ainted with the Templars' blood. Fate seemed to quickly confirm the pre-n. Within months of the murder of Jacques de Molay, Philip and Pope ent both died. King Edward would ultimately be subjected to a death so ble it far surpassed any atrocity ascribed to the Knights. *(For those of you must know, Edward was disemboweled by a red-hot iron thrust through his er parts. Sorry you asked?)*

Meanwhile, the Hospitaliers already owned extensive property on the north of Clerkenwell. They leased the lands of the Templars to a group of lawyers law students to use as classrooms and dormitory housing. The association tinues today under the guise of the Inns of Court's Middle and Inner Tem-London's answer to the medieval university.

◇◇

GEOFFREY DE MANDEVILLE (D. 1144)

Talk about a weathercock! Talk about a fair-weather friend! In a time when political side-switching was as common as the children's game "Red Rover, d Rover," Geoffrey de Mandeville elevated fickle allegiance to a new ight—or, rather, plunged it to a new low. *(If you can't already tell that we really n't like this guy, rest assured: we don't!)*

At the advent of the civil war between Stephen and Matilda, Geoffrey was e castellan of the Tower of London, a position he had inherited from his fa-er. He was also the sheriff of Essex, and held large tracts of land in that shire. These assets, coupled with his holdings north of London, gave him a powerful dge when the opportunity arose to further his own ambitions. The first such pening came in 1140, when he coaxed King Stephen—who was desperate to garner all the support he could—into honoring him as the first Earl of Essex. This bought his loyalty to the king, but only for the briefest period of time.

By 1141, the civil war had reached crisis proportions, and control of London was one of the pivotal issues. As Tower castellan, and now a powerful noble, de Mandeville had the potential to play a crucial role in determining which side the City would back. With Stephen captive in Lincoln, and Matilda's forces showing a temporary surge of strength, de Mandeville quickly changed his allegiance, bartering easy access to London in exchange for the empress's reaffirmation of his titles and accompanying perks. He added to the outrage by holding King Stephen's young daughter-in-law, Constance of France, prisoner in the Tower. However, it would take more than hostages and bad-faith bargaining to assure London's support. True to their tradition of independent thinking, the City leaders were having none of Matilda; so hostile was their response to her presence in London that the empress was literally pressed to flee from her banqueting table at Westminster Hall, disguised as a commoner.

That September, Matilda's short-lived advantage was snuffed at Winchester. Although Stephen would remain in prison a while longer, de Mandeville was

busy setting the purchase price for renewing his loyalty to the Crown. As ever, his allegiance did not come cheap, and, in keeping with his nature, Stephen was willing to pay the price. In addition to being yet again confirmed as Earl of Essex and keeper of the Tower, this time Geoffrey added the roles of sheriff and justiciar of London, Middlesex and Herefordshire to his résumé. Included as part of the "signing bonus" were several of the most important castles in England, including strategic defenses on the outskirts of London. By purchasing the support of such an unreliable knave, Stephen greatly weakened the strength of the sitting government, should de Mandeville change sides again.

Apparently, wiser heads impressed this fact upon their king. In 1143, Stephen sensed a change in the Earl of Essex's wind; a very surprised de Mandeville was arrested (Stephen's delayed reaction to Geoffrey's detaining Constance in the Tower was the "official" reason) and forced to relinquish all of his castles to the Crown. Upon his release, de Mandeville staged a prolonged and particularly violent retaliation, making the fatal error of seizing Ramsey Abbey as his base of operation—an action that alienated the Church, leading to his excommunication and adding to his unsavory reputation. He was killed in battle at the siege of Burwell on September 16, 1144.

His remains rest in the company of far more admirable men at the Temple Church. How they came to be there is an interesting tale. Although de Mandeville died an ex-communicant, and therefore was denied the right of burial in consecrated ground, he was a Knight Templar. Upon his death, the Knights claimed his body and "temporarily" buried him in unconsecrated ground in the orchard just beyond the Temple walls. During the reign of Henry II, de Mandeville's son, the second Earl of Essex, was able to finagle a pardon for his father; the Knights then exhumed the unsavory Geoffrey *(all the more unsavory for having been dead so long)* and gave him a "proper" burial inside the Temple Church. *(We think they should have let this sleeping dog lie.)*

A lost treasure . . . ?

Newgate Prison

Old Bailey at Newgate Street, EC4

Blackfriar's or Holborn Tube

For nearly seven centuries, this site has been closely linked with the administration of justice—or, in the case of Newgate Prison, injustice. From the 13th century until 1902, Newgate was the most infamous of all London prisons. And although penal reforms had greatly improved the jail by the 19th century, the heinous Newgate cast its pall over the entire neighborhood.

Words cannot describe the barbaric treatment felons suffered at the hands of their Newgate gaolers. Those infamous medieval torture devices—conveniently absent from today's romanticized notion of the Middle Ages—were employed in full force here. An appalling lack of light, a dearth of fresh air, infestation by vermin, rampant jail fever, starvation, disease and violence created a hellhole beyond imagination.

If there was a bright side to Newgate, perhaps it was the wealth of literature inspired by incarceration there. The first Arthurian legends were compiled by author (and murderer) Sir Thomas Mallory during his stint at Newgate. Paintings, ballads, plays and satires poured forth as inmates attempted to address, relieve or escape the horrors of this prison.

Both the poet Geoffrey Chaucer and London Mayor Dick Whittington left money in their bequests for improvements to Newgate. They were but a drop in the bucket. Newgate was finally razed in 1902 to make room for the Central Criminal Court—affectionately known as Old Bailey. The prison lives on, however, in the writings of Defoe and Dickens and in the graphic displays at both the Museum of London and the ***London Dungeon Exhibit.***

CONTENTS

+ Sirs, Swells & the Strand + College of Arms
+ Baynard's Castle + Fleet Street & the Printed Word
+ Covent Garden + The Strand + Charing Cross

9
Of Knights & Nobles

Sirs, Swells and the Strand

It is only fitting that the stretch of land that straddles the City and Westminster was populated by a class of people neither mercantile nor regal: the knights and nobles who comprised London's gentry class. Whether drifting down the Thames on a luxury barge, ready for an audience with the king, or navigating the muddy byways en route to close a business deal with some wily merchant, this neighborhood was populated by the rich and famous—too fine to make their home in the congested central city . . . not "fine enough" to claim a chamber in court.

Unfortunately, most vestiges of the ancient nobility's presence in this vicinity have been erased by time and tide. But we assume that you—like us—have a vivid imagination, fueled by countless stories (and movies!) about those colorful, bygone days. So whether you choose to literally stretch your legs on this largely "imaginary stroll," or opt to enjoy the tour from the comforts of an easy chair, join us as we indulge in a re-creation of medieval and Tudor London's poshest addresses.

We think you'll find it a pleasure.

College of Arms

Queen Victoria Street, EC4 (020-7248-2762)

Blackfriar's Tube

OPEN

10:00 a.m.–4:00 p.m. Monday–Friday
Call for an evening tour, by prior appointment

ADMISSION

Free of charge

King Richard III originally established the College of Arms as a home for heralds, whose job was to arrange medieval tournaments, accompany the king on jousts and serve as official scorekeepers and judges of victory. Henry VII, never known for his festive nature, canceled the College's charter and awarded the house (originally in Upper Thames Street) to his mother, Margaret Beaufort. The heralds moved to the present site, former home of the Earls of Derby, when they were re-established by Mary Tudor in 1555.

How blue is your blood? This is the spot to find out. Today, the College of Arms houses a genealogical archive that is truly amazing, and will research and grant arms to those entitled to bear them. Should you want to trace your ancestry, write one month in advance to the Officer-in-Waiting for an appointment.

While you're in the neighborhood . . .

The Tower Royal, off Canon Street at College Hill, marks the site of a minor keep that was used as a residence during the reign of Edward I. Two reigns later, it housed Queen Philippa's wardrobe. While briefly in the good graces of Richard III, the first Duke of Norfolk resided in the keep-cum-mansion. During the Tudor era, it was used as a royal stable, fell into disrepair, and was eventually subdivided into low-income housing. Friday Street recalls the time when the City's Roman Catholics would flock to the nearby fish market in observation of their Friday abstinence from meat. Farther west, Oxford Court was once the London home of the Earl of Oxford. It is entered via Salters' Hall Court in St. Swithin's Lane. Founded in the reign of Edward III, the Salters' Guild was successful due to its close link to the Catholics' meat-free Fridays, when the huge demand for salt fish drove the value of the guild's commodity skyward.

A lost treasure . . .

Baynard's Castle

Queen Victoria Street, EC4

Blackfriar's Tube

LOCATION

Norman Tower: Based on excavations in the area, believed to have been on Godliman Street at Queen Victoria Street, just across from the College of Arms.

Riverside Mansion/Royal Palace: East of Castle Baynard Street, north and west of Upper Thames Street, in the approximate area of the British Telecom Museum.

Note: You'll find blue plaques commemorating Baynard's Castle at 12 and 13 Queen Victoria Street, and a model approximating the original keep is on view in the Museum of London.

Although Baynard's Castle, in all of its various incarnations, has long vanished from the London landscape, its role in medieval and Tudor history is well worth remembering. Seek out the Baynard Castle Tavern, 148 Queen Victoria Street, *and spend an hour or so as close to the original castle site as can be determined. The tavern helps set the stage with three ancient paintings that highlight scenes from our era. Can you identify the action depicted in each? Answers at the end of this section!*

One of the landmarks best known to London's medieval visitors was located at the extreme southwest edge of the City, a focal point for all those entering or leaving Westminster, or approaching the City by water. This was Baynard's Castle *(a.k.a. Castle Baynard)*, the name given to two separate but equally imposing structures: one a fortified Norman keep, the other a glorified 13th-century mansion and royal palace.

Aside from sharing a name, the two had little in common, save for a remote family connection. Their location, although close enough to one another, was not the same. And by the time the second structure rose alongside the Thames, the first had fallen into grave disrepair . . . or perhaps had even vanished entirely.

The original Baynard's Castle was one of three London strongholds built by the command of William the Conqueror after the Battle of Hastings. Together with the White Tower and the short-lived Montfichet's Castle, Baynard provided essential "defense" for *(or, rather, intimidation of)* the newly held territory. The keep was constructed by Ralph Baignard, a Norman noble who distinguished himself in the most violent manner at the Battle of Hastings. This fortress consisted of a crenelated tower, incorporating the City Wall just south of Ludgate. Three generations later, Ralph's descendant William Baynard was convicted of felony, losing his barony and, with it, the London castle. Henry I was quick to award the estate to another powerful baron, Robert de Clare, forbear of the mighty Fitzwalter clan.

Political and emotional intrigue caused the demise of the first Baynard's during the reign of King John. Perhaps you'll recall that Robert Fitzwalter was a primary organizer of the barons' revolt against John. What may be news to you *(and perhaps anti-John propaganda, to boot)* is that John was actively pursuing his rival's daughter, the unwilling Matilda "the Fair." Whether or not he was frustrated in passion as well as in politics, we do know that John vented his fury by destroying Baynard's Castle. Fitzwalter fled to France, and Baynard's remained a gutted eyesore until it was eventually incorporated into the massive holdings of the Dominican Blackfriar's.

Years later, John and Fitzwalter reconciled. Upon his return from exile, Fitzwalter re-established his London residence. Located east of the original site, along the Thames, the new Baynard's *(a.k.a. Old Inn)* was a commanding riverside "town house," with few rivals in size or grandiosity. No longer intended as a fortress, the castle had three crenelated towers that were now for effect. Sprawling for several city blocks, it was convenient to Whitehall, Westminster and St. Paul's. Such prestige did Baynard's carry that the surrounding ward assumed the title Baynard Castle Ward, becoming one of London's most fashionable addresses . . . never mind the tradesmen's hovels, brothels and rank emissions from the Brewer's Company, which crowded the "castle" on all sides.

For the next 400 years, Baynard's would be closely linked to families of influence and to the power of the Crown. As far back as Baignard's time, the senior men of the family that held the castle had been assigned the responsibility for implementing the king's writ. By 1275, these responsibilities were more clearly defined and the lord of Baynard's Castle became the Commander of the Citizenry, the king's standard-bearer and procurator. In time of battle, the lord of Baynard's was to hasten on horseback to St. Paul's, where he would receive the banner of the City, oversee selection of the marshal and issue the call to arms.

The Fitzwalter family held Baynard's until the death of Walter Fitzwalter in 1386. The castle passed to his widow, Philippa, and eventually into the hands of her new husband, Edward, Duke of York, uncle to Richard II. During the minority of

Henry VI, Baynard's was the London home of Humphrey, Duke of Gloucester. This woefully inept duke managed to remain a local favorite—and little wonder! For within the "good" duke's properties was a famous row of "tolerated" or legal brothels, guaranteed to win him undying popularity—at least among the menfolk. In 1428, Baynard's was extensively damaged by fire. Humphrey rebuilt and improved the mansion, only to lose it for his heirs. Upon Humphrey's death and attainder, Henry VI seized the residence and awarded it to Richard, Duke of York, father of two future Yorkist kings. The first, Edward, Earl of March, was in residence at Baynard's when offered the Crown. The scene was replayed years later with his brother, Richard, Duke of Gloucester.

In 1501, Henry VII renovated Baynard's and the newly splendid property became the primary official residence of his mother, Margaret Beaufort, and other early Tudors. Prince Arthur and the young Katherine of Aragon celebrated their wedding with a lavish celebration staged at Baynard's. Alas, Katherine's association with Baynard's would eventually turn grim. It was here that she faced several sessions of the legatine court regarding the divorce forced upon her by Henry VIII. By the time of her imposed exile from court, Baynard's (now the Royal Wardrobe) would be used merely as a warehouse for her precious belongings. *(These treasures were later sold by her "ex" to pay for her funeral and* not, *please note, passed on to her daughter, Mary!)*

What Henry did pass along to his heirs was an enormous royal debt. By the time Mary ascended the throne, it was necessary to divest of key properties in order to raise sorely needed funds. Although Baynard's was the site of the official London proclamation of Mary's ascent to the throne (as it had been for Lady Jane Grey), the mansion was ultimately sold to Sir William Herbert, Earl of Pembroke. It remained the London seat of the Pembroke family until it was destroyed by the Great Fire in 1666.

Answers to the Baynard Castle Tavern picture quiz: 1. Edward the Black Prince and his prisoner, John of France, arriving in London via Temple Bar; 2. Elizabeth I's post-Armada victory procession; 3. A typical late-Tudor inn and coach scene. Winners, buy yourselves another pint!

While you're in the neighborhood . . .

From Queen Victoria Street, take a moment to walk north along St. Andrew's Hill. The first site of interest is the church of St. Andrew's by the Wardrobe, which takes its name from the nearby King's Wardrobe, where Edward I's ceremonial garb was stored. Proceed but a few steps past the church and keep your eyes open for the very tiny Ireland Yard, on your left. Along this block was once property named for John Ireland, who eventually sold the land to William Shakespeare. At the time, the bard had plans for building his own theater in the neighborhood, and Ireland Yard would have proved a convenient residence. Ultimately, he bequeathed the site to his daughter, Sussanah; the deed of transfer is on display in the Guildhall.

FLEET STREET AND THE PRINTED WORD

Fleet Street, home of London's newspaper industry, is named for the River Fleet, or Fleet Ditch, also known as "that stinking abomination." *(No matter how you feel about THE PRESS, you have to admit that's funny!)*

The link between Fleet Street and the printed word dates from around 1500, when Wynkyn de Worde, assistant to London's first printer, William Caxton, relocated his printing press from its original home just outside Westminster Abbey to the Fleet neighborhood. During the reign of Henry VIII, the official royal printer, Richard Pynson, continued to publish works from the banks of the Fleet. In an attempt to control the influx of "heretical" ideas, Henry had effectively banned the import of books from the Continent. This gave London printers a lucrative edge on the English market for reading matter. Unfortunately, it also cut the island off from much of the rich writing that flourished abroad during the Renaissance.

While you're in the neighborhood . . .

Stop in for a light bite at the Olde Cheshire Cheese. The pub was made famous by Dickens, but more to our point, it rests atop the ancient Whitefriars' Crypt. The priory itself was located farther along Fleet Street, about midway down the left-hand side of Bouverie Street. Adjacent to the "Cheese" is the old Wine Office Court, a tiny enclave that was once the monastic gardens and later the home of the Wine Office, which regulated London's fruit-of-the-vine trade. As you continue your approach to the Middle and Inner Temples, you'll pass Fetter Lane, a shortcut to Charterhouse and Ely Place/Hatton Gardens. Fetter Lane dates back to Norman times and may be a variation on the word *fewter,* meaning "vagabond," or *defaytor,* meaning "defaultor." The location, outside the walls of the City and close by the Court of Rolls, makes either interpretation feasible.

COVENT GARDEN

Although the medieval mementos in this area are virtually nil, we know no trip to London is complete without a trip to Covent Garden. As long as you're going to go there anyway, you may as well know a bit about its ancient origins.

Originally belonging to the Abbot of Westminster Abbey, this land was truly the *convent garden,* supplying fruit and vegetables to help feed the extensive clerical personnel of Westminster. Like most church-owned property, the land was separated from the Abbey during the Dissolution; it was then briefly owned by the Duke of Somerset. Upon Somerset's execution in 1552, it was given to the first Earl of Bedford in recognition of his successful defeat of a Cornwall uprising. However, London was notoriously resistant to westward expansion and this valuable land was not significantly developed until the 1630s. Until then, Covent Garden remained a bucolic park for the privileged.

As you nose around the shops or enjoy a night at the theater in the Covent Garden area, you'll happen upon several streets whose names reach back into the Middle Ages. Be on the lookout for Long Acre Street, once lined on either side by the abbot's mighty elms. Drury Lane, which in Tudor times suffered a reputation as one of London's seedier side streets, was part of the ancient "*Hundred of Drury.*" Originally known as Middle Lane, Maiden Lane was the medieval dividing line between two tracts of ecclesiastic land. Russell Street bears the surname of the Earl of Bedford, the area's Elizabethan and Stuart landowners, while Southampton Street bears the title of Thomas Wriothesley, earl of the same, who owned a mansion on this lane in the reign of Elizabeth I.

AN IMAGINARY STROLL DOWN THE STRAND

Separate as they try to be, the City of London and the city of Westminster have been inextricably linked from the minute Edward the Confessor looked outside the Roman wall for his seat of government. Since then, no politician, clergyman or artisan could hope to ply a trade in one jurisdiction without sooner or later crossing into rival territory.

The most popular route for such journeys was a muddy, pitted and perilous bridle path that followed the banks of the Thames. This was the Strand, bustling and noisy, an artery of low social standing that would, in short order, become one of the most-sought-after addresses in residential London.

Little remains to be seen of that medieval byway as you stroll down the Strand today. But if you have had the opportunity to visit the handsome Chelsea manor home, Crosby Place, you'll find it easy to imagine the grandeur of this waterside promenade, where glorious mansions stood shoulder-to-shoulder in a jostle for prestige, position and the most impressive view of the Thames.

Having wandered the neighborhoods of Castle Baynard and the Middle and Inner Temples, follow Fleet Street toward the Strand, once the central enclave of Saxon London. The first residents of prestige to put down roots along the Strand were the bishops and abbots of outlying counties who sought closer access to the Crown. They established grand homes, known as "inns," on the south side of the street. Less affluent landowners would soon develop housing along the north side. Over the next 100 years, noblemen, state officials and courtiers would follow suit. The names associated with the neighborhood read like a medieval "Who's Who" of the prominent and the powerful.

The Dissolution saw an end to the clergy's presence on the Strand. Their homes fell into the hands of "friends" of the Crown, men who took great pride in welcoming their courtly guests as they arrived in private gilded barges at the numerous watergates. By the end of the 17th century—thanks to the Great Fire and Jacobean "urban renewal"—these grand urban palaces had all but vanished.

The Tudor pedestrian would then pass ***Bridewell Palace*** (the current site of the 20th-century Unilever House), located just beyond ***Blackfriar's Bridge.*** Bridewell was built by Henry VIII between 1512 and 1520. There is now a commemorative plaque on ***Bridewell Place,*** between Newbridge Street and Dorset Street at Watergate. Here Bluff Hal entertained with great feasting and merriment and shared his last meal with Katherine of Aragon, just days before Thomas Cranmer issued their divorce decree. Art lovers, take note: on this site the French Ambassador and the Bishop of Lavauer posed for Holbein the Younger's famous painting *The Ambassadors*, now on display at the ***National Gallery.*** Bridewell's days as a royal residence were, however, short-lived. The most particular Edward

VI found it far too noisy, and in 1553 he granted the palace to the City; it was established as a home for destitute persons and a workhouse for "strumpets and idle vagabonds."

A bit farther along, just past Temple Gardens, the unpopular Lord Protector Somerset, guardian of young Edward, established the grandiose Somerset House, England's first Renaissance palace. Appropriating lands east of modern Waterloo Bridge, Somerset went on to demolish a bishop's residence, an Inn of Chancery and the original St. Mary le Strand church in order to have adequate acreage for his lavish scheme. This early version of Somerset House would later be replaced by William Chambers's grand house for civil servants, which now occupies the site.

Proceed along the Westminster side of Waterloo Bridge and on to the premises of the Savoy Hotel, once the site of the Savoy Palace, and for a short time the only residential site on the Strand not occupied by a bishop's inn. Head for the entryway and look at the numerous plaques that outline, in brief, the palace's fascinating history. Originally built in 1245, the mansion was founded by Peter de Savoy, uncle to Eleanor of Provence, the consort of Henry III. Upon his arrival in England, Peter was honored as the Earl of Savoy and Richmond, and was knighted in Westminster Abbey. It is known that King Henry's nemesis, the parliamentary crusader Simon de Montfort, resided for a period of time at the Savoy. The palace was later given to Henry and Eleanor's son, Edmund "Crouchback," founder of the House of Lancaster. Another Henry, first Duke of Lancaster, would lavish a startling £35,000 (millions of pounds, by today's standards!) on the rebuilding of Savoy House between 1343 and 1379. So extravagant was the end product that it was deemed a fitting "prison" for King John of France, hostage of Edward the Black Prince. John was kept at the Savoy in *voluntary* captivity until his death in 1364. *(Either things were really rotten back home in France, or the Savoy was something remarkable!)*

Perhaps the most notorious resident of Savoy Palace was John of Gaunt, Protector of young Richard II. So despised was Gaunt by the common man that when a particularly violent faction of rebels descended upon the Savoy during the 1381 Peasants' Revolt, the commander strictly forbade looting . . . lest the rebels become tainted by association with Gaunt's personal effects. One vagrant caught disobeying the command was put to death on the spot. The mayhem reached its peak when a large barrel, believed to be an ale keg, was tossed onto the flames. It proved, instead, to be gunpowder and the Savoy was blown apart. For 125 years, the massive structure stood in ruins. It was eventually restored by Henry VII and endowed as a hospital.

Hark! In the middle of your imaginary stroll there is something REAL to see! Check out the ***Queen's Chapel of the Savoy,*** located at Savoy Hill and open 11:30 a.m. to 3:30 p.m., Tuesday through Friday. Built in 1516 as part of the Hospital of St. John (Savoy Hospital), most of the original Tudor building is still intact. The stained-glass windows give it an even older feeling—they predate the structure by about 300 years and were presented as a gift in the 1950s. By the way, this was the first London church to be lit by electricity.

Not every lucky landowner along the Strand paid dearly for their home, or felt compelled to spend the extraordinary sums lavished upon the Savoy for renovation and decor. In 1549, the savvy Earl of Arundel paid a mere £40 for Arundel House, and a great many Elizabethan courtiers actually received their homes for "free" . . . although we all know just what kind of strings came attached to Elizabeth's "freebies." Exeter House was awarded to Lord Burghley, and the Bishop of Durham's medieval Durham Place (at times home to Edward VI, Princess Elizabeth and Lady Jane Grey) ultimately went to Sir Walter Raleigh.

Exeter House, now the Outer Temple, was originally the London home of the Bishops of Exeter. Depending on the owner at the time, it may be referred to throughout history and literature as *Paget Place, Leicester House* or *Essex House.* It was at Essex/Exeter that the self-important earl thereof rendezvoused with his fellow rebels and marched into the City on February 8, 1600, hoping to rally support against the queen. When the coup failed, he escaped by boat back to Essex House.

Arundel House also donned a litany of names: *Bath's Inn, Hampton Place, Seymour Place* (after Lord Thomas Seymour) and finally Arundel House. A fine, luxurious home, it was demolished in the late 1600s. And so the "gold coast" aura continued on down the Strand with Carlisle House, Norwich House and St. Mary Runceval (ironically an almshouse!). The last vestige of the Strand's palaces is the landlocked York Watergate, still located at the Victoria Embankment end of Buckingham Street. ***York House,*** a 13th-century mansion, had long been the London home of the Bishops of York. Like its many palatial neighbors, it enjoyed waterside gardens and an impressive river entrance. The mansion was remodeled in the 1600s by the Duke of Buckingham, but the striking watergate remains intact.

Our imaginary walk down the Strand ends here. You will be bearing north toward Charing Cross. The medieval traveler, however, would most likely have headed west, toward the vicinity's most impressive residence of all, the royal palace of ***Whitehall.***

◇◇◇

JOHN OF GAUNT, DUKE OF LANCASTER (1340–1399)

Of all the 14th-century nobles, it is likely that none compares in stature to Edward III's formidable third son, John of Gaunt. Honored from age two as the Earl of Richmond, John married into the duchy of Lancaster in 1362 when he married his first wife, Blanche. His early career is marked with a mighty arrogance, a trait that he, thankfully, tempered a bit with age. An ambitious widower, he took as his second wife Constance of Castile, heir to King Pedro the Cruel, and upon his father-in-law's death, he promptly proclaimed himself King of Castile and León. Spain had other ideas. Gaunt was roundly defeated by the Spaniards in 1388 and forced to relinquish his "kingship" and accompanying realm; two of his daughters, however, would go on to become queens of Castile and Portugal. Still, John did not go wanting for titles. He added "Duke of Aquitaine" to his résumé in 1394, and was, for a short time, Protector of young King Richard II. Unfortunately, Gaunt's insufferable pride made him a resoundingly unpopular choice for regent, and an immature Richard assumed the duties of kingship well before his time.

Despite his ambitions and his haughty demeanor, John of Gaunt never cast his eye upon the throne. He was deeply loyal to the two kings he served—father and nephew—despite the fact that his own son, Henry Bolingbroke, would eventually usurp the crown from Richard II. Gaunt placed great store in traditional virtues such as scholarship, chivalry and piety. Because of his overarching arrogance and vast political sway, Gaunt was never beloved by the Londoners *(to say the least!)*. He was, however, a well-regarded foreign diplomat, wise councilor and a visionary thinker on issues of public policy.

Having twice married for political gain, John's third marriage was for love. In February 1396, he married his mistress of 25 years, Katherine Swynford. Their three baseborn sons were proclaimed legitimate by Richard II, giving the soon-to-be-powerful Beaufort boys a significant career boost. The eldest, Edmund, would become Duke of Somerset, while second son Henry became Cardinal-Bishop of Winchester.

John spent his waning years in ill health, virtually confined to his castles at Kenilworth and Leicester. He died at Leicester on February 3, 1399, and was carried in a princely funeral procession to London. Apparently, the escort took their good sweet time getting there: Gaunt was not buried until March 16, when he was laid to rest at St. Paul's Cathedral beside his first duchess, Blanche of Lancaster.

Charing Cross

The Strand, WC2
Charing Cross Tube

Once a little settlement at the top of Whitehall, Charing Cross has gained notoriety for the presence of its replicated Eleanor Cross. It was in the village of Charing that Edward I erected the last of his 12 monuments that marked the funeral path of his beloved wife, Eleanor of Castile, from Nottinghampshire to Westminster Abbey. The cross on exhibit today can be seen in the forecourt of Charing Cross Station. Although the site is not quite exact, this 1863 replica is largely true to the original structure. The sentimental design, with its flourishes and functionless arches, is believed to have been inspired by similar crosses made for St. Louis of France. Whether English or French, these crosses mark the advent of the "decorative" style of design that so influenced later Middle Ages. Further examples of an Eleanor Cross and similar funereal monuments of the era can be examined up close at the ***Victoria & Albert Museum.***

CONTENTS

IO

Regal London

The Neighborhood of Kings and Queens

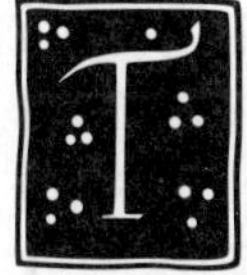

The rocky relationship between the first Norman monarchs and the City of London caused these kings to make the prudent decision of putting a little distance between themselves and the commune. Still, these kings, who were forever in the process of solidifying their control over England, did not want to move too far—they needed the wealth and power of the rich London merchants and they wanted to keep a close eye on the actions of the independent-minded citizens of London. They found the perfect spot in the "west minster," not far outside the City walls, where Edward the Confessor had established a palace and built an abbey.

So, first William the Conqueror and then his sons William Rufus and Henry I made Westminster Palace the center of their governments in the 11th and 12th centuries. Making Westminster the primary seat of their monarchy had the added advantage of subtly underscoring a connection with Edward the Confessor, something the Norman kings needed to strengthen the legitimacy of their claim to the English Crown. That is also why they took up the tradition of holding their coronations in Edward's newly constructed Westminster Abbey and of adopting the Abbey as a particular beneficiary of royal patronage.

The medieval and Tudor rulers who came after the Conqueror and his sons continued these customs, basing royal government in Westminster and making the abbey a focal point of their religious lives. And even when Henry VIII in the 16th century got tired of living in the dilapidated old palace of Westminster, he didn't move far—just down the street into a remodeled Whitehall Palace and adding a back-up palace nearby at St. James. Thus did Westminster become the neighborhood of kings and queens.

WALKING REGAL LONDON

Because there is still so much to see in this royal neighborhood and so much happened here over the course of the more than 500 years we are tracing, this chapter is packed with details about the events that occurred and the daily lives and deaths of the kings and queens who resided in the buildings. As with the Tower of London, we suggest that you read the history before you actually begin your tour, particularly of Westminster Abbey. But if you are pressed for time and want to just do a quick walk around the neighborhood, the following is a brief overview of what there is to see.

Unless you are the type of brave *(or foolhardy)* soul who likes to play chicken with the congested London traffic or are committed to visiting the site of every medieval and Tudor execution ground, we suggest you skip ***Tyburn***, the "commoners'" execution ground, for now. It is marked by a plaque located in the center of an extremely busy traffic island next to Hyde Park. We also suggest that you save your stroll through ***Hyde Park*** until you have a bright, sunny day and the leisure to contemplate the fact that these beautiful grounds were once part of the fields and orchards that belonged to Westminster Abbey.

This means that you are going to start your walking tour at ***St. James Palace***, located on the Mall. Look for the partly Tudor balcony of Friary Court on Marlborough Road. This is where every new sovereign of Great Britain is proclaimed. Around the corner on Cleveland Road, you will find a medieval gatehouse guarded by a red-coated sentry.

Cross the Mall and walk through ***St. James Park*** (said to be the oldest park in London, although the current design dates from 1827) to the corner of Birdcage Walk and Horse Guards Road. You are now in the vicinity of where ***Whitehall Palace*** once stood. Meander on over to the Embankment Gardens (at Richmond Terrace) and you will find remnants of the river wall of the palace and a portion of the terrace.

Now, move back along the Embankment toward Big Ben at the corner of Bridge Street and St. Margaret's. Behind Big Ben is ***Westminster Hall,*** one of the few surviving parts of the medieval Westminster Palace. However, you won't be able to get inside unless you have written ahead for an appointment. Outside, as you walk along the building, you will see ***New Palace Yard,*** which dates from the reign of William Rufus (1087–1100). ***Old Palace Yard*** was the courtyard of an older palace built by Edward the Confessor and is the site where Sir Walter Raleigh was beheaded in 1618. The only ***statue of Richard the Lionheart*** in London also can be found in Old Palace Yard.

Across from Old Palace Yard is the ***Jewel Tower,*** another surviving feature of the medieval palace, which was built in 1365 as a warehouse for Edward III's clothes and jewels. Today the tower has a small display of relics from the old palace.

Next to the Jewel Tower is ***Westminster Abbey,*** but before you bolt inside there, we suggest you make a brief detour into the chapel located to the north of the Abbey. ***St. Margaret's Church*** was consecrated in 1523 and has some interesting Tudor features, including a stained-glass window created to commemorate the engagement of Prince Arthur and Katherine of Aragon.

Here are highlights of some of the fascinating tombs you will stroll past on your walk through the Abbey in the order that you will encounter them.

- ***Aymer de Valence, Earl of Pembroke*** (1270–1324), a cousin of Edward I, whose tomb is located in the sanctuary.
- ***Edmund "Crouchback"*** (1245–1296), second son of Henry III and founder of the House of Lancaster, also buried in the sanctuary.
- ***Edward I*** (1239–1307), the first tomb in the ***Chapel of St. Edward the Confessor.***
- ***Henry III*** (1207–1272), the builder of St. Edward's shrine.
- ***Eleanor of Castile*** (1244–1290), wife of Edward I, buried next to Henry III.
- ***Elizabeth I*** (1533–1603), the monument to the ***"Princes in the Tower," Edward VI, Henry VII, Elizabeth of York*** and ***Mary Queen of Scots,*** all in the ***Chapel of Henry VII.***
- ***Henry V*** (1387–1422), behind the Coronation Chair.
- ***Philippa of Hainault*** (1314–1369), wife of Edward III, whose tomb is next to Henry V's.
- ***Frances, Duchess of Suffolk*** (1517–1559), the mother of Lady Jane Grey, "the Nine Days Queen," who is buried in the Chapel of St. Edmund.
- ***Edward III*** (1312–1377), whose tomb is decorated with statues representing six of his 14 children.
- ***Richard II*** (1367–1400) and his wife, ***Anne of Bohemia*** (1366–1394).

After you pass Richard and Anne's tomb, you are leaving St. Edward's chapel and entering the South Ambulatory. To your right, you will see a plaque to ***Anne Neville,*** wife of Richard III, who is buried in an unmarked grave under the altar. Next to her plaque is the tomb of ***King Sebert,*** who is credited with founding the first church on this site in the 7th century.

Next to Sebert, sandwiched in between two marble monuments, is ***Anne of Cleves,*** Henry VIII's fourth wife.

In ***Poets' Corner,*** you will find the graves of ***Geoffrey Chau-***

cer, Edmund Spencer and ***Ben Jonson,*** as well as a monument to ***Shakespeare.***

In the medieval ***cloisters,*** you can visit the ***Chapter House,*** built between 1250 and 1253, which has the largest existing expanse of original medieval floor tiles in all of England. There also is the ***Pyx Chamber,*** with the oldest altar in the Abbey, and the ***Abbey Museum,*** which has a fascinating display of the funeral effigies of several medieval and Tudor monarchs.

Back in the ***nave,*** you will find a portrait of ***Richard II*** on a pillar outside of ***St. George's Chapel.*** This is the oldest contemporary portrait of an English monarch. The chapel also features a partly medieval stained-glass window with a representation of the ***Black Prince.***

After you have finished your tour of the Abbey, if time permits, you may want to wander across Lambeth Bridge to ***Lambeth Palace***, the ancient seat of the Archbishops of Canterbury. Unless you have written ahead to schedule a tour, you will not be able to get inside the palace. But you can pause to take a close look at the Tudor gatehouse known as ***Morton's Tower*** that still serves as the main entrance to the palace.

You have now completed a rapid review of Regal London.

Tyburn

Located on a traffic island at the junction of Edgware and Bayswater Roads next to Hyde Park

Lancaster Gate, Marble Arch, Knightsbridge or Hyde Park Corner Tube

A plaque on this traffic island marks the location of the Tyburn gallows, London's most infamous execution spot aside from Tower Hill. This is not difficult to find, but it is difficult to get yourself onto the traffic island. Railings blocking pedestrian traffic surround most of the area, and you risk your life to do the dodging and weaving through the fast-moving vehicular traffic necessary to gain access to the island. If you are determined to try, we suggest going very, very early in the morning or late at night, when the traffic will be less heavy.

Tyburn, also sometimes called "The Elms" in medieval records, was where "common" criminals were taken to be hanged. Traitors executed here also were victims of the ghastly sentence "hanged, drawn and quartered." Most were still alive when this barbaric practice was carried out, since hanging simply meant slow strangulation in those days.

No Ghost Alert!

One would think that a place as saturated in blood caused by such horrifying deaths as took place at Tyburn would be crawling with ghosts and evil spirits. But there are no reports of any—at least none from the Medieval and Tudor Ages. The only ghost stories related to Tyburn date from post-Tudor times. *(We didn't think you would care about those any more than we do.)*

While you're in the neighborhood . . .

Between Bayswater Road on the north and Knightsbridge on the south, you will find Hyde Park. One entrance to the park is located near the traffic island with the Tyburn plaque. This has been a royal park ever since Henry VIII confiscated the land from Westminster Abbey during the Dissolution of the Monasteries. He had long coveted it as a hunting preserve. A stroll through some of the park's 340 acres makes for a pleasant walk.

Also while you're in the neighborhood . . .

At the other end of Hyde Park, straight down Park Lane from the Marble Arch, is Hyde Park Corner. This was the site of the ancient manor that belonged to Westminster Abbey . . . before Henry decided he needed the land more than the Abbey did.

St. James Palace

The Mall, SW1

St. James Park, Green Park or Hyde Park Corner Tube

>>

OPEN

Not open to the public

>>

Although he never called it home, St. James was one of the many castles accumulated by Henry VIII during his tumultuous reign. Originally the site of a leper hospital dedicated to St. James the Less that was established by Queen Maude the Good (a.k.a. Matilda, a.k.a. Edith), wife of Henry I, the property came into Henry's possession, as did so many others, during the Dissolution of the Monasteries. *(It certainly was a unique way to become a real estate magnate.)*

Henry acquired this particular piece of property in 1531. He combined it with other land he already held (some of which he had "acquired" from Westminster Abbey) and promptly began to construct a new palace, intended to be a manor house for Anne Boleyn. Unfortunately, that unlucky lady never lived to see the building completed. In fact, the first time St. James was used for a state occasion, Henry was on wife number six, Katherine Parr. The event was the June 1544 wedding of Henry's niece Lady Margaret Douglas to the Earl of Lennox.

☞ Did you know?

At the end of his reign, Henry VIII owned 14 palaces in London alone, houses he either had built or took over during the Dissolution of the Monasteries.

St. James remained a favorite residence of the Tudor monarchs. Mary in particular stayed there often, choosing to retreat there when she knew she was dying. She died at St. James on November 17, 1558, at 4 a.m. while hearing mass. History records that she died at the exact moment the Host was elevated. Her body remained at St. James for a month before anyone could decide what to do with it. Eventually, funeral ceremonies were conducted at Westminster Abbey and she was buried there in the chapel named for her grandfather, Henry VII.

The palace became the official royal residence after Whitehall burned in 1698. It remains the statutory seat of Britain's monarchy and is where ambassadors from other nations are accredited (hence, one can aspire to be the Ambassador to the Court of St. James). It also is the London residence of the Prince of Wales.

Today, there is little left of the Tudor palace. The partly Tudor balcony of Friary Court on Marlborough Road is where every new sovereign of Great Britain is proclaimed. The main entrance to the palace, the gatehouse on Cleveland Row, is guarded now by red-coated sentries rather than knights in armor, but it also is Tudor. The mullioned windows on the right of the gatehouse are part of the Chapel Royal, located between the Color Court and the Ambassador's Court. The chapel's facade is authentic, but the only thing Tudor that survives inside is the ceiling, designed by Hans Holbein in the 1540s. Reportedly, there is a stair turret in the Color Court (behind the gatehouse) that dates from our period. But, alas, there is no way to check, since the public is not allowed entrance to the palace.

☞ Did you know?

The Tudor Rose was "designed," if you will, during the reign of Henry VII (1485–1509) to celebrate the end of the Wars of the Roses. It is a hybrid of the feuding dynasties: the white rose of York and the red rose of Lancaster. Henry VIII was the son of the marriage of Henry Tudor (Lancaster) and Elizabeth of York that united the rival houses.

On very rare occasions, the State Apartments of St. James are opened to the public. Long lines usually broadcast these infrequent events. If you do manage to make it inside, some of the rooms contain bits and pieces of Tudor architecture, and the initials of Henry VIII and Anne Boleyn are carved above the fireplace in the Tapestry Room.

The park across from the palace is reputed to be London's oldest royal park. The original walled park on the site was designed by Henry VIII himself *(certainly a man of many talents—poet, musician, theologian, landscape designer)*. The St. James Park you see today was created by John Nash in 1827.

◊◊

HANS HOLBEIN THE YOUNGER (1497–1543)

Much of what we know today about the way people of the Tudor Age looked, dressed and perceived their world we see through the eyes of the great portrait artist Hans Holbein the Younger. Born in Germany, Holbein moved to England permanently in 1532. He began building his clientele by painting portraits of the members of the Hanseatic League. One of his most famous portraits dating from this time is titled *The Ambassadors* and now hangs in the National Gallery in London.

Holbein became the official court painter in 1536 after producing a portrait of Jane Seymour, Henry VIII's third wife, that Henry particularly liked. From that time on, Holbein was fully engaged in producing portraits of Henry, his potential wives and his courtiers. He also was employed in producing murals for Henry's various castles, the most well known of which is the dynastic mural Holbein created for the Presence Chamber at Whitehall. In his spare time, Holbein designed buildings (i.e., the Holbein Gate at Whitehall), stained glass and jewel settings (many of which can be seen in his portrait work).

Holbein almost lost his cushy job—and came close to losing his head—when he mortally offended Henry by producing a flattering miniature of Anne of Cleves in 1539. Thomas Cromwell, the first Earl of Essex and Henry's chief minister, used the portrait to push Henry into marrying for the fourth time. Cromwell was of the opinion that an alliance with a German prince would be of great benefit to England. When Henry actually met Anne after she arrived in England in December 1539, he hated her on sight and blamed both Cromwell and Holbein for misleading him about the woman's appearance.

Henry never got any happier with his fourth wife and in less than a year (in fact, just seven months after their January 1540 wedding), the marriage was set aside and Anne retired gracefully to live quietly in the country. Cromwell bore the brunt of the blame for the fiasco. His foreign policy was totally discredited, and he was arrested, imprisoned in the Tower of London, attainted and brutally executed in July 1540.

Who knows what saved Holbein. Henry's great love of art, maybe? The important point is that Holbein continued to serve the court until his death (by natural causes) in 1543. Much of his work survives and can be seen in major museums around the world. Windsor Castle also has an excellent collection of his courtier portraits.

◊◊

A lost treasure . . . WHITEHALL PALACE

Whitehall was once the largest palace in all of Europe, containing the royal apartments and another 2,000 rooms for courtiers in a sprawl of buildings spread over 23 acres, stretching from Great Scotland Yard Street in the north, straddling both sides of Whitehall, to Downing Street and Richmond Terrace in the south. From the 1530s until it was destroyed by fire in 1698, Whitehall was the principal seat of the British monarchy.

Today, little is left of this gigantic Tudor palace and what does remain mostly is not accessible to the public. Don't be fooled by the enticement of the Banqueting House. This building was commissioned by James I in 1619. There is nothing Tudor about it or in it.

The most spectacular existing feature of the old palace is a wine cellar built for Henry VIII that is located under the Ministry of Defense building. This room was discovered in the 1940s when the site was being redeveloped. Engineers hoisted the 800-ton, vaulted, brick-built structure and moved it sideways on rollers to preserve it. After a new, deeper basement was constructed, the cellar was rolled back into place. Since that time, the cellar has been used for special events and private parties, but the Ministry of Defense building in which it is located is due for a major renovation and will be closed for the next five years. Therefore, no one is going to be able to see the wine cellar, at least until the construction work is done.

Outside this building, however, in the Embankment Gardens at Richmond Terrace, you will find a portion of the Whitehall Palace wharf. Although the site is officially designated as "Queen Mary's Stairs"—the stairs having been built for Queen Mary II by Wren—a sizable portion of the river wall of the old Tudor palace is still there, as well as a portion of the original terrace.

There are extensive remains of Henry VIII's elaborate tennis courts (he had four, two of which were enclosed). These remains are in and around the Cabinet Office, located at 70 Whitehall, and in the passage linking Downing Street with the Horse Guards parade grounds. But it is very hard for the average visitor to get to see any of them, since the Cabinet Office is not open to the public and access to Downing Street is blocked for security reasons.

The history of Whitehall, although short by the standards of other royal palaces in London, is a fascinating one. Originally known as York House, this site had been the London seat of the Archbishops of York for centuries. It passed into royal hands when Cardinal Wolsey "gave" the house to Henry VIII in October 1529 in an effort to pacify His Royal Majesty.

Wolsey had recently been stripped of the office of Lord Chancellor and had surrendered the Great Seal. He had lost favor with Henry because of his inability to convince Rome that Henry should be granted an annulment from Katherine of Aragon. The unrelenting enmity of Anne Boleyn, the light of Henry's eye *(or should we more accurately say, the fuel firing his lust)* at this point in time, did not help Wolsey's position. Anne had never forgiven Wolsey for his part in preventing her marriage to Henry Percy, future Earl of Northumberland, and ceaselessly worked to undermine Henry's confidence in the cardinal. (For those of you who have forgotten, Anne was about to be betrothed to Henry Percy when she caught King Henry's attention, probably sometime in 1525 or 1526. Henry ordered Wolsey to end the affair, Percy was sent from court and the king began pursuing Anne in earnest.)

Henry eagerly accepted Wolsey's gift of York Place (although he did not restore the cardinal to any of his offices and Wolsey never did regain Henry's confidence). The cardinal had refurbished the palace on a scale to rival Hampton Court (which he had also built and given to Henry) and Henry wanted to use it as a London palace for Anne. He renamed it Whitehall and immediately set about renovating the buildings. He also expanded the site to include all the land between Westminster and Charing Cross and he added a tiltyard (on the site of the present-day Horse Guards parade grounds), cock pit and tennis courts. The street of Whitehall, then called King Street, divided the palace grounds, so Henry linked the halves with a bridge that came to be known as the Holbein Gate, named (of course) for the artist who designed it.

Anne promptly moved into Whitehall, establishing her own court there in competition with that of Queen Katherine. She began presiding over elaborate court entertainments, replacing Katherine as queen in all but name. In fact, much of the drama of Henry and Anne's life together was played out at Whitehall.

It was at Whitehall (still York Place at the time) that they first met. Anne and Henry were both performing in a pageant staged by Cardinal Wolsey after a great banquet hosted by Wolsey in honor of the king and Queen Katherine. This event occurred during Lent, March 4, 1522, soon after Anne returned from her sojourn at the French court. No matter how suave, sophisticated, witty and charming Anne may have been, there is no evidence that Henry paid her any particular notice at this time—he had eyes only for Mary Boleyn, Anne's sister and Henry's mistress at the time *(nothing like keeping it in the family!)*.

Anne and Henry also were married at Whitehall, secretly, just before dawn on January 25, 1533, in the king's private chapel. Secrecy was required because there was some doubt at the time about whether Henry really was divorced from Katherine of Aragon. But any moral squeamishness that either the bride or the groom might have had over the question of possible bigamy was drowned by the need for haste in getting married. Anne was pregnant and both she and Henry wanted to make sure their "son" would be born legitimate. (Of course, the "son" turned out to be the Princess Elizabeth.)

Finally, in a fitting ending to the story of Henry VIII and Anne Boleyn, it was at Whitehall that Henry waited to hear the Tower of London guns signal that Anne was dead before rushing off to his new bride-to-be, Jane Seymour.

Henry had become partial to weddings at Whitehall. He and Jane were married there on May 30, 1536, just 11 days after Anne's execution. This time, the private ceremony was held in the Queen's Closet with Archbishop Cranmer presiding. The wedding was followed by a grand celebration in the great hall of Whitehall over which Jane presided for the first time as queen.

Henry died at Whitehall at 2 a.m. on January 28, 1547. He was 55 years old. Wife number six, Katherine Parr, was in residence at the time. The probable cause of Henry's death was a blood clot that broke loose from a thrombosed vein in his leg and caused a pulmonary embolism. His body was carried to Windsor, where he was buried in St. George's Chapel with Jane Seymour, the love of his life *(probably because she was the mother of his male heir and died young)*.

Henry's successors, Edward VI and Mary I, both spent a great deal of time at Whitehall, but it is with Anne's daughter, Elizabeth, that the palace is most associated. It was her principal residence, the one at which she spent the most time during the 45 years of her reign, and the site of one of the most glorious and extravagant events held annually throughout her reign, Ascension Day, November 17, the anniversary of her inheritance of the Crown.

☞ Did you know?

One of the most famous portraits of the Tudor dynasty was painted by Hans Holbein during the winter of 1536–1537 as a mural for the Presence Chamber of Whitehall. In the painting, Henry VIII is pictured with his current wife, Jane Seymour, and his father, Henry VII, and mother, Elizabeth of York. The painting was one of the first works of art to depict full-length likenesses of royal personages. During her reign, Elizabeth liked to receive visitors to Whitehall standing in front of that mural to emphasize her right to the throne as a direct descendant of Henry VII and Henry VIII. The mural was destroyed when the palace was burned, but fortunately Charles II had had the foresight to commission the Dutch artist Remigius van Leempert to make a copy of it. The copy now hangs in the Renaissance Picture Gallery at Hampton Court. The left-hand section of Holbein's draft for the mural, picturing the two Henrys, can be seen at the ***National Portrait Gallery.***

This was a day of high pageantry during which the code of

chivalry was celebrated. The highlight of the day was the jousts held at Whitehall's tiltyard. The queen would be seated in the gallery that ran through the Holbein Gate, connecting the palace to the tiltyard (now the Horse Guards parade grounds). The young men of the Court would pass before her, presenting her with gifts and challenging her champion in order to prove their knightly prowess. If you stand between the Horse Guards' building and Treasury, you will be approximately in the area where Elizabeth would have sat during the jousting. Close your eyes and you will see the pennants flying, the flash of sun on shining armor and the brightly colored gowns and sparkling jewelry of the women of the Court. You will hear the crack of the lances, the lusty cheers of the crowd of 12,000 spectators and occasional roars of "God Save Good Queen Bess!"

Westminster Palace

Bridge Street and St. Margaret Street, SW1
Westminster Tube

ACCESS

Limited gallery seating on days when Parliament is in session. Tours of Westminster Hall are available by appointment only.
International visitors, write to:
Parliamentary Education Unit
Norman Shaw Building (North)
London, SW1A 2TT
British residents, contact your Member of Parliament for a permit.

The highlight of a visit to Westminster is, of course, a tour of the hall. This is rather difficult, but by no means impossible, to arrange. The trick for overseas visitors is to write ahead and be flexible in your scheduling. Tours for international visitors are officially arranged events, scheduled rather infrequently, so you must be prepared to go whenever the Parliamentary Education Unit says you can. British residents may contact the Member of Parliament for their constituency to arrange for a permit to visit at prearranged times on Monday through Wednesday mornings and after about 3:30 p.m. on Fridays. Permits are limited in number, so it is wise to make a request well in advance of a planned visit. Believe us, this is worth the effort.

If the Tower of London was the symbol of the military might and power of medieval monarchs, then Westminster Palace represented the iron control over government that these mighty kings and queens exercised. The palace was the central seat of the monarchy from the time of Edward the Confessor until Henry VIII moved it to Whitehall in about 1530. It was here that administrative and legal functions were centralized, where the king's council met, where Parliament assembled when called by the monarch, where state trials were conducted.

☞ Did you know?

At the coronation banquet of Queen Mary, a total of 7,112 dishes were prepared. The hungry horde ate only about 2,000 of them, leaving 4,900 untouched to later be given to the poor.

But it was not all dull, bureaucratic routine at Westminster. Many scenes of celebration and high drama were played here. William the Conqueror set the tradition for the elaborate coronation banquets that were held at Westminster throughout the Middle and Tudor Ages. The lavish celebrations surrounding the key church holidays of Easter, Christmas and Pentecost were often staged by the Court at Westminster Palace. One would-be queen, the Empress Matilda, daughter of Henry I, was chased from the hall as she sat down to dinner by the citizens of London, an event that tolled the death knell for her attempt to regain the crown stolen by her cousin Stephen of Blois. Two medieval kings, Edward II and Richard II, were deposed at Westminster, the dramatic trials of numerous noblemen were staged here, and the foundations for the Common Law of England were laid here as kings and barons struggled through medieval and Tudor times to create a balance of power that ensured a stable and just government.

A palace has existed on this site since Saxon times. Although now home to parliament, Westminster officially retains its designation as a royal palace. Sadly, most of the medieval palace was destroyed by a huge fire on October 16, 1834. All that remains of that palace is Westminster Hall, the undercroft and cloisters of St. Stephen's Chapel, which are not open to the public, and the Jewel Tower. The best that can be said is that the Victorians who rebuilt Westminster between 1837 and 1860 did their best to incorporate as many surviving medieval features as possible and constructed the new building in the style of the old palace.

Still, it is a site well worth visiting. The surviving medieval features and the historical echoes that permeate the grounds help conjure vivid images of the sights and sounds of daily life at Westminster Palace throughout the reigns of the Norman, Plantagenet and Tudor monarchs who made this palace the center of control of their kingdom.

On an official tour, you will be entering Westminster through the Victoria Tower, part of the 19th century reconstruction, which is located at the far south end of the complex. This is the sovereign's entrance to the palace. The entryway to the tower is called the "Norman Porch." We're not sure why, because there is nothing Norman about it. However, this tower does house all the Acts of Parliament passed since 1497.

Once you are in the building, you will pass through the sovereign's robing room, various antechambers, the Royal Gallery and the House of Lords. All of these rooms are chock full of statues, portraits and other representations of medieval and Tudor monarchs, barons and archbishops. Don't be fooled. None of them are contemporary. They are all Victorian facsimiles. In fact, unless you have developed a fascination for bad Victoriana and/or the chamber of the House of Lords, you can race right past this stuff, fighting your way through the gaggles of tourists gathered round their all-too-informative guides.

The only room worth a pause on your headlong flight to the hall is the Royal Gallery, where there is an exhibit of a very few of the some three million historical documents stored here. Among those on display is the earliest Act of Parliament kept at Westminster, "An Act for taking of Apprentices to make worsteds in the county of Norfolk," dating from 1497 and signed by Henry VII.

After you have fought your way through the crowded House of Lords, you will eventually reach the central lobby, the chamber that separates the House of Lords and the House of Commons. Again, unless you are captivated by the British system of government and dying to see the House of Commons, you can make a left turn in the lobby and head directly to the breathtaking medieval hall.

The hall you see today is the one constructed by William Rufus from 1097 to 1099, with some renovations dating from the reign of Richard II. Rufus's hall was an extension of the Saxon palace already on the site. William, however, felt that the Saxon hall was not impressive enough to reflect the true power and prestige of the Norman monarchy, so he had a bigger and better hall built. The resulting structure was the largest hall of any court in Europe, measuring about 240 feet by 68 feet. Consistent with his surly personality, William complained when he first saw the hall that it was still too small and vowed to construct one that would make the new hall look like a "bedchamber."

☞ Did you know?

The haughty Elizabeth Woodville, wife of Edward IV, outdid herself in arrogance at the banquet held in Westminster Hall in 1466 to celebrate the birth of her first child with Edward, also named Elizabeth. During the banquet, the queen sat alone in a golden chair at the high table. The banquet lasted three hours. For the entire time, Elizabeth insisted upon complete silence. She also demanded that all of her ladies-in-waiting, including her mother, remain on their knees while they served her. *(And she wondered why she was not popular with the courtiers!)*

Very little was done to change the hall until the reign of Richard II, when he decided this grand space needed some renovation. He hired the famous architect Henry Yevele to do the job. Yevele installed a new hammerbeam roof, said to be one of the finest in all England, strengthened the walls to support the new roof and replaced all of the windows. These improvements opened up the hall, making it seem more spacious by removing the Norman pillars that had supported the old roof, and increasing the available light by enlarging the windows. At the center, the roof is 92 feet high, the highest unsupported timber span in all of England. At least two of Yevele's windows were incorporated into the north and south walls of the hall when the palace was rebuilt in the 19th century. Yevele's work was carried out between 1393 and 1401, but enough of the renovation was completed in time for Richard II to hold his Christmas court at Westminster in 1398.

Architectural improvements were not the only changes Richard II made to the hall. He also set about upgrading the decor, adding intricate carvings and statuary to add an artistic flair to the massive building. Around the hall are elaborate carvings featuring the coats of arms of Richard II, the Plantagenet dynasty and Edward the Confessor (Richard II was a major fan of his).

One of the outstanding features of the hall dating from Richard II's redesign are six stone statues of kings that have stood in the same place, along the south wall of Westminster Hall, since they were first positioned there in 1388. These six statues were part of an original set of 13 commissioned by Richard II and long assumed to represent the kings of England who preceded Richard, from William the Conqueror through Richard's grandfather, Edward III. Larger statues also were commissioned, presumed to represent Edward the Confessor and Richard himself. Seven of the original set of 13, plus the two larger statues, were placed in niches along the exterior stone wall of the north facade of the palace. Altogether, Richard had 23 niches carved along both sides of the doorway, eventually to accommodate statues of future kings *(we guess he thought he would found a dynasty—wasn't that his job?)*. Unfortunately, just eight of the statues that once filled the exterior niches have survived the ravages of time and those have suffered greatly from erosion. Currently, they have been repositioned on the windowsills along the east wall of the hall.

As was typical with medieval living quarters, particularly those of royalty, Westminster Palace actually was an extensive complex of numerous buildings. The hall was the center of social life as well as of major government functions, but a variety of other buildings existed to serve specific functions.

> ☞ Did you know?
>
> Having survived civil wars, numerous major fires and the ravages of time, Westminster Hall almost was lost again during World War II. A bombing raid resulted in yet another fire that threatened both the chamber of the House of Commons and the medieval hall. A Member of Parliament at the time, Colonel Walter Elliot, made the choice to save the hall and let the Commons' chamber go. Three cheers for Colonel Elliot!

Various monarchs felt free to add and subtract features as they believed necessary. Therefore, the layout of the palace was constantly changing. For example, Henry I further expanded the palace after he inherited the Crown following his brother William's unfortunate hunting "accident." One of the first things Henry II did upon his assumption of the throne in 1154 was order his new chancellor, Thomas à Becket, to renovate Westminster Palace. It had been seriously neglected and damaged during the 14-year struggle for the throne that had raged between Henry's mother, the Empress Matilda, daughter and heir of Henry I, and the usurper, her cousin Stephen of Blois. Henry II's grandson, Henry III, added a new "Great Chamber," measuring 80 feet long by 26 feet wide in 1236. The room came to be called "the Painted Chamber" because it was decorated from floor to ceiling with vividly colored scenes from the Old Testament. Edward I began building St. Stephen's Chapel in 1331, but construction was not completed until the reign of his grandson, Edward III. That king's idea of artistic decoration for the chapel was portrayals of himself, his wife, Philippa of Hainault, nine of their children, 40 of their personal servers and 36 knights—another reflection of the size of Edward's ego. By the end of the 14th century, Westminster Palace actually consisted of the hall, St. Stephen's Chapel, a Privy Palace and a Prince's Palace. In addition, a two-story building housed an administrative center, including the Exchequer, and there were facilities for the Courts of Justice, Common Pleas and the King's Bench.

The House of Commons has met at Westminster Palace since 1547, when Henry VIII approved a move from the Chapter House at Westminster Abbey to St. Stephen's Chapel. Although the chapel was destroyed in the great fire that consumed the palace, its size and shape are echoed today in St. Stephen's Hall. The undercroft that did survive the fire has been converted to a private chapel for Members of Parliament, who can be married there and have their children christened there. The cloisters, dating from 1529, are located to the east of Westminster Hall. Neither the chapel nor the cloisters are open to the public.

Outside Westminster Hall, you will find New Palace Yard, a courtyard facing Bridge Street and Parliament Square. Despite its name, New Palace Yard is not so new. In fact, it is more than a thousand years old. The name derives from the "new" palace built by William Rufus. Old Palace Yard, the original courtyard of Edward the Confessor's "old" palace, is in front of the House of Lords. Both Guy Fawkes, who *(boo/hiss)* tried to blow up the hall in 1605 by planting gunpowder in the cellar under the Painted Chamber,

☞ Did you know?

A statue of Richard the Lionheart riding a destrier (a medieval warhorse, for those of you who are light on the lingo) is located in the Old Palace Yard of Westminster. Created by Baron Carlo Marochetti in 1860, the statue is the only one of Richard in all of London. But then, of course, the man only spent about six months in England during his whole 10-year reign, so maybe he doesn't deserve anything but a 19th-century statue.

Richard has one other association with Westminster Hall. Women were banned from his coronation banquet, held here on September 1, 1189. The official reason given was that Richard was unmarried, so it was "inappropriate" for women to be present. The unofficial reason: Richard didn't much like women—except for his mother, Eleanor of Aquitaine.

and Sir Walter Raleigh were beheaded in the Old Palace Yard, Fawkes in 1606 and Raleigh in 1618.

Finally, as you continue your tour around the outside of Westminster Hall, you might want to search out the gardens of the Victoria Tower, where there is a monument commemorating the burghers who surrendered the keys of Calais to Edward III in 1346. It's not medieval—Rodin sculpted it in 1895—but it offers an opportunity to salute Edward's military prowess if one is so inclined.

◇◇

WILLIAM II (1056–1100; REIGNED 1087–1100)

William II, nicknamed William Rufus because of his florid complexion, was number three of the baseborn William the Conqueror's four sons. The second of these sons, Richard, died young, leaving three brothers, Robert, William and Henry, to quarrel over the disposition of their father's vast lands.

Setting a precedent for relationships among future royal families of England, William the Conqueror and his brood were no loving, close-knit family circle. Robert, the eldest and the heir to Normandy, rebelled numerous times against his father. Despite this lack of parental fealty, the Conqueror on his deathbed forgave Robert and allowed his eldest son to keep his inheritance.

However, the wily Bastard did not trust or have enough confidence in the ruling abilities of the unstable Robert to give him England, too. That kingdom the Conqueror willed to his namesake, the future William II. This action kicked off a blood feud between the two brothers. The power struggle lasted from 1087, when the Conqueror died, until 1096, when Robert mortgaged Normandy to William Rufus for three years so that Robert could go on Crusade.

To his third son, Henry, the Conqueror left just £5,000 in silver, even though he believed that Henry was the most capable of the three brothers. Needless to say, Henry was not happy about this state of affairs and brooded about it for years.

William Rufus was a most unpopular king and was considered extremely vicious and cruel even by medieval standards. By reputation, he was not a Christian—a big no-no in that day and time—and was a homosexual—another big no-no. His relations with the Church were horrendous, a state of affairs that made his barons extremely uneasy. Therefore, when he died mysteriously in 1100 while hunting in New Forest, no one mourned.

The mystery surrounding his death centered on the question of how he came to be shot by an arrow from a crossbow. However, since the "accident" was deemed to be fortuitous, no one investigated the matter too closely. Without ceremony or religious rites, William was quickly bundled into a grave in Winchester Cathedral and brother Henry, who happened to be a member of the hunting party, seized his chance, hastily claiming the throne and having himself crowned King of England as Henry I before brother Robert could return from Crusade.

KING-MAKING AT WESTMINSTER

Richard II was deposed at Westminster Hall by a parliament summoned to meet at the end of September 1399. Although the parliament was called in the king's name, power was already in the hands of Henry Bolingbroke, soon to be Henry IV. While the peers of the land ponderously debated the momentous issue of what to do about the king's misrule (as they saw it), Bolingbroke grew impatient. He boldly stepped forward and claimed the throne. (Incidently, he spoke in English when he did so, becoming the first king since the Norman invasion to claim the throne of England speaking the native tongue of its people.) Even then, the lords might have ignored Bolingbroke's effrontery, but his bluster was backed by a large crowd of potentially riotous Londoners who were stationed at the door to Westminster Hall. The lords wisely acceded to Bolingbroke's claim. They had learned their lesson from history.

This was not the first time the Londoners had played a role in king-making at Westminster. In 1141, the Empress Matilda had gained the upper hand in the struggle she had been waging against Stephen of Blois ever since he usurped her crown upon the death of her father, Henry I, in 1135. Stephen's ineptitude as king had steadily eroded his support, leading to the outbreak of full-scale civil war in 1139. After Stephen was captured during a great battle at Lincoln on February 2, 1141, Matilda quickly gained control of the royal treasury and marched to London to prepare for her coronation at Westminster Abbey. Then the trouble began.

Matilda, by all accounts a haughty and arrogant woman (something hard to tolerate in an age of rampant male chauvinism, when women were chattel, the property of their husbands, fathers or brothers), decided to exact revenge for the solid support the City of London had provided Stephen. She levied a heavy tax on the city and announced that she planned to revoke the commune status granted the city by Stephen. Needless to say, the surly citizens of London did not take kindly to these actions. Instead of complying with Matilda's demands, they entered into secret negotiations with Stephen's wife, another Matilda, who was rallying support for his cause.

One day, just as Empress Matilda was sitting down to dinner in Westminster Hall, the citizens of London opened the city gates to Queen Matilda's forces and themselves stormed Westminster. Warned by the clamor of the multitudinous church bells of London, the empress, along with her closest supporters, fled the hall, barely escaping before the Londoners broke in and plundered the place (hence the need for repairs when Henry II inherited the property).

This event abruptly halted Matilda's coronation plans and helped turn the tide of war in Stephen's favor again for a while. Their struggle over the crown raged on for another 12 years.

Londoners also played a role in wresting power from Edward II. Hundreds of them crowded into Westminster Hall on January 7, 1327, to hear parliament debate whether the king should be deposed. Their vociferous support of Isabella, the "She-Wolf of France," and her son, soon to be Edward III, helped seal Edward II's fate. No poll was necessary to measure the opinion of the Londoners on this question. Three days after the scene at Westminster, Isabella and the Prince of Wales appeared at the Guildhall where people from all walks of life from all over London came to swear their allegiance to the future Edward III. Then a prisoner at Kenilworth Castle, Edward II was forced to abdicate his throne in favor of his 14-year-old son on January 16. Edward III was proclaimed king on January 24, 1327, and crowned at Westminster Abbey a week later.

◇◇◇

RICHARD II (1367–1400; REIGNED 1377–1399)

Richard II is one of the more unfortunate medieval kings. The son of the Black Prince Edward, who died in 1376, and Joan of Kent, Richard inherited the throne at age 10 when his grandfather Edward III died in 1377. Early in his reign, many people thought Richard had the potential to be a great king after he demonstrated tremendous courage and leadership in confronting the Peasants' Revolt in 1381 when he was just 14 years old.

But Richard soon grew into a petulant, arrogant, impulsive man whose effeminacy and excessive fastidiousness were offensive to his nobles. (The invention of the handkerchief is accredited to him in a time when most men blew their nose between their fingers or on their sleeves.) Tone-deaf politically, Richard was an extreme autocrat who took counsel from the wrong people, insulted those he should have befriended and dispensed favors upon the undeserving, to the chagrin and anger of powerful lords.

One of these disgruntled lords was Richard's cousin Henry Bolingbroke, the Duke of Hereford and son of John of Gaunt, the third son of Edward III. Bolingbroke took umbrage when Richard accused the earl of treasonous acts and banished him from England. Richard further alienated his cousin when he attempted to deny Bolingbroke his inheritance of the dukedom of Lancaster upon the death of John of Gaunt in February 1399. That was the last straw for Bolingbroke, who returned from France at the head of an army in July 1399.

Richard was no soldier and Bolingbroke was one of the best of his time, so the battle for control of the throne was over almost as soon as it began. Richard fell into Bolingbroke's hands at Flint Castle in Wales in August 1399 as the king was returning from a fruitless campaign in Ireland. Bolingbroke, who in Richard's absence had been busy consolidating support in England, promptly escorted the king to London and imprisoned him in the Tower. At a raucous gathering of parliament at Westminster Hall on September 30, Bolingbroke claimed the throne of England as Henry IV and Richard was forthwith deposed.

Now known as Richard of Bordeaux, the former king was eventually moved to Pontefract Castle, where he died early in 1400. The cause of his death has variously been attributed to murder or self-starvation *(does anyone believe that?)*. Originally, Richard was buried with little ceremony at Kings Langley, a Dominican priory located in Hertfordshire. After his accession to the throne, Bolingbroke's son Henry V, who apparently had a genuine affection for Richard or perhaps to make up for a guilty conscience caused by his father's usurpation of the Crown, had Richard's body moved to Westminster Abbey to lie in resplendent state with the other kings and queens of England.

Jewel Tower

Abbingdon Street, SW1 (020-7222-2219)
Westminster Tube

OPEN

10:00 a.m.–6:00 p.m. April–September
10:00 a.m.–5:00 p.m. October
10:00 a.m.–4:00 p.m. November–March
Closed December 24–26 and January 1; also closed for state occasions

ADMISSION

£1.50 Adults
£1.10 Students and senior citizens
£0.80 Children (under 5 free)
15 percent discount for groups of 11 or more

CONVENIENCES

Gift shop

Located across the street from the non-Norman "Norman Porch" of the Victoria Tower, the Jewel Tower is one of the other surviving features of the medieval Westminster Palace. The three-story moated tower was built by Henry Yevele in 1365 as a giant safe for Edward III's treasure. Although the coronation regalia never was housed here, great hordes of jewelry, fur, gold and silk were kept safe in this impenetrable stronghold. In time, it would become the Tudors' Royal Wardrobe.

Although you won't find the Crown Jewels here, you also won't suffer the horrendous lines and showy baubles that mar the *other* "Jewel Tower." What you will find is a small museum with relics from the old palace.

☞ Did you know?

At the time it was built on the southwest corner of the Westminster Palace grounds, the Jewel Tower encroached considerably on the lands of Westminster Abbey. The Keeper of the King's Palace, one William Ussheborne, added insult to injury when he went on to stock the moat with freshwater fish that he culled for his own use. Alas, one afternoon, Ussheborne choked on his *poisson du jour* and died without absolution. Not a tear was shed on his behalf by the Abbey monks.

St. Margaret's Church

St. Margaret Street, Westminster, SW1 (020-7222-6382)
Westminster Tube

OPEN

9:30 a.m.–3:45 p.m. Monday–Friday
9:30 a.m.–1:45 p.m. Saturday
2:00–5:00 p.m. Sunday

WORSHIP

11:00 a.m. Sunday, Sung Eucharist

ADMISSION

Donation appreciated

In your haste to beat a path to the Abbey's "dead kings," don't overlook the charming parish church of St. Margaret's, which is right next door. The detour will take but a minute and will be especially rewarding for those with a "Tudor" bent.

The original St. Margaret's Church was founded here in the 12th century, making it one of London's oldest houses of worship. It was established to provide the laymen of Westminster with a place to worship, where they could hear mass and receive the sacraments, without disturbing the religious devotions of the Benedictine monks of the Abbey. The religious needs of the people of Westminster were ministered to by one of the monks appointed to this duty by the abbot.

Because St. Margaret's was a monastic church, Pope Clement III issued a Papal Bull on St. Margaret's Day, July 20, 1189, specifically exempting the church from the jurisdictional authority of the Diocese of London. In 1212, it also was excluded from the authority of the Archbishop of Canterbury. After the Reformation, Elizabeth I continued the tradition by designating Westminster Abbey as a "royal peculiar" and including St. Margaret's in that designation as an appendage of the Abbey. That is the status of the church today.

The present building is the third on this site. Designed by Robert Stowell, this church was consecrated in 1523.

Try, if you can, to enter St. Margaret's on a bright, sunny day. You will be dazzled by the rainbow of colors cast from the magnificent Flemish window at the rear of the church. This was commissioned as a gift from King Ferdinand and Queen Isabella to celebrate the engagement of their daughter, Katherine of Aragon, to Prince Arthur, eldest son of Henry VII. By the time the window arrived, Arthur had met his untimely death, his brother was king and Katherine was, for the time being, enjoying life as Henry VIII's consort and queen.

Other medieval and Tudor features of the church include a 15th-century statue of the patron saint St. Margaret of Antioch and memorials to Blanche Parry, who was nurse to Princess Elizabeth and her personal maid after she became queen, and Lady Dorothy Stafford, who served Elizabeth as a Lady of the Bedchamber for 40 years. Those tombs are located on either side of the door to the nave. There also are memorial windows to William Caxton, the father of Britain's publishing industry who, as a parishioner, was buried in the churchyard, and Sir Walter Raleigh, who was buried under St. Margaret's altar after he was executed in the Old Palace Yard of Westminster Palace. The windows themselves are not of our period, just their subjects. Look for the plaque on the stone wall next to the rear entrance with the epitaph penned by Raleigh in which he pleads, *"Reader, should you reflect on his errors, Remember his many virtues and that he was a mortal."*

Westminster Abbey

Broad Sanctuary, SW1 (020-7222-5152)
Westminster Tube

OPEN

Abbey:

9:00 a.m.–4:45 p.m. Monday–Friday (last admission 3:45 p.m.)
9:30 a.m.–2:45 p.m. Saturday (last admission 1:45 p.m.)
Note: You may want to call ahead because the Abbey is sometimes closed to visitors for special services or events.

The Old Monastery (Chapter House, Pyx Chamber and Westminster Abbey Museum, East Cloister):

10:00 a.m.–5:30 p.m. daily, April 1–October 31 (last admission 5:00 p.m.)
10:00 a.m.–4:00 p.m. daily, November 1–March 31 (last admission 3:30 p.m.)

Chapter Library, East Cloister:

11:00 a.m.–4:00 p.m. Wednesday only, May–September

College Garden:

10:00 a.m.–6:00 p.m. Tuesday–Thursday, April–September
10:00 a.m.–4:00 p.m. Tuesday–Thursday, October–March

SERVICES

Morning Prayer: 7:30 a.m. Monday–Friday
9:20 a.m. Saturday

Holy Communion: 8:00 a.m. and 12:30 p.m. Monday–Friday
8:00 a.m. only Saturday and Sunday

Evensong: 5:00 p.m. Monday–Friday
3:00 p.m. Saturday and Sunday
Matins: 10:00 a.m. Sunday
Sung Eucharist: 11:15 a.m. Sunday
Organ Recital: 5:45 p.m. Sunday
Evening Service: 6:30 p.m. Sunday

ADMISSION

Whole Abbey, including the royal chapels:
£5.00 Adults
£3.00 Students and UK OAP cardholders
£2.00 Children (11–18)
£10.00 Family
Super Tour (includes guided tour of the whole Abbey, plus free entry into the Chapter House, Pyx Chamber and Westminster Abbey Museum): additional £3.00
The Old Monastery: £2.50
£1.00 with Abbey tour ticket
Free with Super Tour ticket

TOURS

Tours depart the enquiry desk in the nave at the following times:
April–October
10:00 a.m., 10:30 a.m., 11:00 a.m., 2:00 p.m., 2:30 p.m. and 3:00 p.m. Monday–Friday (no 3:00 tour on Friday)
10:00 a.m., 11:00 a.m. and 12:30 p.m. Saturday
November–March
10:00 a.m., 11:00 a.m., 2:00 p.m. and 3:00 p.m. Monday–Friday (no 3:00 tour on Friday)
10:00 a.m., 11:00 a.m. and 12:30 p.m. Saturday
You may book a tour in advance:
By telephone: 020–7222–7110
By letter: Super Tours
20 Dean's Yard
Westminster Abbey
London SW1P 3PA

CONVENIENCES

Audio guides are available in several languages at a cost of £2.00.
The Abbey Bookshop is located at the west end of the Abbey.
Coffee stalls are located in the North Cloister and in the sanctuary outside the west end of the Abbey.

Note: Several free brochures about the Abbey are available at the information desk. You should pick up one with a map of the Abbey in it. This will help you greatly on a self-guided tour, since the layout of the chapels can be somewhat confusing.

Note 2: There are no public bathroom facilities in the Abbey itself, so make sure you visit the loo before you enter. Public bathrooms are located on Broad Sanctuary opposite the west entrance to the Abbey.

Now that you have plowed through this daunting list of logistical information, let us reassure you that a visit to Westminster Abbey is well worth the time and effort. In fact, the logistical information is very detailed because there is much to see and do there. We suggest that you try to set aside a couple of hours to tour the Abbey. Trust us—once inside, it's hard to leave. There are just too many sites that capture and hold the attention of the true medieval and Tudor era enthusiast. We also recommend, particularly if this is your first visit to the Abbey or you are traveling with children, that you indulge in the Super Tour. The vergers who conduct them are great at making history come alive for kids.

»»

Directly across the street from Westminster Palace is the awe-inspiring church-cum-mausoleum of Westminster Abbey. A glorious structure that was built over centuries, Westminster Abbey was integral to the religious and political life of medieval and Tudor kings and queens. Through the coronation ceremony, the Abbey has provided the religious backing that supported the absolute divine right to rule of the monarch claiming the throne of England—regardless of how that particular king or queen came to be in possession of the Crown—ever since William the Conqueror defeated Harold "Harefoot" at the Battle of Hastings.

Tradition has it that there has been a church on this site since the 7th century. The story is that Sebert, King of the East Saxons, built a church on Thorney Island that was consecrated by Mellitus, the first Bishop of London, in 604. Lending credence to the story is the fact that Sebert (d. 616) was a nephew of Ethelbert, the King of Kent, who had received St. Augustine when he came in 597 on a mission ordered by Pope Gregory.

The first historical record of a religious complex on the site dates from the 8th century. King Offa of Mercia (d. 796) founded a Benedictine abbey that was dedicated to St. Peter and called "West Minster," meaning "western monastery," because of its position west of the City of London. Hints of what the Abbey would become and its relationship to the monarchy also can be found in records that indicate St. Dunstan, Bishop of London, brought about a dozen monks to live at Westminster in about 960 and that King Edgar, who reigned from 957 to 975, granted land to the Abbey in 961 to help support the monks in their religious lives. In addition, there is evidence that ancient kings and queens, including Athelstan (924–939), Ethelred the Unready (979–1016), Canute (1016–1035) and his queen, Emma, all supported this early abbey with the donation of relics.

It was Edward the Confessor, though, who put Westminster Abbey on the course that would make it what it is today. A saintly but rather strange man who was a pretty bad king, Edward had sited a palace at Westminster and then decided that the charming little abbey across the road would make a fine burial place. While he was entranced by the modest monastery, he decided that it was not grand and glorious enough to house the tomb of a king. Therefore, he launched a rebuilding program.

Construction began in 1050 and continued for the next 15 years. The new church was to be larger than any known contemporary Norman church. Its features would include a long nave with six bays, aisles, a wooden roof, a lantern tower and a presbytery with two bays. In a magnificent celebration, the new church was consecrated on December 28, 1065. Sadly, Edward was not able to attend the ceremony. He fell ill on Christmas Eve 1065 and died on Twelfth Night 1066. He was buried under a plain gravestone in the rebuilt Abbey. The same day that Edward died, his brother-in-law, Harold Godwinson, stepped forward to claim the throne and was crowned king, reportedly in the new Abbey.

As we all well know, Harold was not the only claimant to the

English throne. He had formidable competition in William, Duke of Normandy. William didn't wait for diplomatic negotiations to resolve the dispute . . . he didn't even try them. He just promptly assembled an army and invaded England before Harold had time to properly enjoy being king.

We all know the outcome to that. Just three days shy of the first anniversary of the new Abbey's consecration, on December 25, 1066, William was crowned King of England at Westminster Abbey, thereby establishing a tradition that continued through the 20th century, and earning himself the sobriquet "the Conqueror."

Now William was no fool. Actually, he was a very savvy politician. He was well aware that big chunks of the population of England did not much care to have him as their ruler. Therefore, he launched a propaganda campaign designed to bolster the legitimacy of his claim by capitalizing on the saintly reputation of Edward, who William said had named him heir to the English throne.

☞ Did you know?

When William the Conqueror was crowned, the crowd gathered in Westminster Abbey was asked in English to acknowledge him as their king. The responding shouts alarmed the nervous Norman guards waiting outside. They thought their liege lord was under attack. Immediately, they set fire to all the buildings surrounding the Abbey. Who knows what they hoped to achieve with this maneuver. One would have thought that they would have rushed into the church to save their leader. At least they created a spectacular bonfire in celebration of his coronation.

Stories began circulating almost as soon as Edward was buried that miracles were occurring at his gravesite. An anonymous author of *Vita Aedwardi Regis* wrote that "the blind receive their sight, the lame are made to walk, the sick are healed, and the sorrowing are refreshed by the comfort of God." William made sure that these stories were circulated far and wide. A portion of the Bayeux Tapestry that tells the story of William's conquest of England was devoted to illustrating the burial of the "saintly" Edward in Westminster Abbey.

The cause of establishing Edward's sainthood was taken up

by each of the Conqueror's successors. They all understood that linking themselves to the Confessor helped establish the legitimacy of the Norman claim to the throne. They also recognized that having such a predecessor declared a saint would vastly increase the prestige of the English monarchy. First Stephen of Blois tried to have Edward canonized in 1140 and then Henry II succeeded in 1161. Thus was the reputation of Westminster Abbey as a significant holy site, home to a major saint, established and the glory days of the Abbey launched.

> ☞ Did you know?
>
> Another future saint, Archbishop of Canterbury Thomas à Becket, presided at the first translation of the body of Edward the Confessor. The solemn ceremony was witnessed by Henry II, his fiery wife, Eleanor of Aquitaine, and several of their children, possibly even including Henry III's father, the future King John.

Henry III picked up where his grandfather, Henry II, had left off. By this time, St. Edward had become a cult hero for England's ruling monarch. Henry III, a great lover of beauty and art, decided that the simple Norman abbey and rather plain tomb to which Edward's body had been moved on October 13, 1163, were not elaborate enough to truly honor such a great saint. Therefore, he decided that a whole new church and tomb were needed.

There was a second motivation behind Henry's decision to move ahead with the construction of a new abbey. The monarchy needed a new burial place for its dead. Up until the reign of John (1199–1216), most of the Norman kings and queens were buried in their continental lands, many—including Henry II and Richard I—in Fontevrault Abbey in Loire. Fontevrault was lost to the French during the wars waged in John's reign and, therefore, was no longer available as a burial site for English monarchs. An alternative was needed.

And so the long-term—and extravagantly expensive—project of rebuilding Westminster Abbey began in 1245. By the time Henry died in 1272, he had spent about £45,000, the equivalent of millions of pounds today, on the reconstruction, nearly bankrupting the royal treasury several times and forcing him to sell royal plate and jewels to keep construction going. Despite the fact that only a short section of the nave (five of 12 planned bays were finished) and the Confessor's shrine were complete, work stopped when Henry died (his son Edward I, being of a more militaristic frame of mind, had different interests and ways to spend money, such as the conquest of Wales). Construction was not resumed until 1375 when Abbot Litlyngton, using funds left to the Abbey by his predecessor, Cardinal Simon Langham, and with the support of Richard II, picked up the task again. He contracted with the famous architect Henry Yevele (who rebuilt Westminster Hall for Richard II) to continue the rebuilding.

Somewhat amazingly, Yevele stuck with the master plan created by Henry III, resisting the temptation to put his own creative stamp on the project and thereby preserving consistency in the design of the new building. Work would continue for another four centuries, with various monarchs and abbots adding and subtracting chapels and making other improvements according to their political and religious needs and interests at the time. The nave itself was not finished until 1517—the same year that Martin Luther first spoke of reformation. The Abbey as it stands today was essentially finished in 1745 when Christopher Wren *(you knew he was going to show up somewhere in this story)* completed construction of the West Towers.

Even construction that continued over the centuries did not prevent the ruling kings and queens from making Westminster Abbey a focal point of their religious lives—and deaths. Every monarch since William the Conqueror, except the young Edward V and Edward VIII, has been crowned at Westminster Abbey. Edward V, in fact, was born there while his mother, Elizabeth Woodville, was in sanctuary. She had fled to the protection of the Abbey when Edward IV was forced to flee England because of a revolt led by the Earl of Warwick and Edward's brother George, Duke of Clarence. Many of the medieval and Tudor monarchs, their consorts and children are buried here.

Until the 14th century, burial at Westminster was pretty much reserved for abbots and members of the royal family.

Richard II changed that in 1395 when he permitted John de Waltham, Bishop of Salisbury, to be buried in St. Edward's chapel. That caused great consternation at the time, but Richard made sure the Abbey was well compensated for the inconvenience and embarrassment. Today, there are about 3,500 people known to be buried in the Abbey, but you can rush right past most of the monuments and markers, since they are tacky things from the 17th century forward. Rest assured, we'll let you know when you should stop and take notice.

☞ Did you know?

Henry IV was crowned in Westminster Abbey on St. Edward's Day, October 13, 1399, the anniversary of the translation of St. Edward. You would have thought this was a lucky omen. But it didn't turn out to be. Sacred relics were dropped during the coronation ceremony. And when the Archbishop of Canterbury went to anoint the new king's head with the sacred oil of St. Edward, the poor guy found that Bolingbroke's head was crawling with lice. In the end, Henry died at Westminster Abbey on March 20, 1413. After collapsing while at prayer, he was carried to the Jerusalem Room of the abbot's quarters. Thus was a prophecy fulfilled that Shakespeare immortalized in a scene in *King Henry IV, Part II*. In that scene, the king is quoted as saying, "*It hath been prophesized to me many years, I should not die but in Jerusalem; which vainly I supposed the Holy Land:—but bear me to that chamber; there I'll lie, in that Jerusalem shall Harry die.*"

Such lavish royal patronage established Westminster as one of the most important monasteries in England despite the fact that it was not a cathedral because it had never been the seat of a bishop. In medieval times, the monastery was home to 30 to 60 monks with up to 300 people supporting day-to-day life in the Abbey. It also was a rich facility, owning about 216 manors scattered all over England. By the beginning of the Tudor Age, Westminster had 25 monks, making it the 17th-largest monastery in England, and an annual income of £2,409, making it one of the richest. In comparison, the priory of Christchurch in Canterbury, the largest monastery in the country, had 70 monks and an annual income of £2,374.

Westminster also enjoyed a special status that distinguished it even more from other monasteries. In 1222, an Award of Papal Judges was issued exempting the Abbey from the authority of the Bishop of London and Archbishop of Canterbury. Thus the Abbey bypassed the Church's chain of command and reported directly to the pope.

For all practical purposes, Westminster ceased to exist as a monastery in 1540 when Abbot Boston was compelled by Henry VIII's enforcers of the Dissolution to sign a deed of surrender. Many of the medieval treasures kept at the Abbey were sold to beef up the depleted royal treasury of Henry VIII, and the Shrine of St. Edward was despoiled. There was a brief effort during the reign of Mary I to restore the Benedictine community, but it was not successful and did not last long. The monks left Westminster for good in 1560 when Elizabeth I issued a Royal Charter designating the Abbey as a collegiate church, again bypassing Church hierarchy and setting it so the Abbey was responsible directly to the Crown.

> ☞ Did you know?
>
> Elizabeth I's coronation ceremony was the last to be performed in Latin. The change in custom to come was signaled by the fact that some parts of the service were read in English, too.

Still, when you visit Westminster Abbey today, it is very easy to imagine the black-clad monks moving silently about the church and the cloisters or assembling in the choir for the various services of the day; to see the thousands of pilgrims who came to pay homage at St. Edward's shrine; to conjure up the glory and spectacle of a medieval coronation.

When you enter the Abbey today, you enter through the door that provides access to the North Transept. The layout of the Abbey can be rather confusing, so we are going to try to take you through according to what you will be seeing on the official tour route rather than according to historical development, although we'll try to explain some of that as we move along.

THE NORTH TRANSEPT

As you turn the corner from the entryway to begin your walk up the North Transept, immediately to your left is what is now the east aisle. This once was three chapels dedicated to St. John the

Evangelist, St. Michael and St. Andrew. Since most of the people buried here are of no interest to us *(being the pure medievalists that we are)*, you could skip this part of the tour if you so desire. But if you, like us, are compelled to poke into every nook and cranny that might contain a morsel of medieval or Tudor history, here are a couple of the notable personages whose tombs can be found in this area.*

- ***Sir Francis Vere*** (1560–1609); buried in the Chapel of St. John the Evangelist, the first space you enter when moving into the east aisle. Sir Francis was one of Queen Elizabeth's greatest soldiers and served as commander-in-chief of the English forces in the Low Countries.
- ***Sir Henry Norris,*** first Baron Norris of Rycote (1525–1601); buried in the Chapel of St. Andrew at the very end of the space as it is laid out today. Sir Henry was the son of the Henry Norris who was one of the five charged with having an affair with Anne Boleyn. Norris went to his death proclaiming the queen's innocence and denying the charge. As a reward for this loyalty, Elizabeth I knighted the younger Norris in 1566 and appointed him ambassador to France. Norris was raised to the peerage in 1572.

Across from the east aisle, you will start to see the tombs of the royal personages buried around the sanctuary and the Chapel of St. Edward the Confessor. If you, like us, are burning to get up close and personal with these ancient historical personages, their tombs and effigies, you may be somewhat disappointed in this part of the Abbey tour. The sanctuary and shrine are high up and close access to the tombs is blocked. Still, it is an awesome experience to look on these centuries-old tombs and know that they hold the remains of people who had a major impact on history.

*Throughout this segment, we do not attempt to mention every medieval or Tudor grave, monument or feature. There are simply too many of them. We have tried to identify the most memorable or fascinating—at least from our point of view.

First up on your right is ***Aymer de Valence, Earl of Pembroke*** (1270–1324). A cousin to Edward I, the earl stood high in the king's favor because he defeated Robert the Bruce in a vicious campaign that brought Scotland to its knees. His honor and reputation suffered greatly in the reign of Edward II when Piers Gaveston, the king's "favorite," was killed while in the earl's custody. But Edward II forgave him and the earl died while on an ambassadorial mission to France on the king's behalf.

Below Pembroke is ***Sir John Harpedon,*** who died in 1438 and whose claim to fame is that he was the fifth and last husband of Joan de la Pole, Lady Cobham (fairly unusual in a time when women generally died young and it was the men who had multiple marriages).

Across the North Ambulatory from Pembroke's tomb is the grave of ***Abbot John Esteney*** (d. 1498). Abbot Esteney governed Westminster Abbey from 1474 until his death and so was abbot when Elizabeth Woodville fled into sanctuary at the Abbey for the second time after Richard, Duke of Gloucester, captured her son Edward V on his way to London for his coronation. Abbot Esteney also was William Caxton's patron and therefore can claim some credit for the establishment of the printing press in England, since it was he who gave Caxton permission to set up the press within the Abbey's precinct in 1476. Esteney's tomb once was surrounded by an iron railing and was covered by a canopy. All of this was destroyed and the abbot's tomb moved in the 18th century.

Next to Pembroke in the sanctuary is ***Edmund "Crouchback"*** (1245–1296). He was named Earl of Lancaster by his father, Henry III, in 1267. His second marriage, through which he founded the House of Lancaster, was to Blanche, the widow of Henry, King of Navarre, and daughter of Robert, Count of Artois. Edmund died in 1296 at Bayonne during the Siege of Bordeaux.

Below Edmund is ***Brian Duppa*** (1588–1662), who served as Dean of Christ Church, Oxford, and got around as a bishop as well, serving successively as Bishop of Chichester, Salisbury and Winchester. He also was a tutor to Charles II. *(Not that we really care about any of this, but the tomb looks like it might be our period so we thought that we would answer the question before you asked it.)*

Next to Duppa is the tomb of ***Thomas Millyng, Bishop of Hereford*** (d. 1492), who was Abbot of Westminster from 1469 to 1474. He was abbot when Elizabeth Woodville first took sanctuary at the Abbey. Her son, the future Edward V, was born and baptized in the abbot's house, which he had generously turned over to Elizabeth. His appointment as Bishop of Hereford was a reward from Edward IV for the abbot's service to Elizabeth.

Now you are about to view the "*holy of holies*" of Westminster Abbey—the Chapel of St. Edward the Confessor.

The first tomb you come across when you enter the chapel is that of ***Edward I***, a.k.a. "Edward Longshanks" (1239–1307). He *(depending upon how you look at it)* became one of the most effective but ruthless rulers of England. He conquered the Welsh in a merciless campaign and wanted his epitaph to be "Hammer of the Scots." 'Nough said.

THE CHAPEL OF ST. JOHN THE BAPTIST

Across from Edward's tomb is the entrance to the Chapel of St. John the Baptist. This large, rounded chapel is a treasure trove of tombs and monuments for medieval and Tudor enthusiasts.

On your right as you enter the chapel is the tomb of ***George Fascet***, abbot from 1498 to 1500. Beneath him on the floor is a marker to ***Richard Harounden***, abbot from 1420 to 1440.

Next to Abbot Fascet is ***Thomas Ruthall, Bishop of Durham*** (d. 1523), who served Henry VII as his private secretary and Henry VIII as a member of the Privy Council. Legend has it that Bishop Ruthall died of grief after sending, by mistake, an accounting of his private financial holdings rather than a sheaf of state papers to Henry VIII. The accounting records were discovered by Cardinal Wolsey, who turned them over to Henry, saying "he knew now where a man of money was in case he needed it."

On the other side of Ruthall is ***William de Colchester***, abbot from 1386 to 1420. Colchester was implicated in a plot to restore Richard II to the throne and incarcerated in the Tower of London in 1400 by Henry IV. Henry V restored the abbot to power and used him extensively as a roving ambassador.

This chapel also has the highest monument in the Abbey. Standing 36 feet tall, the monument was erected in the memory of ***Henry Carey, first Baron Hunsdon*** (1525–1596), a cousin to Queen Elizabeth and her Lord Chamberlain. Buried along with the baron are his wife Anne (d. 1606/7) and various other family members.

Other personages buried here who are worth noting are as follows.

- ***Sir Thomas Vaughan*** (d. 1483) was Edward IV's private treasurer. He quickly followed his liege lord in death when Richard, Duke of Gloucester, ordered his execution. He was beheaded at Pontefract Castle along with Elizabeth Woodville's father, Earl Rivers.
- ***Thomas Cecil*** (1542–1623) was the son of William Cecil, the Baron Burghley who was Queen Elizabeth's longtime confidant and close advisor. He served Elizabeth militarily and was rewarded by being made Governor of Hull. He is buried with his first wife, ***Dorothy Neville*** (d. 1609).
- ***Robert Devereux, Earl of Essex*** (1591–1646), was the son of *that* Robert Devereux, Earl of Essex, who rebelled against Elizabeth I after years of taking advantage of her favoritism.

THE CHAPEL OF ST. EDWARD THE CONFESSOR (PART I)

Crossing the North Ambulatory from the Chapel of St. John the Baptist, you are back in the Chapel of St. Edward the Confessor and gazing upon the tomb of ***Henry III***, the man responsible for creating this magnificent shrine. Henry died at Westminster Palace on November 16, 1272. He had been a pitiful character for many years. At the Battle of Evesham in August 1265, Henry's son Edward had proved himself the better strategist and warrior; henceforth, Edward, in effect, ruled the kingdom. His father continued to hold the title, but the truth is that Edward wielded the power from 1265 until his father's death *(and for a few years before that, Simon de Montfort, Earl of Leicester, had)*. Still, Edward did appear to love and honor his father . . . Henry III's funeral, held on St. Edmund's Day, was a magnificent event. In addition, in a symbolic action that Henry would well have appreciated, he was buried in the same tomb from which the Confessor's bones had been translated three years previously.

☞ Did you know?

While it was Henry III who recognized the need for and provided the impetus to establish a grandiose mausoleum for Norman kings of England, he still had emotional ties to his ancestral lands (even if he didn't possess them anymore). His will may have provided for his body to be buried in England, close to the revered body of his favorite saint, Edward the Confessor, but it also stipulated that his heart be buried at Fontevrault in France, where many of his ancestors had been laid to rest.

Behind Henry's tomb, you can catch a glimpse of the Confessor's shrine, located in the middle of the chapel. Henry III lavished a lot of attention—and money—on this shrine. It took 20 years to construct. The original shrine, according to the 13th-century chronicler Matthew Paris, was made "of purest gold and precious stones." The casket containing the Confessor's bones was decorated with jewels and golden images of kings and saints.

☞ Did you know?

Every year on St. Edward's Day, October 13, modern pilgrims revive the medieval custom and kneel at Edward's shrine to offer prayers to the Confessor and bless Henry III.

Only the base of the shrine survived the wrecking of the monasteries and religious icons sanctioned by Henry VIII and

Edward VI. The wooden structure now on top of the marble base was built in 1557 when Queen Mary attempted to restore the shrine, but the effort fell seriously short of recapturing the glory of the original structure.

Edward in his shrine is surrounded by his near and dear and by those who revered him —or at least parts of them. Although no markers exist, medieval records state that ***Edith*** (d. 1075), Edward's wife, is buried to the left of the shrine. At the time of Edward's translation, she must have been moved along with him from her original burial site near him in the old church before the high altar. Also in an unmarked grave, but supposedly to the right of the shrine, is the Confessor's great-great-niece ***Edith/Matilda, a.k.a. "Good Queen Maude,"*** wife of Henry I, who died in 1118.

☞ Did you know?

Also located close to the shrine of Edward the Confessor, and preserved in its own golden heart shrine, is the heart of ***Henry of Almayne,*** the son of Richard, Earl of Cornwall, and nephew of Henry III. Henry—the nephew, not the king—was murdered before the altar in the Church of San Silvestro at Viterbo in 1271 by his cousin, Guy de Montfort. Guy was taking revenge for the nasty death of his father (Simon de Montfort) at the Battle of Evesham (1265), which ended the rebellion against Henry III and earned Edward I his reputation for duplicity and soldiery. Guy earned himself a place in Dante's "Rings of Hell" for this sacrilege.

Next to Henry III is his daughter-in-law, ***Eleanor of Castile*** (1244–1290), Edward I's dearly beloved wife . . . remember, he had all those crosses constructed for her on the stopovers when her body was being transported back to Westminster for burial. Unlike the tombs of the kings, Eleanor's does not have a nameplate identifying whose tomb it is.

THE CHAPEL OF ST. PAUL

Across from Eleanor of Castile is the entrance to the Chapel of St. Paul. It also is chockablock with medieval and Tudor tombs. A couple of the most notable are as follows.

- ***Sir Thomas Bromley*** (1530–1587) presided at the trial of Mary, Queen of Scots. He died two months after her execution.
- ***Sir John Puckering*** (1544–1596) served Queen Elizabeth as Lord Keeper of the Seal and twice was selected Speaker of the House of Commons. He also took part in the trial of Mary, Queen of Scots. It was his secretary, Davison, who was later prosecuted for getting Elizabeth to sign the order for Mary's execution.
- ***Giles Daubeny, first Baron Daubeny*** (1452–1508), was raised to the peerage in 1486 as a reward for his help in seating Henry VII on the throne of England. After Henry's ascension, Daubeny served as Lord-Lieutenant of Calis and Lord Chamberlain.

At the peak of the Confessor's chapel is the Coronation Chair. Edward I had that chair made to enclose the Stone of Scone, the legendary and mystical coronation stone of the Scots. For centuries, England's kings were crowned seated over that stone despite the fact that Scotland did not become part of the English kingdom until James VI of Scotland inherited the throne from Elizabeth I. When he was crowned James I, the new king became the first with the true right to be named King of England, Ireland, Wales and Scotland. The Stone of Scone was returned to the Scots in 1996 and now rests in Edinburgh Castle. You'll get a better look at the chair when you exit the Henry VII Chapel and re-enter the Confessor's chapel.

THE CHAPEL OF HENRY VII

For you Tudor fanatics, your turn has come. The Chapel of Henry VII is where you are going to find most of your heroes and heroines, villains and traitors. Here you will find buried Henry himself, Mary Tudor, Elizabeth, Mary, Queen of Scots, and so on.

Henry originally started this chapel with the intention of making it a shrine to Henry VI. Somehow, he conceived the idea that if he could have Henry VI canonized, it would add legitimacy to his very weak claim to the throne and justify his actions in usurping the usurper Richard III *(he must have been taking a page out of William the Conqueror's book).* But Henry VII was too tight to offer Rome enough money to get the job done, so that plan fell through and Henry VI's body was never moved from its tomb in Windsor. Instead, the chapel became a mausoleum for the Tudors and various hangers-on.

Construction of the chapel began in 1503. Two others had to be demolished to make room for it: the Lady Chapel built as part of Henry III's restoration of the Abbey and the Chapel of St. Erasmus, which had been endowed by Elizabeth Woodville in gratitude for Abbot Millyng's support during her first spell in sanctuary at the Abbey. Contrary to his usual tight-fisted policy, Henry VII spent liberally on the construction and to endow the chapel munificently for prayers and masses for his soul "perpetually and for ever while the world shall endure." *(Was a guilty conscience at work here?)* Henry's frugality did show up in the recycling of some materials from the demolished chapels. For example, the misericords used by the monks to support their tired legs and feet during long services in the Lady Chapel were attached to the stalls in the new chapel. The misericords are decorated with intricate carvings.

The lavishly decorated chapel is splashed everywhere with signs and symbols designed to underscore the legitimacy of the Tudor claim. Royal badges, red and white roses, some joined, some not; the lions of England, Welsh dragons and other regal and ancestral symbols can be found everywhere you turn. The chapel also is adorned with elaborately carved niches in which stand statues of saints. Ninety-five of the original 107 statues remain. The superlative fan vaulting and carved pendants add their own splendor to the decor.

The new chapel was consecrated in 1519. Henry VII could

not have anticipated when he was ordering perpetual masses that his son, Henry VIII, would dissolve all the abbeys and confiscate the treasure of his father's carefully designed chapel, stripping it of its finery and destroying some of its magnificence *(anyone see anything Oedipal here?)*. After that, the chapel was badly neglected and nothing done to restore it until 1807, when a parliamentary grant for its repair was obtained. The work was completed in 1822. What you see today is largely a result of that effort, although the chapel has been cleaned and periodic repairs have been made since then.

Now we're getting to the good stuff. As you move down the north aisle of the chapel, the first tomb you come to that will thrill your soul is the tomb of "***Good Queen Bess***" (1533–1603) and her sister, "***Bloody Mary***" (1516–1558). Never close in life, they are now sharing eternity, thanks to James I. Perhaps because of Mary's nasty reputation, Elizabeth had never gotten around to building a tomb for her sister. For all the years of Elizabeth's long reign, Mary's grave was covered with the broken stones of the altars that used to abound in the Chapel of Henry VII. For who knows what reasons, James had Elizabeth's tomb constructed on top of Mary's grave and inscribed "*Partners both in throne and grave, here rest we two sisters, Elizabeth and Mary, in the hope of one resurrection.*" One could only hope that his intention was to help bridge the still-wide gap between Protestants and Catholics in England. Elizabeth's, though, is the only effigy to adorn the tomb and is a good one. You probably will be pressed out of the room by the crowds always milling in Westminster Abbey before you have gotten your fill of this monument.

> ☞ Did you know?
>
> The last requiem masses ever sung in Westminster Abbey were for Queen Mary and the person she always viewed as her bulwark in life—Emperor Charles V, who preceded her in death by just a few days.

Sharing space in the alcove that holds Mary and Elizabeth's tomb is a small monument dedicated to the "Princes in the

Tower." It was placed here by order of Charles II after the bones of two children were discovered in 1674 under an excavated staircase at the Tower of London. The bones were presumed to be those of ***Edward V*** and his younger brother, ***Richard, Duke of York.*** Of course, no one has ever proved that to be the case. Still, that's what the monument reads.

After paying your respects to Elizabeth and Mary, cross over into the nave of the chapel and look in front of the altar for the floor marker covering the grave of their brother, ***Edward VI*** (1537–1553), the long-desired heir of Henry VIII, born to wife number three, Jane Seymour. Edward was a devout Protestant—almost as fanatical a Reformist as his sister Mary was a Catholic—and it was at his funeral that, for the first time, the English Prayer Book and its burial service were used at a funeral for an English king.

Moving on around the altar, you will find the magnificent tomb and effigies of ***Henry VII*** (1457–1509) and his queen, ***Elizabeth of York*** (1465–1503). Their marriage at the Abbey on January 18, 1486, helped end the Wars of the Roses by uniting the Houses of York and Lancaster. It was a brilliant political move on Henry's part, engineered, many thought, by his equally astute and politically adept mother, Margaret Beaufort, a descendant of John of Gaunt. Supposedly, it was a happy marriage. Certainly, Elizabeth fulfilled her role as queen and provided adequate heirs to the throne as well as enough daughters to meet foreign relations needs as marriage pawns. (She was already pregnant with the future Prince Arthur at the time of the royal wedding.) The grandiose funeral Henry gave her was interpreted to represent the affection and regard in which he held his wife.

You can ignore the five small chapels that form the apse of the Henry VII chapel. Most of the graves and monuments in them date from the 17th century forward. The only one you might be interested in searching out is that of ***Anne, Duchess of York*** (1472–1481), the child bride of Richard, Duke of York, younger son of Edward IV and one of the "Princes in the Tower." Anne and Richard were married when they were both just 5 years old. She is buried in the northeast chapel near Queen Anne of Denmark, wife of James I.

Once you are in the south aisle, the first tomb you are going to find is that of ***Margaret, Countess of Lennox*** (1515–1578). Margaret was a piece of work—she was Tudor through and through, in spirit and temperament. She was a niece of Henry VIII, daughter of his sister Margaret through her second marriage to Archibald Douglas, Earl of Angus; and mother to Henry Stuart, Lord Darnley, husband of Mary, Queen of Scots, and father of the future James I of England. Throughout her life, Margaret—the daughter, not the mother *(we know, it gets confusing at times)*—who was willful, ambitious and very beautiful—schemed and plotted to place a descendant of hers on the throne of England. This earned her the enmity and distrust of her cousin Elizabeth and so Margaret died in poverty, alone and neglected. It was her grandson James I who built the elaborate tomb for her that you see now.

Next to Margaret is her daughter-in-law ***Mary, Queen of Scots*** (1542–1587). After her execution, Mary originally was buried in Peterborough Cathedral. Her son, James I, had her remains brought to Westminster after he ascended the throne. This lady has one magnificent tomb. Maybe her son was redeeming himself for having abandoned her while she was imprisoned by her cousin Elizabeth I. Throughout Mary's 19 years of confinement in England, James did nothing to try to help her. Of course, he never knew his mother. He had no contact with her from the time he was less than a year old. He had been reared by people who did everything in their power to poison him against her. But isn't it interesting *(probably Freudian)* that James raised an impressive monument to the mother he never knew and stinted Elizabeth, the woman from whom he inherited a great and glorious kingdom.

The last major tomb in this area is that of ***Lady Margaret Beaufort,*** mother of Henry VII. Now, let's talk about a formidable woman. This lady *(excuse us—child)* was married at age 12 to Edmund, Earl of Richmond, one of the children of Henry V's widow, Katherine of Valois, and Owen Tudor and a half brother of Henry VI. Margaret herself was a descendant of John of Gaunt through one of his children by Katherine Swynford, later legitimatized by Richard II as "Beauforts" . . . so we're talking backhand—or, as they say, "left side of the bed"—royalty from the start here. Edmund died before their child, Henry, was born, when Margaret was just 13. She formed a close alliance with Edmund's brother Jasper and, together, they set out to protect the interests and well-being of her child, Henry. Despite his tenuous claim to the throne, Margaret schemed and plotted for years to place him there. She went through several husbands in order to stay close to the Yorkist monarchy and keep tabs on what they were doing. She adopted an extremely pious attitude so that she could send clandestine messages through priests and monks to her son, who had taken refuge abroad. And she worked tirelessly behind the scenes to build support and allies for her son. Ultimately, it all paid off. Her son was crowned Henry VII, she was honored as the pious and righteous Queen Mother and she got a magnificent tomb in Westminster Abbey.

As you circle through the room, coming out on the opposite side of these tombs, take note of the floor markers between the tombs of Mary, Queen of Scots, and the Countess of Lennox. The two that touch on our period are those of ***Henry Frederick, Prince of Wales*** (1594–1612), the eldest son of James I, and ***Lady Arabella Stuart*** (1575–1615), another pawn in the plans of her grandmother Margaret, Countess of Lennox, to win the throne of England for one of her descendants. Arabella was the unhappy child of Margaret's son Charles, Earl of Lennox, and Elizabeth Cavendish, daughter of another ambitious lady who thought she could take on Elizabeth I. Unfortunately, Arabella exhibited no more sense than her royal grandmother had . . . she married without the queen's permission and ended her life—insane—as a prisoner in the Tower of London.

THE CHAPEL OF ST. EDWARD THE CONFESSOR (PART II)

As you exit the Chapel of Henry VII, dead ahead of you is the Coronation Chair. This used to be behind the altar, but has been moved to where it is now blocking the view of the tomb of ***Henry V*** (1387–1422), hero of Agincourt *(remember your Shakespeare: "We few, we happy few, we band of brothers . . ." that immortalized the battle in which a few thousand English archers defeated 30,000 French knights on St. Crispin's Day, October 25, 1415)*. Henry's will ordered that a high Chantry Chapel be erected over his tomb, so the relics stored at the end of the Confessor's shrine were cleared out to make room. When completed in 1431, the tomb and chapel were a marvel to behold. Henry's wooden effigy was covered entirely in plates of silver gilt and all of his regalia was of silver. Everything was stolen in 1546 during the Dissolution and Henry's head was chopped off. The head you see today was actually made of polyester resin in 1971. It was modeled after a contemporary portrait of the king. The gates that guard the tomb were part of the original structure.

☞ Did you know?

The relics that were moved to make way for Henry V's chapel were the most precious the Abbey owned. They included the Virgin Mary's girdle that had been presented by William the Conqueror, a stone marked with a print of Christ's foot at the Ascension, Christ's blood in a crystal vase, a piece of the True Cross, set in jewels, that had been acquired by Edward I during his pillaging in Wales, and the head of St. Benedict, brought from France and presented to the Abbey by Edward III. When the relics were moved, they were packed into a chest that was placed between the Confessor's shrine and Henry III's tomb. There they remained until the Dissolution.

Buried beneath the altar slab in Henry's Chantry Chapel is ***Katherine of Valois*** (1401–1437), the daughter of Charles VI of France, who was Henry's queen and the mother of the future Henry VI. After Henry's death, Katherine secretly married one of her servants, a Welsh squire named Owen Tudor, with whom she had several children. The eldest of these, Edmund, later was named Earl of Richmond by his half brother Henry VI and was the father of Henry VII. Katherine died at Bermondsey Abbey while giving birth to a daughter by Owen Tudor. Henry VI gave his mother a magnificent funeral and she was buried in the Lady Chapel behind the Confessor's shrine. When Henry VII tore down that chapel to build his own, he had his grandmother's body moved and placed in an open coffin that remained aboveground near Henry V's tomb until 1778. Apparently, visitors got quite a thrill from this rare view of the mummified corpse of an English queen. When it was first moved in 1778, Katherine's body was placed beneath the Villiers monument in the Chapel of St. Nicholas. In 1878, it was moved again to its present resting place.

Next to Henry V is the tomb of ***Philippa of Hainault*** (1314–1369). Philippa was married to Edward III for 42 years and exercised great influence over him. She was credited with taming some of the worst aspects of his character that, after her death, went unchecked. Like the tomb of Eleanor of Castile, Philippa's is not marked.

☞ Did you know?

The third son of Katherine of Valois and Owen Tudor was born at Westminster Abbey when Katherine went into premature labor during a visit in about 1435 to Henry VI, who was staying at Westminster Palace. The child, who was named Owen after his father, was taken from Katherine at birth (these children by a commoner were seen as a threat to the succession by Henry VI's councilors). Owen was reared at the Abbey as a monk under the name of Edward Bridgewater. He died and was buried there in 1502 in what later became known as Poets' Corner.

THE CHAPEL OF ST. NICHOLAS

Across from Queen Philippa's tomb is the entrance to the Chapel of St. Nicholas. This chapel contains the private vault of the Percy family, one of the power-broking families of the Middle and Tudor Ages whose descendants still have the right to be buried in that tomb. In addition, a host of other fascinating artifacts and folks can be found here *(you'll be amazed at how many of them are women—in fact, all the interesting ones are).*

- The firestone screen separating this side chapel from the main one probably was erected by Henry VII. One big clue: the whole thing is decorated with royal badges and roses.
- The first tomb on the right is that of ***Philippa, Duchess of York*** (d. 1431). The really interesting fact about this thrice-married lady is that after the death of her third husband, Edward, second Duke of York, grandson of Edward III, at the Battle of Agincourt, the duchess was permitted to hold the Lordship of the Isle of Wight in her own right. *(What a victory for women's rights!)*
- ***Winifred, Marchioness of Winchester*** (d. 1586), the daughter of Sir John Brydges, Lord Mayor of London, is buried in this chapel—a clear indication of how high the daughter of a leading figure of the merchant class could rise by the 16th century.
- A large monument against the south wall, comprised of different types of marble stones, was constructed by William Cecil, Lord Burghley, Queen Elizabeth's chief advisor for many years, in honor of his second wife, ***Mildred Cecil*** (d. 1589), and their daughter, ***Anne, Countess of Oxford*** (d. 1588).
- ***Anne, Duchess of Somerset*** (d. 1587), was the wife of Edward Seymour, Duke of Somerset, who was chosen as Lord Protector of the realm for the minority of Edward VI, son of Henry VIII, who inherited the throne at age 10.
- ***Elizabeth Cecil*** (d. 1597) was the wife of Robert Cecil, who inherited the post of his father, William Cecil, Lord Burghley, as chief advisor to Queen Elizabeth. Elizabeth herself was a Lady of the Bedchamber.

THE CHAPEL OF ST. EDMUND

Next to St. Nicholas is the Chapel of St. Edmund. You'll find a few names you recognize as you stroll around the monuments in this room.

- ***William de Valence, Lord of Pembroke and Wexford*** (d. 1296); de Valence was one of the pesky half brothers and other near relatives who came to England and were embraced by Henry III that so infuriated Henry's nobles and caused them to rise up in rebellion against their liege lord. De Valence's particular crime was that Henry had married him off to the heiress of the Earls of Pembroke even though the king never invested his brother with the title that went with the lands. De Valence's tomb is the only one in England with Limoges champlevé enamel work.
- ***Frances, Duchess of Suffolk*** (1517–1559), whose major claim to fame is that she was the mother of Lady Jane Grey, "the Nine Days Queen." It was through Frances that Lady Jane's claim to the throne was based. Frances was the granddaughter of Henry VII through his daughter Mary's second marriage to Charles Brandon, Duke of Suffolk. After the attempt to place Lady Jane on the throne failed and first her daughter and then her husband were executed, Frances lived in poverty and obscurity. In 1557, she married her groom of the chamber, Adrian Stokes. It was he who erected the monument in her honor, complete with an effigy of the duchess wearing her royal coronet.
- ***John of Eltham, Earl of Cornwall*** (1317–1336), second son of Edward II, whose name derived from his birthplace, the Palace of Eltham. Despite his youth, John served as regent several times when Edward III was out of England.
- ***Sir Humphrey Bourgchier*** (d. 1471) was killed fighting for the House of York at the Battle of Barnet.

- ***Eleanor, Duchess of Gloucester*** (d. 1399), was the wife of Edward III's youngest son, Thomas (who is buried next to his mother, Philippa of Hainault). After Thomas's death, Eleanor spent the two years she had remaining on earth in the nunnery at Barking. Her effigy has her dressed in widow's clothing.
- ***Richard de Berkyng*** (d. 1246) was Abbot of Westminster from 1222 until his death. Abbot Berkyng was one of the signatories of Magna Carta.

THE CHAPEL OF ST. EDWARD THE CONFESSOR (PART III)

Across from the Chapel of St. Edmund, back in St. Edward's chapel, is the tomb of ***Edward III*** (1312–1377). He is buried in a tomb built by Henry Yevele of Purbeck marble. Edward was quite proud of the numerous children he sired and reared to healthy adulthood with Philippa of Hainault. *(Of course, not being soothsayers, they had no idea of the trouble their fertility and good gene structure would bring to England over the next couple of hundred years as their descendants battled for control of the Crown in the Wars of the Roses.)* Reflecting this pride *(or maybe boastfulness in a time when, no matter how many times the woman conceived, children often died at birth or in infancy),* the tomb was decorated with niches around the sides to hold images of 12 of the 14 children they had. Six of the little bronze statues that once filled these niches are still in place on the south side of the tomb. The statues, from left to right, represent Black Prince Edward (1330–1376); Joan of the Tower (1333–1348); Lionel, Duke of Clarence (1338–1368); Edmund, Duke of York (1341–1402), founder of the House of York; Mary of Brittany (1344–1362); and William of Hatfield (d. 1336).

☞ Did you know?

The coronation of Edward III marked the first time the shield and sword of State were carried before the sovereign during the procession. Today, they are kept in St. Edward's shrine.

Next to Edward III is St. Edward's other big fan, ***Richard II*** (1367–1400). Richard's burial here took some time to achieve. After he was deposed by Bolingbroke, Richard was moved around, under close guard, to several different castles. Just a few months after his deposition, he died—most likely he was murdered—at Pontefract Castle. He was buried without ceremony at King's Langley in Hertfordshire (ironically, once a favorite private retreat of that other deposed king, Edward II). Upon Henry V's ascension, rumors began flying that Richard II was still alive. Henry, who apparently had genuinely liked his cousin Richard and felt remorse for his father's usurpation *(although not enough to cede the throne)*, had Richard's body brought back to Westminster and reburied in an elaborate state ceremony. *(Need we say that Henry also had a great understanding of political reality, public relations and power politics.)*

☞ Did you know?

Richard II was so distraught by the death of his wife Anne of Bohemia that he had the palace where she died, Sheen, pulled down. During the funeral in Westminster Abbey, the king was so enraged by what he thought was insolent and disrespectful behavior on the part of Richard Fitzalan, Earl of Arundel, that he grabbed a staff from a church official and hit Arundel over the head. Arundel collapsed and lay bleeding on the floor of the Abbey while the shocked courtiers stood gaping. This action further alienated Richard from his barons, who were now firmly convinced that the king was deranged.

Richard is buried with his beloved first wife, ***Anne of Bohemia*** (1366–1394), in the tomb that he had built for her. The original effigy that decorated their tomb had Richard and Anne holding hands. The effigy was defaced in the Cromwellian era; Richard and Anne's hands were chopped apart.

Others who are buried in St. Edward's chapel but whose tombs are not visible or accessible to the public are as follows.

- ***John de Waltham*** (d. 1395) was Bishop of Salisbury and a favorite of Richard II. His burial in the chapel caused a stir and began opening the Abbey for burials of people other than royalty and Church aristocrats. Waltham's grave is located behind Edward I's tomb in the interior of the shrine.

- ***Princess Elizabeth Tudor*** (1492–1495) was a daughter of Henry VII and Elizabeth of York who died at age 3.
- ***Thomas, Duke of Gloucester*** (1355–1397), was the youngest son of Edward and Philippa. A haughty man who thought he knew better than his nephew Richard II how to rule England, he mortally offended the king, who went himself to arrest his uncle at his castle of Pleshy. The duke was taken to Calais, where he was smothered under a featherbed.
- ***Princess Margaret*** (1472) was an infant daughter of Edward IV and Elizabeth Woodville.

THE SOUTH AMBULATORY

Beneath Richard and Anne's tomb in the floor of the South Ambulatory is the grave of ***Sir John Golofre*** (d. 1396). Golofre was a great favorite of Richard II, who had the knight's remains moved to the Abbey from their original burial place in Wallingford.

Across from Richard and Anne beneath an arch dividing the chapels of St. Edmund and St. Benedict is a small altar tomb containing the remains of ***Katherine,*** the dearly loved deaf-mute child of Henry III and Eleanor of Provence, who died in 1257 when she was just 5 years old. Eventually, four other children of Henry and Eleanor who died young were buried in this same tomb, as were four of Edward I's.

Back across the ambulatory, on your right, next to the altar, is a painted wooden screen erected during the reign of Edward I. The recently cleaned and restored paintings have suffered much from the ravages of time, but are believed to include images of Henry III, Edward I, the Confessor holding out a ring to a pilgrim and a saint, possibly St. Peter. The screen is on top of the tomb of ***King Sebert,*** who legend holds founded the first church on the Abbey site in the 7th century.

Near the door leading from the altar into the Confessor's chapel is the unmarked grave of Richard III's wife ***Anne Neville,*** who died in 1485. A pawn used mercilessly by her father, the Earl of Warwick, during the latter phases of the Wars of the Roses, Anne was first wed to Prince Edward, son of Henry VI and Margaret of Anjou, and then given to Richard after the Battle of Tewkesbury on May 4, 1471, in which the prince was killed. A bronze tablet to this unlucky lady's memory was erected on the wall by Sebert's tomb.

Next to Sebert, between two marble monuments, is ***Anne of Cleves,*** Henry VIII's fourth wife, whom he divorced because he thought she was ugly. She, alone of all his wives, was sensible *(perhaps terrified might be a better description)* and rapidly agreed to a divorce so that they "could remain friends."

☞ Did you know?

Anne of Cleves was the only one of Henry VIII's six wives to survive well into the reigns of his children. Always welcome at court, the luckiest of Henry's wives was a witness to Edward VI's short reign and early death and was present at Mary's coronation, even riding in the same litter as Princess Elizabeth in the procession to and from the Abbey. Anne died on July 16, 1557, at Chelsea Old Manor at age 41 *(apparently, being a wife of Henry VIII did not lead to longevity; the strain on the heart and nerves must have been enormous).* She was buried on August 3 with great ceremony by the order of Queen Mary.

THE CHAPEL OF ST. BENEDICT

The last chapel in this walk around the sanctuary, altar and chapel of St. Edward is St. Benedict's, dedicated, of course, to the founder of the Benedictine monastic order of which the Abbey originally was a part. Here you will find the tomb of ***Cardinal Simon de Langham*** (d. 1376), the only Westminster abbot ever to be appointed Archbishop of Canterbury. Langham, who served as Abbot of Westminster from 1349 to 1362, was made Bishop of Ely and Chancellor of England in 1362 by Edward III and served in that capacity until 1366, when he was named Archbishop of Canterbury. He willed the Abbey the money needed to finish the reconstruction started by Henry III.

Also buried in this chapel is ***William Bill*** (d. 1561), who served as the first Dean of Westminster after the Abbey was established as a collegiate church by Elizabeth I. A mural on the wall to your right depicts the kneeling figure of Bill's successor, ***Gabriel Goodman*** (1529–1601), who served as dean for 40 years during the reign of Queen Elizabeth. Also on that wall is a memorial to the monks who served the Abbey.

POETS' CORNER

Turning from the entrance to St. Benedict's chapel, you find yourself in Poets' Corner. The corner first got its name—and its reputation—because the body of ***Geoffrey Chaucer*** (c. 1343–1400) was moved around 1550 from St. Benedict's chapel to a special tomb constructed for him in the east aisle of the South Transept.

> ☞ Did you know?
>
> ***Abbot Nicholas de Litlyngton*** (d. 1386), the abbot who was responsible for picking up the job of restoring the Abbey that was left unfinished because of the death of Henry III, is buried in an unmarked grave somewhere in Poets' Corner.

Then ***Edmund Spenser*** (1552–1599), author of *The Faerie Queen,* which was dedicated to Queen Elizabeth, was buried not far away. Spenser's funeral was a great literary event. All the leading authors of the time, Shakespeare included, attended the funeral, wrote elegies on the spot and then threw the tributes and the pens they had used into the grave with Spenser. *(Were they hoping for creative inspiration from the grave?)*

Ben Jonson (1574–1637), one of history's greatest dramatists, was buried in the nave of the South Transept after he died in great poverty in a house that was located between the Abbey and St. Margaret's. Jonson was a spendthrift who, despite the fact that he was tremendously admired by James I and had received significant financial support from the king over the years, was not able to hang on to any of the wealth he earned as the author of such still famous plays as *Volpone, Every Man Out of His Humour* and *Bartholomew Fair.*

These interments—and the ceremonies that accompanied them—made this corner "the place to be" in death if you were a man of letters. ***Shakespeare*** (1564–1616), however—always one to follow a different drummer—is *not* buried here . . . his tomb is in Holy Trinity Church in Stratford-upon-Avon. There is a monument to him, though, that dates from 1740 *(how could there not be?).*

At the southeast door of the transept, you will find a plaque about ***William Caxton*** and the first printing press set up in the Abbey precincts in 1476. Caxton was a great favorite with the Tudors. Among his most influential patrons were Henry VII, who commissioned *Feats of Arms,* and Henry's mother, Margaret Beaufort. His best-selling print jobs were such classics as Chaucer's *Canterbury Tales,* Mallory's *Mort d'Arthur* and other chivalric romances and religious works.

On the other side of the door, you will see wall paintings entitled *St. Christopher* and *The Incredulity of St. Thomas.* They are attributed to Walter of Durham and date back to about 1280.

If you are into English poetry and literature, you will find many familiar names on the monuments and tombs in this corner.

THE SANCTUARY AND ALTAR

When you are done wandering around Poets' Corner, you may want to move to your right to stand in front of the sanctuary, where the high altar is located. Except for the brilliantly colored and intricately designed 13th-century tiles with which the sanctuary is paved and the tombs that you can see, there is nothing medieval or even Tudor about this space anymore. But we are confident that the ghosts of past kings will come alive for you here, since this is where every king of England since Harold, the last Saxon king, has been crowned. The exceptions were Edward V, whose throne was usurped by his uncle Richard III before the young king was coronated, and Edward VIII, who abdicated to marry the love of his life *(that's a 20th-century story, so we won't go into details).*

As you stand facing the altar, to your left you will see the tomb of ***Aveline, Countess of Lancaster,*** the wife of Edmund "Crouchback." Edmund was the younger son of Henry III. Aveline and Edmund's wedding in April 1269 was the first royal wedding to be held in Westminster Abbey. Aveline was heiress to great swathes of land in England and on the Continent, but she died childless in 1274, so Edmund lost out on the inheritance. Still, she got to be buried in her father-in-law's sumptuous new church . . . and in the sanctuary, close to the altar at that.

Two former abbots also are buried in the sanctuary: ***Abbot Richard de Ware,*** who ruled Westminster from 1258 until his death in 1283, buried closed to Aveline, and, on the other side of the altar, his successor, ***Abbot Walter de Wenlock,*** who governed the Abbey from 1283 to his death in 1307.

THE CLOISTERS

When you turn the corner from the South Transept, you will be guided into the East Cloister. This is not a bad thing. The cloisters are truly a sight to delight the soul of any amateur historian interested in medieval history. First of all, the walks themselves date from at least the 13th century and the chapels emanating from the East Cloister in particular are chock full of medieval and Tudor treasures.

Be alert when you stroll through the cloisters . . . there are hidden gems everywhere. Representations of the heads of Henry III and Queen Eleanor of Provence are on either side of the East Cloister door, while those of Abbot Litlyngton and Richard II can be found decorating the archway leading to the Dean's Yard. The grave of ***Abbot Simon de Bircheston,*** who died of the plague in 1349 along with 26 other monks of the Abbey, can be found in the East Cloister. The other monks are in the South Cloister Walk next to the effigies of three Norman abbots: ***Abbot Laurence*** (d. 1173), who helped Henry II secure the canonization of Edward the Confessor; ***Abbot Gilbert Crispin*** (d. 1117), who has the oldest effigy in the Abbey; and ***Abbot William de Humez*** (d. 1222), who was abbot when the foundation stone for the new Lady Chapel was laid by Henry III.

☞ Did you know?

The floor of Westminster's Chapter House is the largest surviving set of medieval tiles to be found in England. Each of these tiles was fired with different shades of clay and is engraved with a scene of palace life. Depictions are of performing musicians, Queen Eleanor of Provence hunting with a falcon, Henry III's coat of arms and numerous royal symbols such as leopards, wyverns and centaurs.

When you emerge into the East Cloister, the first room you will find open to the public is the Chapter House, a spectacular medieval structure with a fascinating history. This is an octagonal room with a central pillar, built between 1250 and 1253, and is one of the largest of its kind still existing in England . . . it is 60 feet in diameter . . . and is incredible. You have no trouble here imagining the monks of Westminster gathering every morning after Prime to discuss the daily business of the monastery. They would have filed in silently, taking seats along the stone benches that surround the walls, eyes downcast out of humility but possibly also to drink in the incredible beauty of the brilliantly colored, intricately designed, hand-painted tiles that decorate the floor. The burdens of confession, punishment and logistical drudgery that were part of these daily gatherings had to have been lightened by the atmosphere created by the six great windows (40 by 20 feet) that flood the room with light and the resplendent murals that decorated the walls. Traces of these incredible works of art still remain to help fire the imagination. This is a room in which you are going to want to spend some time, drinking in the atmosphere and being transported back in time.

Starting in the 14th century, the Westminster monks had to share their Chapter House with the House of Commons. The center of England's government was firmly established in Westminster Palace, but no space had been provided for the "commons" (remember, they were not part of the equation when the Norman kings began to base government in Westminster). This situation continued until the 16th century when Henry VIII abandoned Westminster as a royal palace in favor of Whitehall. Westminster then became the seat of parliamentary government—rather than monarchial *(isn't the evolution fascinating?)*—and the House of Commons then was assigned its own space in the hall.

Next to the Chapter House is a doorway that leads to the Abbey Library, formerly the monks' dormitory. It is open to the public on a limited basis (see our logistical notes at the beginning of this segment).

If you skip—or miss—a visit to the library, you will be moving on to the Pyx Chamber. This 11th-century structure was used as a strong room for the royal treasury. This is where the money was kept and tested *(sort of a Bureau of the Mint for medieval times)*. The "trial of the Pyx" was an annual event held to make sure that all newly minted coins met the set standards. This event is still held—only it takes place now at the Hall of Goldsmiths in the City. The room was commandeered by the Crown at the time of the Dissolution *(probably only Henry or Cranmer knows why)* and has never been returned to Abbey control. This is now a museum managed by English Heritage.

After you have dipped into this museum to see the oldest altar in the Abbey, you are going to strike gold in the Westminster Abbey Museum. This is where the good stuff is. Here are a few examples of the cool artifacts you will see there.

- The shield, sword and saddle purchased for Henry V's funeral and a contemporary tournament helm that all were once on display on a bar above his Chantry Chapel have been moved to the museum for better preservation.
- The painted funeral effigy of Katherine of Valois, Henry's wife, the mother of Henry VI and grandmother of Henry VII through her marriage to Owen Tudor.
- The wooden effigy of Edward III that was carried at his funeral; this is the earliest death mask in the museum, dating from 1377. It is a wood carving covered with a thin coat of plaster.
- The remains of Edward I's funeral effigy.
- The painted wooden head of Anne of Bohemia (d. 1394), the queen of Richard II.
- The wax funeral effigies of Henry VII and Elizabeth of York.
- The head of Mary I's funeral effigy.

You can keep wandering around the cloisters and the Dean's Yard to your heart's content. This is all early medieval stuff—the buildings, gardens, school, culture, etc.—dating back 800–900 hundred years. Let us know if you want more specific details or are content, like we are for the most part, to absorb the atmosphere of a place that throbs with the spirits of all the people who lived—and then were buried here—and the electricity of all the dramatic events—the weddings, coronations, funerals and tribulations of people who populated and ruled England for more than a millennium.

THE NAVE

Once you have finished roaming through the cloisters, you can re-enter the Abbey to tour the nave, a medieval structure with soaring arches and great stained-glass windows. After you have stood in the middle and admired the sweeping grandeur of the space, wander up to the choir and ruminate on the thought that services have been sung continuously on this spot for 900 years even though there is nothing medieval about the current structure.

Then stroll over to the North Aisle and look for the painted shields hanging on the wall. These date from the time of Henry III's reconstruction and represent the arms of the men and families who contributed financially to the rebuilding of the Abbey. Originally there were 16 shields, eight on the wall of the North Aisle and eight on the south. Because access to the South Aisle is now blocked, it is easier to view the shields up close on the north side. There you will find the shields of the Holy Roman Emperor; the King of France; Richard de Clare, Earl of Gloucester; Roger Bigod, Earl of Norfolk; Simon de Montfort, Earl of Leicester (Henry's brother-in-law who late in the reign led a rebellion against the king); John de Warrenne, Earl of Surrey; and William de Forz, Count of Aumale. On the south side are the arms of Edward the Confessor, the King of England; the Count of Provence (uncle to Henry's consort Eleanor of Provence); Roger de Quincy, Earl of Winchester; Richard, Earl of Cornwall (Henry's brother); and an Earl of Ross. The missing shields are reportedly those of the King of Scots and the Bohuns, Earls of Hereford.

At the end of the South Aisle, to the left as you face the west entrance, you will find the Chapel of St. George. In there is a stained-glass window that is partly medieval and partly more modern. The figure in the window represents Edward "the Black Prince," eldest son of Edward III and father of Richard II, who died before inheriting the throne. On a pillar just outside the chapel, you will find a portrait of Richard II. This is the oldest contemporary portrait of any English monarch.

That completes your tour of Westminster Abbey. Now, rush right next door and visit the Abbey gift shop, where you can find a great supply of medieval and Tudor literature.

EDWARD THE CONFESSOR
(C. 1005–1066; REIGNED 1042–1066)

While William the Conqueror gets much of the blame—or credit, depending upon how one looks at it—for the Norman conquest of England and the resulting dramatic change in the course of history, there are many who think that Edward the Confessor should share the honor. After all, it was mainly because Edward took a saintly vow of chastity and thus failed to even try to secure the succession that there were even more contenders for the Crown of England than usual.

Edward was actually a very weak and ineffectual king. He was driven from England by the Danes, who then proceeded to rule his kingdom for 27 years while Edward spent his time in exile, tooling around Normandy, becoming buddies with a relative by marriage, William, Duke of Normandy. Legend has it that Edward vowed during this time that if he ever returned to England, he would make a pilgrimage to St. Peter's in Rome. More practically, William, Duke of Normandy, later claimed that it was also during this time that Edward promised that he, William, would inherit the throne of England if Normandy would lend its support for Edward to reclaim . . . and then hold his crown *(a much more iffy proposition, given Edward's command and leadership abilities)*.

Whatever Edward did or did not pledge in terms of a religious vow—or promise his cousin William in terms of the English Crown—he found upon his return to England in 1041 that there was way too much trouble in his kingdom for him to ever leave (a problem many future English kings found when they took vows to go on Crusade). So Edward needed to hedge his bets politically to stay in charge of his kingdom. The pope released him from his vow to make a pilgrimage in exchange for Edward building a monastery dedicated to St. Peter. This Edward promised to do and the expanded Westminster Abbey was born.

The problem of the succession was a bigger one. Edward had taken a vow of chastity, something that was pretty incomprehensible in a day and time when feudal lords were expected to sire sons *(or, rather, their wives were; of course, with their cooperation)* in order to secure the succession. This was called stable government in a time when chaos and anarchy generally reigned. Edward was being derelict in his duty.

Even more important, this lack of clarity in terms of the succession fueled the ambitions of a number of claimants, most notably William, Duke of Normandy, and Harold Godwinson, Edward's brother-in-law. Clearly, the situation was ripe for civil war and/or physical conquest at the time of the Confessor's death in 1066.

Despite his political ineptness, Edward was revered by his Anglo-Saxon subjects as a pious and just king. Therefore when he died, reports of miracles occurring at his tomb began spreading almost immediately . . . particularly when word got around that William, Duke of Normandy, who had a fearsome reputation, was not going to accept Harold's assumption of the crown without a fight. The search for miracles escalated once the Battle of Hastings had been won (by William) and lost (by Harold).

One miracle that was reported to have occurred involved Wulfstan II, the Saxon Bishop of Worcester. The story goes that Wulfstan appealed for help to the dead Edward when William the Conqueror demanded that the bishop resign his see (William was forcing all Saxon bishops to resign so he could appoint Normans in their place). Apparently in a fit of anguish, Bishop Wulfstan stuck his staff into Edward's tomb. And lo and behold, the staff remained upright and could be removed by no one but Wulfstan himself. *(Did Merlin teach him this trick?)*

When William heard about the miracle *(no fool, he),* he allowed Wulfstan to retain his bishopric and built a sparkly new tomb, studded with expensive gems and gold, to cover the Confessor's grave, then located before the high altar of the church Edward had built. William quickly understood the value of having a saint as a predecessor on the throne of England, especially if that predecessor was assumed to have expressly chosen the current wearer of the crown. William wasted no time in bolstering Edward's pious reputation. Thus was the legend of St. Edward the Confessor born.

◇◇

HENRY III (1207–1272; REIGNED 1216–1272)

One of England's longest reigning monarchs, Henry III, the son of the deservedly infamous King John, inherited the throne at age 9 in the middle of a civil war. John had so infuriated his barons that a good many of them invited Prince Louis of France to try for the throne with their support. John's most recent sin—among many others—was that he had signed Magna Carta and then reneged on it, turning to the pope for help and making England a fiefdom of Rome, thus putting all of his barons at the risk of excommunication if they failed to yield to his will. It was a close call as to whether England would become a fiefdom of the kingdom of France, but then John died of dysentery during the fighting. The child Henry became king.

Henry was a lucky guy at first. John's death pretty much brought an end to the war—not to say there weren't some heavy-duty battles before it was over. The barons were fighting against John, not for Louis. So after John's death, barons began deserting the rebel's cause right and left. They preferred to be on the side of such righteous folk as William the Marshall, the new Protector of the Realm for Henry's minority, and the saintly Archbishop of Canterbury Stephen Langton, a member of the council.

Life rolled along pretty smoothly, at least for the times, during Henry's minority. The competent councilors managing the kingdom for him were able to bring order out of the chaos that had marked the last few years of John's reign. So when Henry reached his majority in 1227, he inherited a stable government in a peaceful and prosperous realm. That was when the trouble started.

Henry was a poor ruler who was temperamentally unsuited to be king. He was a lover of beauty and art and a lousy battle commander—a bad combination in a time when military prowess was how a man, especially a king, was judged and when few men could read and write. He could be warm and generous, particularly to those he loved, but stubborn, petulant and spiteful when he did not get his way. He was extravagant, spending huge sums to create monumental buildings, buy works of art and deck himself, his wife and his family in luxurious and rare clothes and gems, so the government was always strapped for funds for essential functions and services. He was devoted to his wife and family, an odd quirk in a man whose male ancestors were notorious lechers and whose power lust drove them to myriad attempts at usurping each other's kingdoms and/or killing each other. In fact, Henry took family love to new extremes, warmly embracing a foreign horde of his wife's relations and his own half brothers and sisters from the second marriage of his mother, Isabella of Angoulême, to Hugh de Lusignan. He lavished these relatives with honors and rewards, appointed them to powerful positions and relied heavily on their advice and counsel, much to the chagrin of his English lords and barons.

It was this extreme nepotism, combined with all of the other faults and failures of Henry's long reign, that ultimately led to a major baronial rebellion that began in about 1257. It started mildly enough with a group of barons and clerics attempting to force Henry to live up to Magna Carta, the division-of-power agreement signed by his father, and to expand the baronial rights and privileges defined in that document through a new agreement, referred to as the Provisions of Oxford. Henry had no more desire than his father—or any other absolute ruler—to see his power restricted. He balked at agreeing to the Provisions.

Henry's greatest misfortune was that the leader of the baronial party—and the strongest advocate of the Provisions—was his brother-in-law Simon de Montfort, Earl of Leicester, the greatest soldier of the time. Simon also had an ego and a moral certitude that matched his military prowess—a bad combination for Henry. When Henry refused to agree to adhere to the Provisions, Simon led an active revolt against the king. In a battle at Lewes in May 1264, Henry was captured and taken prisoner; de Montfort effectively ruled in his name for the next year and a half.

But de Montfort's own personality, particularly his inability to foster a spirit of teamwork among his friends and supporters, ultimately doomed his cause. Other barons defected in droves back to the king's banner, now hoisted by Prince Edward on his father's behalf. Mistake after mistake, primarily by de Montfort's incompetent, arrogant and overconfident sons, allowed Edward to gain the upper hand in the military campaign and, through treachery and trickery, crush de Montfort's army at the Battle of Evesham in August 1265. De Montfort and his eldest son, another Henry, were killed and the earl's body was shamefully mutilated.

But the whole episode effectively brought an end to Henry III's rule. While he remained king in name, from the Battle of Evesham until his death, Henry's kingdom was governed by his son, the future Edward I. Henry died a sick, old man of little influence in November 1272. However little credit his contemporaries gave him, it is worth noting that Henry's achievements, most notably the expanded Tower of London and Westminster Abbey, stand today as symbols of his time.

◊◊

SANCTUARY

The ancient right of sanctuary—whereby people in fear of losing their lives sought refuge and protection behind the skirts of the Church—was exercised often at the medieval Westminster Abbey. Perhaps because of its proximity to Westminster Palace and its close ties to the ruling families, the Abbey frequently was the place to which people fled when they found themselves on the losing side, at least momentarily, in the numerous dynastic battles over the throne that raged throughout medieval and Tudor times.

One of the most celebrated sanctuary guests of the Abbey was Elizabeth Woodville, the consort of Edward IV, who actually enjoyed two different lengthy stays at Westminster. The first time Elizabeth decamped to the Abbey was in October 1470. She had been staying at the Tower of London, awaiting the birth of her fourth child by Edward, when she learned that the fortunes of war had turned against her husband.

Richard Neville, Earl of Warwick and Salisbury, a.k.a. "the Kingmaker," and Edward's brother George, Duke of Clarence, had joined forces with Margaret of Anjou, Henry VI's queen, in an effort to reseat Henry on the throne of England. Backed by King Louis of France, these erstwhile enemies, now allies, invaded England in Henry's name in September. Lancastrian supporters raced to join the invading forces and disaffected Yorkists went along with them. The tide of power had shifted in the ongoing Wars of the Roses—this time against the House of York—and Edward knew it. He promptly fled the country, leaving Elizabeth to fend for herself.

A shrewd and resourceful, although not very likable, woman, Elizabeth reacted immediately on learning the news of Edward's flight. She gathered her three young daughters and went straight to Westminster Abbey to seek sanctuary, taking very few possessions and no money with her. Abbot Thomas Millyng granted her request and surrendered three rooms in his house for Elizabeth's use. He also generously provided food and financial support during the five months that Elizabeth remained in sanctuary and stood as godfather when the new Prince Edward was born at the Abbey on November 2, 1470.

Edward IV invaded England in March 1471 with an army backed by the support of his brother-in-law, Charles of Burgundy, and this time, fate was on the Yorkist side. Edward reclaimed his capital on April 11 and immediately had Elizabeth and their children brought from sanctuary to join him in Westminster Hall.

In gratitude for Abbot Millyng's protection and support, Elizabeth later endowed the Chapel of St. Erasmus at the Abbey. The chapel was demolished to make way for the Chapel of Henry VII. Edward also rewarded Abbot Millyng, appointing him Prince's Chancellor on July 8, 1471, and elevating him to the see of Hereford in 1474.

Elizabeth availed herself of the right of sanctuary at the Abbey again at midnight on May 1, 1483. This time the news that precipitated her action was that her brother-in-law Richard, Duke of Gloucester, had intercepted the retinue of her son, Edward V, as the new king was on his way to London for his coronation following the death of Edward IV. Richard had taken the young king into his custody, an action Elizabeth found very threatening since she and her family had long been Richard's enemies. Once again, she gathered up her daughters and the young king's brother Richard, Duke of York, and moved over to the Abbey, adding to her entourage a son from her first marriage, Thomas Grey, Marquis of Dorset; her brother Lionel, Bishop of Salisbury; and a great deal of luggage, including, according to some, the Crown's treasury. *(She must have learned the first time how tough life in sanctuary is without money and the comforts of home.)* Again, the abbot at the time, John Esteney, surrendered his house to her.

The whole situation was very embarrassing for the Duke of Gloucester. The fact that Elizabeth had felt compelled to seek sanctuary for herself and her children was a very clear signal that she did not trust the brother whom Edward IV had named "Protector" of the realm for the minority of Edward V. Richard and his council went to great lengths to entice Elizabeth to leave the confines of the Abbey, but she steadfastly refused.

In particular, Richard wanted Elizabeth to release his other nephew, the Duke of York. As long as she had a "spare heir" to the throne in her custody, Elizabeth had a powerful bargaining chip with Richard. No one knows why she eventually yielded and surrendered the 9-year-old duke to his uncle. It may have had something to do with the ring of armed men with which Gloucester had surrounded the Abbey. Rumor had it that Richard had ordered the troops to violate sanctuary and seize his nephew if the pleas of a delegation to Elizabeth, led by Cardinal Bourchier, Archbishop of Canterbury, were not successful in convincing the queen to let her son go. Whatever the reason, Elizabeth did allow the Duke of York to leave sanctuary in June 1483. He was never seen alive outside of the Tower of London again.

Elizabeth and her five daughters—Elizabeth (the future wife of Henry VII), Cecily, Anne, Catherine and Bridget—remained at Westminster Abbey. They were there, still living in the abbot's house, when Richard and his wife, Anne, were crowned king and queen on July 6, 1483. They did not leave sanctuary until March 1, 1484, after Elizabeth wrung an oath from Richard III that he swore to in front of a crowd of witnesses gathered for the occasion in Westminster Hall.

> *I, Richard, by the Grace of God King of England etc., in the presence of my lords spiritual and temporal, promise and swear on the word of a king that if the daughters of Dame Elizabeth Grey, late calling herself Queen of England, will come to me out of Sanctuary at Westminster, and be guided, ruled and demeaned after me, then I shall see that they be in surety of their lives, and also not suffer any manner hurt by any manner person, nor any of them imprison within the Tower of London or any other prison, but that I shall put them in honest places of good name and fame, . . . and shall see . . . [that they] have all things requisite and necessary as my kinswomen . . .*

In this oath, Richard also promised to find good husbands for his nieces and to provide Elizabeth with a home and financial support. After this, the girls left sanctuary and joined Richard's court, a piece of evidence many people cite to try to debunk the theory that Richard had killed their brothers, who had not been seen for months by this time. *(Thank you, Thomas More and William Shakespeare.)*

Not everyone who sought sanctuary at the Abbey was as lucky as Elizabeth Woodville. The right was regularly violated and people were often dragged from the church to their executions. Three particularly sordid episodes of this date from the turbulent reign of Richard II.

A squire named Richard Hauley was actually murdered in the church in August 1378 after he and another squire, Richard Shakel, had sought sanctuary there. The two squires had been holding a hostage while awaiting payment of a ransom they were promised by a great Spanish nobleman they had captured when warring with the Black Prince in Spain. Spain wanted the hostage back. Richard II's council agreed to the demands and ordered the squires to release the man. They refused, and were arrested and imprisoned in the Tower of London. Somehow they managed to escape and took refuge at Westminster Abbey. The Constable of the Tower pursued them with 50 soldiers, sacrilegiously invading the church. Shakel was arrested, but Hauley resisted and was killed, along with a sacrist named Richard, in the Abbey choir during high mass. Hauley was buried in what is now Poets' Corner. Everyone involved in the murder was excommunicated.

Sanctuary at the Abbey also was violated during the Peasants' Revolt when Richard Imworth, Steward of the Marshalsea, was dragged screaming from St. Edward's shrine, where he had been found clinging to the columns. Imworth was beheaded without trial at Cheapside.

The third time sanctuary at Westminster Abbey was violated during Richard II's reign occurred during the Merciless Parliament of 1388 when Richard's unhappy barons tried to replace his court officials with their own choices. One of the most hated of these was Sir Robert Tressilian, the Chief Justice, who ran to the Abbey when he recognized which way the wind was blowing. He was arrested in the Abbey by Thomas, Duke of Gloucester, and then dragged to Tyburn, where he was stripped, his throat was cut and he was hanged. So much for the protection of the Church.

Lambeth Palace

Lambeth Palace Road, SE1

Lambeth, Westminster or Vauxhall Tube

OPEN

In order to visit, apply in writing to the Social Secretary several months in advance. This will secure you a spot on the Wednesday or Thursday guided tour, the only days that tours are conducted.

ADMISSION

Free of charge

To approach Lambeth Palace from Westminster, proceed along Dean Bradley Street and turn left onto Horseferry Road. Cross Lambeth Bridge and follow Lambeth Palace Street to the gatehouse.

Okay, we know. Lambeth Palace never was a royal castle, although it did play host often enough to various reigning monarchs. We put it into this chapter because it made the most sense to include Lambeth with a walking tour of Westminster. Besides, as the London seat of the Archbishop of Canterbury, Lambeth certainly was a site where many key events impacting the monarchy occurred.

Located across the Thames from Westminster Palace, Lambeth was conveniently close enough to the seat of government for the archbishops to keep a close eye on royal doings, but separate enough to maintain a safe distance between the reigning monarch and the head of the Church in England. Construction of the palace actually was begun by Hubert Walter, who served as archbishop from 1193 to 1205. But it was the saintly Archbishop Stephen Langton, arch-foe of King John, who selected it for his in-town address in 1207 and established Lambeth as the London seat for the Canterbury bishopric.

Relations between Archbishop Stephen Langton and King John were ever tumultuous. A prolonged struggle over the Crown's right to appoint the Archbishop of Canterbury ended with Pope Innocent's imposed selection of Langton—a surprisingly good choice for England; a decidedly painful outcome for John. Langton consistently challenged John, even going so far as to side with the mutinous barons who were attempting to define the limitations of monarchial power, earning himself a rebuke from the Pope, and serving as a mediator between John and his barons to negotiate Magna Carta. After John's death, the archbishop loyally supported the ascendency to the throne of the king's son, Henry III, and became part of the ruling council that governed England during Henry's minority.

As the political role of subsequent Archbishops of Canterbury expanded, so Lambeth Palace grew, although it never reached truly grand proportions—never took on the swagger of, say, Wolsey's York Palace or Hampton Court. Instead, Lambeth claimed the spotlight not for its physical stature, but for the grand scale of events that took place within its close. From Lambeth, the archbishops zealously guarded the rights, privileges and hegemony of the Church, confronting both king and commoner whenever they concluded that a breach in the Church's iron control over religious and social life was threatened.

The oldest part of the palace is *(need we say it?)* the crypt. Dating from Langton's time, the crypt is a crypt, but this one has original doorways and windows dating from the 13th century. The most interesting thing about it, unless you are seriously into crypts and Norman architecture, is that this is where the official hearing ending Henry VIII's marriage to Anne Boleyn was held in 1536.

Above the crypt is the chapel. Cromwell's soldiers and Hitler's bombs both did a number on this 13th-century structure, so very little is left that dates from the original construction. But you will pass through it on the official tour, so while there, close your eyes and imagine what it must have been like when Archbishop Cranmer sat in his box above the altar and listened as his Book of Common Prayer was first used in a service.

The Great Hall actually is a 17th-century reconstruction of the old medieval hall. It was rebuilt after Cromwell's troops destroyed the palace *(it clearly was a favorite target for anyone who had a grudge against the Church)*. But once again, if you apply your imagination, you can envision Henry V feasting with his courtiers when he moved the court to Lambeth so that the Holy Roman Emperor Sisamagund could have Westminster Palace to himself when he visited England in 1416. Or you can imagine Henry VIII conferring endlessly with his chief ministers over the monarch's break with Rome, masterminding a strategy to make the sovereign the Supreme Head of the Church of England and the Archbishop of Canterbury his prime spiritual consultant. The first to claim that honor was Thomas Cranmer, who succeeded in annulling Henry's marriage to Katherine of Aragon.

Today, the Great Hall serves as the library of Lambeth Palace and is stuffed with treasures to thrill the soul of any amateur

☞ Did you know?

Ironically, when Katherine of Aragon first came to London as the bride-to-be of Henry VIII's elder brother, Prince Arthur, she was welcomed at Lambeth Palace on November 9, 1501. She stayed there until her marriage day, November 14. After the ceremony and celebration, she and Arthur spent their first night of wedded bliss at the lost treasure of Baynard's Castle and whatever happened—or did not happen—that night provided the grounds for Henry's divorce from Katherine 27 years later. Katherine maintained until her death that nothing happened and therefore her marriage to Henry was not incestuous, as he claimed. But then Henry was ingenious at coming up with reasons to back his desires to discard wives.

historian of medieval and Tudor lore. It has one of the most extensive collections of medieval manuscripts and books in the world. Among these gems are the illuminated 9th-century Macdurnan Gospels, an 11th-century Lambeth Bible, a Gutenberg Bible, a Book of Hours that belonged to Richard III and passed to Margaret Beaufort after her son ascended the throne as Henry VII *(Richard must have been rolling in his grave)*, six of the first books printed by William Caxton, a first edition of Thomas More's *Utopia*, Edward VI's Latin grammar, Elizabeth I's prayer book and Francis Bacon's letters. In addition, even though it is a little past our period, we thought we would mention that the library also has a first edition of the King James Bible, much of which was written at Lambeth. If you don't have time to take the tour that includes the library, you can write to the Lambeth Palace librarian and obtain advance permission to visit this treasure trove. It's worth the effort.

☞ Did you know?

The Peasants' Revolt was not the first time Lambeth Palace was sacked. The de Lusignan brothers, Henry III's half brothers by his mother, Isabella of Angoulême, and her second husband, Hugh de Lusignan, got there first in 1252. Their desecration of the palace was one of the inflammatory actions that enraged Henry's barons and caused them, under the leadership of Simon de Montfort, to rebel against their anointed king.

The palace guardhouse was constructed out of necessity after the rebels of the Peasants' Revolt ransacked the buildings in 1381. Archbishop Sudbury fled to the "safety" of the Tower of London from which he was subsequently dragged and beheaded by the angry mob. The guard chamber today contains portraits of various archbishops painted by Holbein, Van Dyck, Hogarth and Reynolds.

Several of Lambeth Palace's tower buildings date from our period. According to tradition, Archbishop Cranmer added the tower that sits northeast of the chapel, although no documentary evidence exists to prove this. The tower at the west end of the chapel is variously known as Chicele's Tower, because it was built by Archbishop Chicele in the 15th century; the Water

Tower, because it led to the quay on the river; and Lollards' Tower, because, legend has it, the small prison in the turret at the top was used to confine Wycliff's followers. That the room was used as a prison there is no doubt. The walls still are decorated with iron rings used to restrain prisoners. The only mystery is whether Lollards really were imprisoned there.

The most impressive tower, called Morton's Tower, was built by Archbishop Morton between 1486 and 1501 during the reign of Henry VII. It is one of the best examples of Tudor brickwork in London, if you're into Tudor brickwork, that is. The new tower replaced an old medieval gateway and remains today the main entrance to the palace. Morton's Tower actually consists of two towers flanking a central room over the gateway. The room was once an audience chamber. On the ground floor of the left tower, Friar Peto was imprisoned for preaching against Henry VIII's impending marriage to Anne Boleyn. Arm irons cast into the walls are reminders of his captivity and that of royalist prisoners held here during the Commonwealth.

◇◇

THOMAS CRANMER (1489–1556)

Thomas Cranmer, Archbishop of Canterbury from 1532 until 1555, was one of the single most important figures in the establishment of the Anglican Church, and one whose fingerprints are still all over the liturgy, services and style of worship of the church today.

Born in 1489, Cranmer was a brilliant scholar, entering Cambridge at age 14 and moving quickly toward a divinity degree. Early on, however, he exhibited a willingness to challenge—even to rebel against—established church doctrine. He ruined his career in the church in 1515 by marrying a barmaid, Black Joan. He was promptly thrown out of Cambridge *(remember those vows of chastity?)*. The marriage didn't last long, though; Joan died within a year in childbirth. Cranmer was readmitted to Cambridge and shortly took holy orders, vowing to devote his life to study.

Cranmer first came to the attention of Henry VIII in 1529. Cranmer had told a couple of Henry's court officials that the matter of the king's divorce from Katherine of Aragon was not something to be decided by the pope, but by doctors of divinity at leading universities. Henry, who had by now been struggling with this problem for several years, was overjoyed to hear Cranmer's opinion and immediately summoned him to court to write a treatise on the subject. Cranmer so impressed the king with his intellect and abilities that Henry appointed Cranmer Archbishop of Canterbury in August 1532. Cranmer thanked the king by promptly declaring Henry's marriage to Katherine of Aragon "null and absolutely void" as well as "contrary to divine law."

The new archbishop was eager to take up the mitre, viewing the appointment as a great opportunity to begin implementing major ecclesiastical reforms. Still, he had to move slowly. Although willing to set himself up as the Supreme Head of the Church in England so that he could marry Anne Boleyn, Henry VIII continued to view himself as a Catholic and resisted the reformist changes that the more Protestant-leaning of his secular and clerical lords favored.

Cranmer was at Henry's bedside when the king drew his last breath on January 28, 1547. A secret Lutheran since the 1530s, Cranmer was now free to begin serious church reform, secure in the knowledge that the new young king, Edward VI, had already embraced Protestantism and would support the archbishop's efforts. He also was supported by the Lord Protector, the Duke of Somerset, who had long been a reformist.

No time was wasted. By the end of 1548, Latin had been banned from services at St. Paul's and the Chapel Royal, the doctrine of transubstantiation had been publicly denounced, churches had been ordered to remove images of saints, the carrying of candles during services was forbidden, the bearing of palms and creeping to the Cross on one's knees during Good Friday services had been prohibited and clergy were free to marry. In December, the reformists submitted to parliament a Bill of Uniformity that banned the Catholic mass and dictated that the new Book of Common Prayer written by Archbishop Cranmer was to be used for services in all churches. The bill was passed by parliament in March 1549.

Cranmer's troubles began when Edward died on July 6, 1553. Panicked at the thought of the Catholic Mary wearing the crown of England, the archbishop was one of the few councilors of the realm who supported the Duke of Northumberland to the bitter end in his effort to seat Lady Jane Grey on the throne. He paid dearly for this.

Mary forgave many of the men who had supported the duke in his effort to usurp her crown, even appointing some of them councilors . . . but not Cranmer. She blamed him—and hated him—for her father's divorce from Katherine of Aragon and marriage to Anne Boleyn. The archbishop soon gave her an excuse to take her revenge when he criticized the re-establishment of the Catholic mass in church services. He was arrested and taken to the Tower of London on September 14, 1553. Along with Lady Jane Grey and her husband, Lord Guilford Dudley, Cranmer was tried for treason at the Guildhall on November 14. All three pleaded guilty and were condemned to die.

For a time, Mary stayed her hand and the three condemned traitors were left to languish in the Tower. Cranmer even continued to hold his title of Archbishop of Canterbury. But on September 30, 1555, Cranmer was tried for heresy in Oxford and his case referred to the pope for a decision. In December, Cranmer received word that the pope had declared him guilty of heresy, excommunicated him and stripped him of his archbishopric.

Great pressure was put on Cranmer to renounce his Protestant beliefs. He was forced to watch Bishop of Worcester Hugh Latimer and Bishop of London Nicholas Ridley die at the stake for refusing to renounce their beliefs and endured endless harangues by Catholic bishops urging him to recant. He finally buckled under the pressure and did make several statements renouncing his faith. Mary was having none of it. Cranmer was sent to the stake on March 21, 1556, in Oxford.

The night before his death, he spent writing another recantation. Sometime before he was taken to the execution site, Cranmer had yet another change of heart and instead of reading his final recantation, he issued a ringing statement of his faith in Protestantism. He told the assembled crowd that his right hand, which had so offended God by signing the recantations, would be the first part of his body to burn. Thus, Cranmer died a martyr's death, proclaiming to the end his Protestant faith.

◇◇

CONTENTS

·····II·····

Shakespeare's Southwark

Southwark

Before you read any further, get this one straight: it may be spelled "South Wark," but give that destination to any London cabbie and who knows where you'll wind up! The "proper" pronunciation of this south-of-the-Thames neighborhood is "Suthick." Feel like a local now, don't you?

Too often relegated to the role of the ugly stepsister, Southwark played a vivid, fascinating part in the history of medieval and Tudor London. In fact, the local history stretches even further back, to the earliest days of Roman occupation. Amateur historians will know that there are references to significant activities in this village "over the river," starting with the moment William the Conqueror sent London its first smoke signal by setting Southwark to flame. By 1086, Southwark was recovered sufficiently to make its way into the Conqueror's *Domesday Book*, with about 40 households and a major church to serve its residents.

By 1295, Southwark had grown substantially. Technically under the jurisdiction of the City of London, the borough was deemed large enough—and important enough—to be granted its own representation to parliament, the first London district outside the City to enjoy this right. Despite its ties to the City, Southwark was seldom closely supervised, and the ancient neighborhood soon developed a reputation *(not altogether undeserving!)* as a haven for ne'er-do-wells and a den of iniquity known for its illicit—and often violent—pastimes. Yet the "second-class" residents of Southwark often lent crucial support to the City and, at times, served as an uncomfortable foil for events across the Thames. Bear in mind the glory (or the ignominy) with which the Empress Matilda, Simon de Montfort and the Peasant Rebels crossed London Bridge . . . then, thank or curse Southwark! From Chaucer's very real Tabard Inn to the Bishop of Winchester's all-too-real Clink prison, Southwark wasted no time in establishing important landmarks, many of which can be enjoyed *(with the help of your vast knowledge and keen imagination)* today.

As Shakespeare groupies, we believe Southwark's most valuable contribution to London was the fertile welcome it gave the burgeoning theater industry. Although there were several popular theaters on the north side of the Thames, these were at the constant mercy of the humorless City fathers and subject to arbitrary fines, strictures and closings. Southwark's transient visitors, whores, pimps, thieves, rat catchers, ditch diggers and dung collectors may have been sneered at as ignorant dolts, but the raucous appreciation of these "groundlings"—coupled with Southwark's independence from City authorities—allowed for a rich theatrical legacy that otherwise may have withered and died.

Enjoy your visit to Southwark. It will be brief, colorful, and—for theater buffs like us—totally engaging!

A lost treasure . . .

✠ Bermondsey

East of London Bridge at the junction of Bermondsey Street and Tower Bridge Road, SE1

>>

If antiquing is one of your favorite London pastimes, chances are you are already familiar with the world-renowned Bermondsey Antique Market, held every Friday in Bermondsey Square. If not, you're certain to find the history of this medieval neighborhood well worth note.

One of the earliest mentions of Bermondsey appears in the Domesday Book compiled in 1086. At that time, the property was the site of a royal manor home, although it had lent its name to the better-known Bermondsey Abbey, founded in 1082 on the site of an ancient (c. 700 CE) monastery dedicated to St. Saviour. William II granted the royal manor to the Abbey in 1094, and its valuable landholdings were further increased when Henry I deeded additional properties in Rotherhite, Dulwich and Southwark. By the reign of Henry II, Bermondsey was one of the most prominent English abbeys and His Grace honored the monks in residence by spending Christmas 1154 in their company. He was not alone in making the pilgrimage to Bermondsey; the monks were enjoying visitors from far and wide, come to pay homage to the Rood of St. Saviour, dredged from the Thames in 1117, but "marketed" as having fallen from heaven.

Religious gimmicks, superstitions and wealth made all abbeys vulnerable to the wrath of Henry VIII and Bermondsey was no exception. The confiscated abbey was purchased by Sir Thomas Pope, who tore down the ancient structure and used the stones to build his own ostentatious manor, Bermondsey House. The home was fancy enough to suit the Earl of Sussex, who, upon several occasions, opened Bermondsey's doors and larder to entertain Queen Elizabeth.

Bermondsey Square is a good distance from our proposed Southwark walking tour. However, if you find yourself in the neighborhood—in search of antiques or out of mere curiosity—you will be able to trace the inner courtyard of the Abbey. A home in nearby Grange Walk still bears the hinges of the Abbey's east gates.

While you're in the neighborhood . . .

Look for the ruins of Edward III's moated royal manor. We have heard that they are near the Bermondsey Market, but despite our most diligent efforts, we have been unable to track them down. If you're successful, let us know!

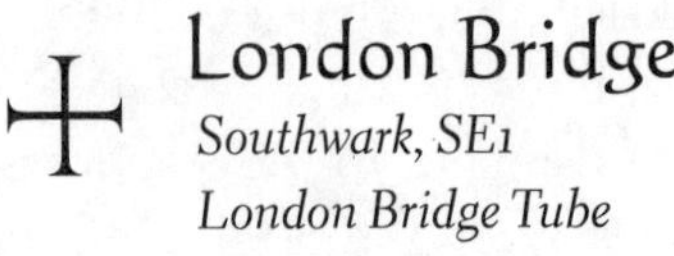

London Bridge

Southwark, SE1
London Bridge Tube

> *. . . London Bridge is broken down,*
> *gold is won and bright renown, my fair lady . . .*
> —Ottar Svarte

The history of London Bridge is as old as the history of London itself, dating back to 75 CE when the Romans first sought to span the Thames. This ancient wooden structure burned and was rebuilt many times over the course of its early years. In 1014, the bridge was literally "broken down," when the Norwegian supporters of King Ethelred, under the command of Olaf of Norway, pulled the bridge into the Thames in an attempt to thwart Danish invasion. The heroic enterprise inspired the Norse poet Ottar Svarte to pen the lines that would evolve into one of the best-loved children's nursery games.

Construction began on the bridge of our particular interest in 1176, under the supervision of Peter de Colechurch; it was completed in 1209. This was a noble structure, befitting the only link between the southern regions and the majestic City of London. Kings and queens, merchants and monks, rebels and religious pilgrims, all would venture over London Bridge to fulfill a mission in the outlying shires, or to seek their fortune at London's door. The bridge was built atop 19 narrow arches, through which boat captains would valiantly strive to meet the challenge of shooting the Thames's mighty rapids. A drawbridge and massive stone gate limited access and egress on the Southwark end. Above hovered a seemingly airborne community, virtually a city unto itself. The heavily traveled bridge was chockablock on both sides of its roadway with looming wooden houses. On the ground floor of these structures were shops: precursors of today's tacky tourist shops. The requisite taverns and churches—including an important tribute to St. Thomas à Becket—completed the hodgepodge. Unfortunately, the narrow streetscape with its timber and thatch-roof structures posed a significant fire hazard. Indeed, the village atop the bridge was leveled in the devastating fire of 1212 . . . only to be rebuilt in a remarkably similar fashion!

☞ Did you know?

The Honorable Company of Watermen established their hall near London Bridge. In addition to leasing sculls and oars for cross-river passage, they enjoyed the grander employment of rowing the gilded barges for livery parades. From 1422 to 1856, they rowed the Lord Mayor–elect to Westminster, there to secure the monarch's approval of his election. This thoroughly ritual ride was given added sparkle in 1452 with an ostentatious new barge, adorned with sterling silver oars.

In the coldest winters, the bridge's restricted tidal flow created ideal ice conditions and seemingly all of London would congregate for a merry "Frost Fair." Booths selling hot food and gewgaws, skating and sliding competitions and savory barbecues provided a splendid break from the season's dark doldrums. Apparently, the mood was not in the least dampened by the vacant stares from the various traitors' heads that adorned the bridge's highest spheres.

Naturally, London Bridge was a favored approach to the City, and little time would pass between the pageants and parades, the cheers for heroes and the jeers for villains. Even the most important of these events comprise a list far too long to detail here, although an unusual on-the-bridge jousting tournament in 1325 bears note. By 1760, the houses that had provided ringside seats for so many spectators disappeared from along the bridge. The medieval structure itself was razed in 1831 and replaced with a fanciful incarnation some 20 meters upstream. That Victorian bridge was deconstructed in 1977 and rebuilt in Lake Havasu City, Arizona, USA.

◇◇

THOMAS À BECKET (1118–1170)

The memory of Thomas à Becket will forever be closely linked to Canterbury. It was there, at the seat of the Church in England, that the archbishop wielded his greatest influence, took his most dangerous risks and met his scandalous demise in front of Canterbury Cathedral's high altar. Yet Becket was London born and raised; he was welcomed to the world in Ironmonger Lane, Cheapside. Indeed, in his own lifetime he was known as "Thomas of London," Becket being his father's surname and "à" Becket a conceit that was added after the Reformation. For all his ties to Canterbury, medieval London jealously guarded their attachment to the martyred saint, their native son.

Born of Norman parents, Matilda and Gilbert, Thomas enjoyed the affluent lifestyle his merchant father's success ensured. His mother, who had long yearned for a son, was so overjoyed by Thomas's arrival that she made annual donations to her parish church in the amount equal to Thomas's birthday weight. Doting parents, an entrepreneurial upbringing and the independent spirit of his hometown all seem to have helped form Thomas into the confident, ambitious and clever man known to history.

Although by no means a brilliant scholar, Thomas was well educated, first at London grammar schools, then at the Augustinian priory at Merton, and later abroad. He was not, however, trained with an eye toward a church career; that would come much later in Thomas's life—after he had sown more than his share of wild oats! Rather, Thomas's first profession was as an accountant—first in the household of Osbert Huitdeniers, and later in the service of Archbishop Theobold of Canterbury. It was through this auspicious connection that Thomas found his entry into the world of politics and embarked upon a path that would eventually lead to his remarkable religious calling.

Of course, Thomas of London's pivotal relationship would be with England's new king, Henry Plantagenet. Thomas was appointed chancellor to young Henry II in 1155 and remained the king's closest friend and advisor until Thomas was elevated to the see of Canterbury in 1162. This was a tremendously lucrative period for Thomas; the king's special favor bestowed upon him extensive lands, vacant bishoprics and secular baronies. Thomas lived like a noble—a noble with rich taste and a propensity for flaunting his perks.

In 1161, Archbishop Theobold died, and in a very controversial move, Henry appointed Thomas to fill his role. Traditionally, monks formed the pool from which the Archbishop of Canterbury was chosen; this fact, coupled with Thomas's less-than-devout lifestyle, created a considerable stir in the ecclesiastic community. Yet fill the shoes of Theobold Thomas did—and he took his new role as head of the church in England very, very seriously, indeed.

It is not our task here to give you a complete biography of Thomas à Becket, nor to outline in detail the complicated issues that would form the famous riff between Thomas and his king. *(We will, however, tell you much more in our next book, when we lead you on a tour of Canterbury!)*

Suffice it to say that from this point on, the honeymoon between the two mighty men was over. Years of discord and unpleasantry ensued; in 1164, Thomas embarked upon a six-year exile, and his typically ostentatious return to Canterbury in 1170 drove an irate Henry to hurl the words that sealed Thomas's *(and in a sense, Henry's)* fate: ". . . Will no one rid me of this turbulent priest?"

On December 29, 1170, four of Henry's knights did, in fact, rid their king of the thorn in his side—at least physically. Thomas was confronted before the high altar in Canterbury Cathedral and, upon refusing to submit to arrest, was murdered in cold blood.

For one who had such a stellar rise, sainthood seems a fitting end. And so it would come to be. Within a matter of days, the devout of England were flocking to Canterbury Cathedral, where miracles were already reportedly taking place; over 700 of them would be attributed to the martyred Becket in the decade after his death alone. He was canonized in 1173, and became the most popular cult figure of the medieval era. It would take the Reformation to fuel a decline in the Becket frenzy.

Next to Canterbury itself, London became the home of the second-most-important Thomas à Becket shrine. A church was erected in his honor, smack in the middle of London Bridge; it was also believed to be the site of many Thomas-granted miracles and attracted huge numbers of pilgrims throughout the Middle Ages. Somewhat later, one of London's leading hospitals would bear the martyr's name; St. Thomas's Hospital is still a Southbank landmark, although it was long ago relocated from its medieval Southwark location. A second hospital was founded in 1190 by Thomas's sister Agnes and her husband.

This one, housed in Becket's former childhood home, was called St. Thomas of Acon.

Becket also left a secondhand legacy to the City of London: a scribe in Becket's household, William fitz Stephen, wrote one of the most informative and evocative descriptions of medieval London (c. 1180). It has inspired historians and travel writers—including yours truly!—for nearly 900 years.

London Dungeon

Tooley Street, SE1 (020-7403-0606)
London Bridge Tube

OPEN

10:00 a.m.–6:00 p.m. daily

ADMISSION

£8.50 Adults
£5.50–£7.50 Concessions
Under 5, free of charge

Warning: The portrayals in the London Dungeon are far too graphic for young children. We rate this attraction "R."

We don't mean to imply that *your* taste is this low-brow and macabre, but perhaps someone else in your party has a hankering for something out-of-the-ordinary. A bit off our Southwark tour (to the east of London Bridge), the London Dungeon allows you to actually observe the more horrific medieval (and later) tortures . . . rather than simply imagine them. As with Madame Tussaud's, there is nothing "scholarly" about these depictions. Then again, we did say "amateur," did we not?

☞ Did you know?

At the advent of the Tudor era, there were six separate prisons in Southwark. Painfully small and terribly overcrowded, they were a breeding ground for disease and death. Although gruesome in their detail, the tortures portrayed in the London Dungeon are not atypical of the times.

Southwark Cathedral

Montague Close, SE1 (020-7407-2329)
London Bridge Tube

OPEN
9:00 a.m.–6:00 p.m.
(Touring restricted if service is in process)

WORSHIP
Cathedral Eucharist: 11:00 a.m. Sunday
Evening Prayer: 5:30 p.m. daily

ADMISSION
Donation suggested

CONVENIENCES
Restaurant open 10:00 a.m.–4:00 p.m. daily
Bookshop operates during cathedral open hours

Chances are, as you've savored the tales of medieval history, you've happened upon a reference or two to St. Mary Overie (or, Overy: "over the river"), the Augustinian priory and primary church of the parish of Southwark, erected here in 1106. Although the roots of this church date much, much earlier—mid 7th century*—it is the medieval house of worship that remains, in part, on view today.

In truth, it is remarkable that any of the ancient building has survived at all. A devastating fire in 1212 severely burned a major portion of the church and priory, and a second fire in the 1390s undermined much of the newly renovated buildings. Through the benefice of the influential Bishop of Winchester, Cardinal Henry Beaufort (son of John of Gaunt), funds were raised to once again restore the church's beauty. The tower and south transept reflect the munificence of Beaufort, who wanted to be certain that an impressive stage was set for the marriage of his niece, Joan, to King James I of Scotland. The Beaufort arms decorate the south transept's east wall.

*Even older are the traces of a Roman villa that once stood on this site. Pavings from this residence have been incorporated into the south choir aisle.

Although Henry VIII confiscated the church during the Reformation, his nod of royal favor allowed St. Mary's sanctuary to continue, under the name of St. Saviour of Southwark, as the parish church for the borough. In keeping with the nature of the neighborhood, St. Saviour suffered an embarrassment of riches. So down-at-the-heels did the former priory become that parts were eventually rented out as cottages, a bakery, even a pigsty before being reclaimed (and renamed) in the 19th century.

Although most of the building has been restored numerous times since the 13th century, distinct sections of the original architecture can readily be identified, once inside. This was London's first fully Gothic church, and this is best appreciated in the ancient choir and in the east end chapels. Because there are so many fragments of medieval construction partnered with renovations and innovations, you'd be best to engage the help of a docent while strolling through the main body of the church.

To scout out the rather sentimental tribute to Shakespeare, turn right upon entering the cathedral and proceed down the south side aisle. The most interesting feature of this "shrine," erected in 1912, is the frieze behind the statue depicting Southwark as it "probably" looked when the Bard was "probably" a neighborhood resident. The brightly hued window above the statue pays tribute to Shakespeare's comedies, tragedies and histories *(we know you've already purchased a ticket to a performance for each day of your stay!)*. There is also a recently added memorial in honor of the American actor/artistic director Samuel Wannemaker (1919–1993), whose vision and leadership led to the reconstruction of the Globe Theater, just a short walk from the cathedral. Duck inside the Harvard Chapel for another Shakespeare memorial, this to younger brother Edmund Shakespeare, who died of the plague in 1607 and was buried in the cathedral . . . although not necessarily where this stone marker indicates.

Back in the main sanctuary, pass through the gate and you'll find, on your right, one of the cathedral's earliest monuments, the Effigy of a Knight. This was carved in 1275, and although it is officially designated as "anonymous," there is some speculation that the gent may have been a member of the de Warrene clan. Keeping him company are Shakespeare's friendly rival and manager of the Rose Theater, Philip Henslowe, as well as John Gower, a personal friend of Chaucer's and Poet Laureate to both Richard II and Henry IV. Look, too, for the memorial to Mayflower captain Christopher Jones, who is buried in the Southwark Cathedral churchyard.

☞ Did you know?

St. Mary Overie's dock was the site of many an escape from the nearby Clink prison. Hundreds of small craft received and discharged freight before returning to the Continent, and it was relatively easy for an escapee to hide amongst the hordes of sailors passing along the waterway.

At the time of our most recent visit, Southwark Cathedral was in the midst of an exciting rejuvenation. Included in the extensive plans will be an archeology chamber displaying a major portion of the old Roman road, the early cloister foundations, the Norman church wall and the cellars and warehouses of Winchester Palace. The east churchyard will be relandscaped to include a historically accurate medieval apothecary herb garden *(Cadfael fans, take note!)*. And a second churchyard will be added, with flower beds created around biblical and Shakespearean themes. Finally, the old refectory will be converted into an interactive high-tech exhibition where the history of Southwark will be brought to life. We can't wait to go back!

Tip!

For a total Southwark experience, visit the cathedral on Shakespeare's birthday, April 23. The celebratory service offered in his honor is enchanting.

A lost treasure . . . St. Thomas's Hospital

Among the many significant buildings at the Priory of St. Mary Overie was the 13th-century St. Thomas's Hospital. Originally named the Hospital of St. Thomas the Martyr, the facility was a tribute to Thomas à Becket. Although of vital service to the community, the hospital was subject to numerous relocations. Destroyed by fire in 1215, it was rebuilt in Borough High Street, ending its association with the priory. Despite its separation from St. Mary, it was closed by Henry VIII during the Dissolution of the Monasteries. Reopened in 1551, the newly named Hospital of St. Thomas grew to become one of the leading hospitals in the London area. It was eventually moved to make way for the expansion of the London Bridge Tube station and is now located near the base of Westminster Bridge.

The *Golden Hind* Replica

St. Mary Overie Dock, Cathedral Street, SE1 (020-7403-0123)
Monument or London Bridge Tube

OPEN

10:00 a.m.–sunset daily

ADMISSION

£2.50 Adults
£1.50–£1.90 Concessions

New to the Southwark neighborhood is a handsome full-sized reproduction of the *Golden Hind.* The dashing Elizabethan courtier, Sir Francis Drake, made his famous 'round-the-world sail in the original ship from 1577 to 1580. When you see how small a vessel he captained, you will be amazed how daring a venture this truly was! This replica duplicated that journey, circumnavigating the world as a floating museum, before coming to dock between Southwark's two landmark bridges. You may take a tour of this painstaking reproduction, while guides in period clothing tell tall tales of life at sea in the 16th century. This is an adventure that the children in your party will particularly enjoy.

Winchester Palace

Pickford's Wharf off Clink Street, SE1
London Bridge Tube

As any historian, amateur or otherwise, can attest, the Bishop of Winchester played an intriguing—if not always scrupulous—role in English politics for more than half a century. From King Stephen's turncoat brother, Henry of Blois, to William of Wykeham, founder of the English public school system, the collective bishops were a group of true medieval power players. Befitting of their influence was their spectacular Thames-side home, close enough to Westminster to ensure a ringside seat as important events unfurled. Unfortunately, the only view you'll have of the ancient Winchester Palace is through an imposing steel fence. Oh well, that's a whole lot more than you would have seen 20–25 years ago, before 1970s redevelopment efforts exposed the ruins of the palace's banqueting hall.

Did you know?
Although no one would argue that Southwark ever rivaled the Strand as the "gold coast" of London, the Bishop of Winchester did have stiff competition for grand riverside accommodations. The Bishop of Rochester kept an exceedingly impressive residence in this neighborhood as well, located on the site of the current Borough Market. The Duke of Suffolk also built sumptuous quarters in the vicinity of Marshlea Road and Borough High Street. Unfortunately, no trace of either manor still exists.

Winchester Palace was the London seat of the Bishops of Winchester from the early 13th century until the bishopric was suppressed, some 500 years later. Built in 1109, the palace was a convenient meeting place for conferences between church and state. It is believed that at one such meeting, Henry VIII was first introduced to Catherine Howard. Alas, even this second-hand connection to Heaven couldn't quite confer sufficient blessings upon Henry's fifth marriage.

In 1642, the venom of parliament caused a dramatic reincarnation from palace to prison for Winchester House. From there, the tumble toward decay continued unchecked. In its heyday, however, Winchester Palace was magnificent. As you look at the west wall, you'll see the great oriel rose window, c. 1330, for which the palace was renowned. The three doors beneath the window led to the pantry, buttery and kitchen. The barricaded first floor doorway was once the main entrance.

Partially exposed as it is, there is more to Winchester Palace than meets the eye: beneath the medieval ruins are the remains of a substantial Roman villa!

Clink Prison Museum

1 Clink Street, SE1 (020-7378-1558)
London Bridge Tube

OPEN

10:00 a.m.–6:00 p.m. daily

ADMISSION

£3.50 Adults
£8.50 Family ticket; children must be accompanied by an adult
£2.50 Concessions

Warning: Some of the displays in the Clink Museum may be too sexually explicit for youngsters. We rate this attraction PG-13.

Americans associate "in the clink"—slang for jail—with B-grade gangster movies. For Londoners, the phrase was meant literally. A Southwark institution since 816, the Clink was the common name for the prison attached to Winchester Palace. Until the early 1600s, Southwark's thriving red-light district was within the Winchester liberty, with the holier-than-thou bishops collecting regular income from the neighboring brothels. Although it was frequently used as a penitentiary for religious malefactors, the Clink also had the distinction of being one of the few London prisons to incarcerate women. It was typically filled to capacity with "Winchester Geese," prostitutes who violated the arbitrary laws governing their profession. Today, these "Ladies of the Night" are remembered in the Clink Museum's display on prostitution, along with other memorabilia from the old prison and a working armory.

> ☞ Did you know?
> Bitten by the "Winchester Goose"? Better head to the chemist for a healthy dose of penicillin!

While you're in the neighborhood . . .

Keep an eye out for Redcross Way. This street was once the site of a dismal burying ground commonly referred to as the "Crossbones," an unconsecrated cemetery where the wretched Winchester Geese were laid to rest after finally surrendering to the perils of their profession.

Borough High Street

Southwark, SE1

London Bridge Tube

One continual ale house . . .

—Anonymous

Famed for its drinking, whoring and other forms of debauchery, Borough High Street was the scene of the Elizabethan barcrawl. As you stroll along, you'll see that each street and yard that you pass is named for one of the alehouses that served the rowdy carousers. Most taverns were three-sided structures with courtyards that opened directly onto the roadway, making them convenient way stations for out-of-town coaches, as well as for City rowdies hoping for an evening's diversion. Look closely, and you'll note that parts of one ancient tavern, The George, still exist. Four blocks down, search out White Hart Yard. Possibly named for Richard II, whose crest bore a white hart, the inn that stood here until 1889 is mentioned in Shakespeare's *Henry VI.* Further along, you'll discover the marker for Talbot Yard, formerly the Tabard Inn, point of embarkation for Chaucer's Canterbury pilgrims.

Anchor Tavern

34 Park Street, SE1 (020-7407-1577)
London Bridge Tube

OPEN

11:00 a.m.–11:00 p.m. Monday–Saturday
Noon–10:30 p.m. Sunday

While in the Southwark neighborhood, pay a visit to the oldest pub site in London, once home to a 15th-century tavern, Castle Upon the Hoop. So what if the Anchor is an 18th-century newcomer: the tradition of hoisting a pint goes back much further! Rest a while—perhaps on the lovely riverside deck—and offer a toast to the thespians, playwrights and stage crews who enjoyed their après-theater refreshment with the colorful Southwark residents at the "Hoop" . . . or one of the numerous incarnations to follow.

The Historic Bankside Theaters

Whether or not you're a theater aficionado, most visitors to London recognize the city's status as one of the leading theater cities of the world, and chances are you've included at least one performance on your London itinerary. What you may not appreciate is the very rocky start suffered by London theater . . . and just how instrumental the Southwark region known as "Bankside" became in establishing deep roots for the city's performing arts.

Although Elizabeth I was known to greatly appreciate a good performance and enthusiastically supported key players and playwrights of her time, the Elizabethan era was not a particularly friendly period for the burgeoning business of stagecraft. Playing on people's fear of widespread disease, the Master of the Revels would frequently close a theater at a moment's notice. In fact, the harsh disapproval and intense moral lobbying by puritanical sects was, more often than not, the real reason behind the anti-theater movement.

During the late 1500s and early 1600s, several theaters managed to eke out a precarious existence north of the Thames. Among them were The Curtain and James Burbage's first single-purpose playhouse, (imaginatively named) The Theatre—which would later be dismantled, moved to Southwark and renamed The Globe.

Southwark had several distinct advantages over the City as a site for fledgling theaters. Bear baiting and cockfighting were spectator sports well established in the vicinity, and many of the future Bankside theaters, such as The Rose, actually began by offering plays as additional entertainment for an eager audience. The audience itself was also favorable south of the river; even though the residents of Southwark were by and large looked down upon as "lumpen," the area was a thriving way station for stagecoaches from the south of England and vessels from the Continent—sources of travelers with a few spare coins in their pockets and some spare time on their hands. But perhaps the greatest advantage of all was Southwark's independence from the eagle-eye and iron fist of the City aldermen, the firebrands and moralists eager to see the theater business strangled once and for all.

The combined resources of actor Edward Alleyn and theater impresario Philip Henslowe laid the groundwork for what would soon become London's first legitimate, relatively stable "Theater District." The Rose Theater staged its first performance in 1592; it was quickly joined by The Swan, The Hope, The Bear Garden and the Curtain's new incarnation, The Globe. The talents of William Shakespeare, Christopher Marlowe, Ben Jonson, Richard Burbage and John Fletcher were magnets for playgoers of every ilk. It soon became fashionable for gentry from the City, Westminster and close-in suburbs to spend an afternoon cheek-to-jowl with the Southwark commoners and transients enraptured by the tragedies, romances, histories and comedies brought to life on the Bankside stages. If the location was a tad inconvenient, it only added to the audience's sense of adventure—naturally the ferrymen were thrilled!

Despite this fertile climate, the Bankside theaters lasted a relatively short time. The increased furor of the Puritan movement, coupled with numerous plague scares, greatly undermined the last stubborn vestiges of the Elizabethan and Jacobean theater. Orders were given in 1642, at the height of the Cromwellian uprising, to demolish all remaining theaters. By 1660, no traces of the Bankside playhouses remained and, until quite recently, amateur historians and theater aficionados had to content themselves with a handful of dated site markers as the remaining link to the pinnacle of early theater. Luckily, development activity in the area, coupled with the vision and drive of theater supporters worldwide, have brought to light vestiges of several of the most important stages of that time.

We hope you'll take the time to visit the site of the newly discovered Rose Theater and the painstakingly re-created Globe

Theater—where you can appreciate classical performances in an atmosphere nearly identical to that enjoyed by Tudor audiences.

The Rose Theater Site

Southwark Bridge Road at Park Street, SE1 (020-7593-0026)
London Bridge or Blackfriar's Tube

OPEN

10:00 a.m.–5:00 p.m. daily except Christmas and Boxing Day

ADMISSION

£3.00 Adults
£2.00 Children 5–15
£8.00 Family tickets
£2.50 Concessions

One of the most influential playhouses of the Elizabethan era, Philip Henslowe's Rose Theater enjoyed a remarkably brief life span—less than 20 years. Still, with the exception of the Globe, few playhouses premiered a more important canon of work: Shakespeare's epic *Henry VI* (1592), *Titus Andronicus*, and Marlowe's magnificent *Dr. Faustus* (1594), to name but a few. However, the Rose was relatively small, and the advent of the nearly adjacent, and much larger, Globe gave the Rose more competition than the market could bear. It presented its last production in 1606.

Unlike William Shakespeare, Philip Henslowe left a considerable number of valuable documents and artifacts behind as testimony to the impact of the Rose. Henslowe's fairly detailed construction notes proved to be of immense value in 1989, as Museum of London archeologists set about the task of excavating the Rose and reconstructing the theater to an as-close-as-possible approximation. To date, the outline of the stage and substantial portions of the inner and outer gallery walls have been unearthed. Pending the successful conclusion of the Save the Rose building campaign, a protective layer of sand has been placed over the excavation site. For now, you can enjoy a comprehensive video on the excavation and assumptions being made, based on the earliest findings on the site. Long-range plans include a modern museum-style exhibit on the importance of the Rose in Elizabethan theater, and a viewing gallery from which visitors can appreciate the 400-year-plus remains of the original playhouse. As you tour Southwark, you'll easily be able to locate the Rose site, read the current information on the building plans and progress, and maybe make a cash contribution to this important historic undertaking.

Shakespeare's Globe

New Globe Walk, Bankside, SE1 (020-7902-1500)
London Bridge Tube (if following Southwark tour)
Cannon Street or Mansion House Tube
(if attending a performance)

OPEN
9:15 a.m.–12:15 p.m. daily, May–September
Museum and tours 10 a.m.–5 p.m. daily, October–May

MUSEUM ADMISSION
£6.00 Adults
£15.00 Family ticket
£4.00–£5.00 Students and senior citizens

PRODUCTION SEASON
May–September (dates and times vary; call box office for details)

BOX OFFICE (IN SEASON)
10 a.m. — 7 p.m.

There are, obviously, two ways to enjoy Shakespeare's Globe, and both of them are well worth your while, schedule and weather permitting. The first is to follow this book's walking tour of Southwark, timing your visit to coincide with one of the fascinating guided tours of the Globe. For anyone interested in drama, literature or architecture, this is one of the very best tours around. You will learn an amazing amount about Shakespeare, the early years of theater and the challenges of historic preservation/re-creation, presented in a friendly, fast-paced format.

The second option, which requires a second visit, is to attend a live performance at the Globe. The season, as one would expect for an open-air theater, is relatively short—late spring through early autumn—and your experience will be enhanced *(or dampened),* weather depending. Productions at the Globe are very true to the original staging: casts are frequently "all male," costumes and props are minimal, groundlings swell the attendance for a mere pittance, while river noises from the neighboring Thames *(and 21st-century London streets)* add to the atmosphere. In short, there is no better way to get a firsthand feeling for Elizabethan entertainment *(and yes, that includes those tourist-popular "merrie olde banquets" you'll see hawked about town).*

> ☞ Did you know?
>
> Bardolatry aside, Shakespeare was known for making great use of his poetic license. "This wooden O," a reference to the Globe from the prelude to *Henry V,* is a case in point. In fact, the Globe was not an "O" but a polygon. Not that we delight in nit-picking, but we've known editors who would do the same to us.

Although the Bankside Globe opened in 1599, its roots stretch across the Thames to the Shoreditch neighborhood. Originally established in 1577 by James Burbage as The Theatre, the playhouse was subsequently dismantled and moved to the theater-friendly Southwark area by Burbage's son Richard. Among the shareholders of the new theater was actor and resident playwright William Shakespeare. Indeed, many of Shakespeare's greatest works—*Hamlet, Macbeth, King Lear, Othello* and *Henry V*—made their debut on the stage of the Globe. Unfortunately, so did the Bard's *Henry VIII;* a cannonball fired from this 1613 production set the thatch of the Globe on fire and the theater burned to the ground. The owners were smarter the second time 'round. The Globe was rebuilt with a tile roof and remained a tremendously popular venue until its demolition during the Civil War (1644).

Unlike the Rose, Shakespeare's Globe is a reconstruction. As such, it does not sit on the identical site of the original Globe Theater, but close enough. The construction is loyal to the times, and every possible detail has been re-created to mirror the building materials, finishes and general ambiance of a Tudor playhouse. In addition to the museum and theater, Shakespeare's Globe features an active actors' training program, special education presentations, a café and a very pleasurable gift shop: perfect for picking up Bardish baubles and books.

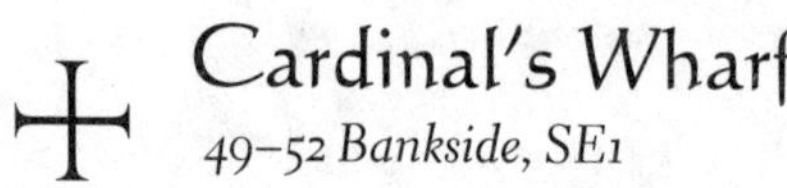

Cardinal's Wharf

49–52 Bankside, SE1

Nearly hidden in the shadows of the defunct Southwark power station is a precious collection of red brick homes, amongst which are some of the oldest residences of the area. The name "Cardinal's Wharf" is believed to be a nod to the former Bishop of Winchester, Cardinal Wolsey . . . as was the brothel (favored by theater types), which stood on this site, known as "The Cardinal's Cap." Local legend tells the tale that in 1501, the teenaged princess Katherine of Aragon made the Cardinal's Cap her temporary London home. One can only imagine the reaction the fanatically straitlaced Katherine must have had to sisters-in-residence!

QUEEN MATILDA (1080—1118)

Wife of Henry I, good Queen Matilda left her majestic imprint all over the City, building public lavatories, founding lazar houses and endowing monasteries. Originally named Edith, she opted later in life for one of the most popular names of her day: Matilda. This would have been perfectly fine, had she not complicated matters by answering to the nickname Maude. The daughter of Scotland's Malcolm II, Matilda *(and all her alter egos)* is buried at Westminster Abbey. We suppose that since she had three names, Londoners found it easier to simply name these stairs the ambiguous "Queen"hithe.

Queenhithe Stairs

West of Southwark Bridge at the Thames, just east of Stew Lane
Bankside, SE1

Note: Although Queenhithe Stairs are located on the opposite side of the river, they are closed to public access. You can, however, view them clearly from this Southwark vantage point.

The moment you've been waiting for! This is the site of London's very first public loo, commissioned by one of the earliest public health officials, Queen Matilda, in 1100. The stairs may have been named for her, or perhaps for Queen Eleanor of Aquitaine, whose commercial shipping fleet was known to dock here. For years, this was London's primary wharf and the stairs provided access for disembarking sailors.

☞ Did you know?

Hold it! The first public loo may have been at Queenhithe, but the "Loo of the Year" award, for several years running, has been bestowed upon the public facilities at the Tower of London. Worth waiting for.

Queen Matilda was not the first person to recognize the need at this very location for public facilities that would accommodate private rituals. The Romans used the site for one of the largest Roman baths in Londinium, allowing bathers to view—and be viewed by—Thames River traffic.

CONTENTS

12

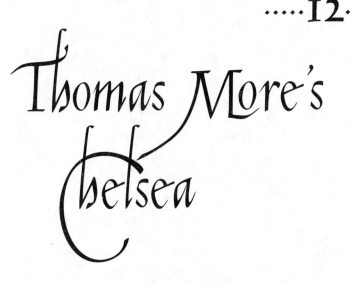

Thomas More's Chelsea

A Taste of Tudor Times

To enjoy a stroll down Cheyne Walk is to experience a slice of Tudor life. More specifically, it is a slice of Thomas More's life. The sites and history of this Chelsea enclave are directly linked to Sir Thomas More, Henry VIII's onetime close friend and ill-fated chancellor.

Cheyne Walk is particularly lovely on a sunny day, with the Thames on one side and the sheltering bows of ancient trees on the other. If you're looking for a retreat from the jostle of in-town London, this tourist-free respite is just the thing. You can easily complete the tour in an hour . . . but we imagine you'll find yourself wanting, as we did, to linger and absorb the serenity. Either way, we think you'll find Chelsea and the tales of those troubled Tudors evocative, indeed!

Cheyne Walk at Chelsea Mews

Chelsea, SW3

Long one of the most-sought-after addresses for London's wealthier artists, musicians and literary types, the history of Chelsea is very much a Tudor history. The homes that line numbers 19–26 Cheyne Walk today sit on the grounds of a large, lovely estate built by Henry VIII in 1536, which stood on the site until 1753. A blue plaque marks the location. In a rare fit of generosity, he gifted the property to his sixth wife, Katherine Parr, in 1543. It was the favorite home of Parr's stepdaughter, Princess Elizabeth, who lived here with her stepmother until 1547. Apparently the property was ripe with sweet-smelling mulberry trees, around which Elizabeth was rumored to be chased by her lecherous stepfather, Thomas Seymour (giving rise, we wonder, to *Round and Round the Mulberry Bush?*). You will still find some of these bountiful trees beneath the archway of home number 24, which sits on the old manor grounds. Careful where you step—mulberry stains are difficult to remove!

Crosby Hall (Crosby Palace)

Cheyne Walk, SW3 (020-7352-9663)

Sloane Square Tube, then bus or taxi to King's Road

OPEN

10:00 a.m.–noon and 2:30–5:00 p.m. Monday–Saturday
2:30–5:00 p.m. Sunday
Often closed for private functions; phone ahead

ADMISSION

Free of charge

By the mid 15th century, the textile trade was one of the most lucrative professions available to the merchant class. Perhaps the best illustration of the wealth that could be gleaned from such enterprises comes to us from the sumptuous mansion Crosby Hall (a.k.a. Crosby Place).

In 1466, Sir John Crosby leased a fine but modest home in Bishopsgate, and promptly set about to enlarge and improve upon it—the better to reflect his well-heeled position as a trader of silk and wool, alderman and sheriff of the City of London. Described by John Stow as "the highest house in London," the mansion passed, upon Crosby's death, to Edward IV and became the favored London residence of the Yorkists. Indeed, this was Richard of Gloucester's preferred address while serving as Protector of the Realm in 1483. The home is referred to three times in Shakespeare's *Richard III*. In an ironic turn of events, Crosby Hall was later owned by Sir Thomas More, whose scathing biography of Richard saddled the "white boar" with much of his dreadful reputation.*

☞ Did you know?

Although Thomas More is most closely associated with the neighborhood of Chelsea, there are several other London locales that played important parts in More's rise to fame. Young Thomas began his education at St. Anthony's school in Threadneedle Street. Upon his graduation from Oxford, he read law at the Inns of Court, first at New Inn and then, in 1496, at Lincoln's, where he maintained his lifelong membership. Although he was England's first lay chancellor, More was a profoundly spiritual person and for a brief time considered an ecclesiastical career. For four years he resided at Charterhouse, studying theology and living a semi-monastic lifestyle with the brothers there. More became a member of Parliament in 1504 and was elected Speaker of the House of Commons in 1523.

In 1907, Crosby Hall was dismantled, each stone and beam numbered, and the entire home transported to Chelsea. It was reassembled in a corner of Thomas More's Chelsea Gardens, where it stands today. In the past century, it has been the home of the East India Company

*Never one to let even a *saint* get off scot-free, Sarah would like to remind you that it was Sir Thomas More whose poison-pen biography of Richard III first burdened the king with the sinister reputation with which he is still yoked. You may argue that he did this just to please the Tudors, but that is highly unlikely. After all, standing up to Henry is what More is known for. No, either More's sense of morals teetered on the maniacal or More was a very amateur historian, indeed!

and a restaurant, before becoming a less-well-known attraction for amateur historians!

As you tour Crosby Hall, note the striking hammerbeam roof, the exquisite carving on the ceilings, the beautiful oriel window and the minstrel's gallery—a merchant he might have been, but Crosby intended to live like royalty! Study, too, the Holbein painting of Thomas More and his family. This is one of three Holbeins commissioned by More, and it is said to give clues as to the fate of the "little prince," Richard, Duke of York.

◇◇

SIR THOMAS MORE (1478–1535)*

If England had its fair share of "king-makers," the kings of England did more than their fair share of "saint-making." Henry II's rash comment "Will no one rid me of this turbulent priest?" led to the foul murder and subsequent canonization of Thomas à Becket. So, too, did Henry VIII have his St. Thomas.

Author of the famed *Utopia* and one of the great humanists of all times, Sir Thomas More was born on Milk Street, in the London neighborhood of Cheapside, the son of a well-regarded barrister. A man of outstanding education, talent and opportunity, he was placed at a relatively young age in the household of the Archbishop of Canterbury, a revealing education for one who would eventually need to navigate the waters between church and state.

Upon Wolsey's fall from favor in 1529, More became the first layperson to hold the powerful job of Chancellor of England. Henry seemed to truly like and admire More, finding himself drawn to Sir Thomas's keen wisdom, refined taste and cultural sophistication. More rapidly became Henry's closest confidant. The honeymoon between monarch and chancellor was, however, doomed to be short-lived. Like Thomas à Becket, Thomas More took great pride in standing on principle . . . at all costs. He first refused to accept the validity of Henry's marriage to Anne Boleyn, ultimately resigning the chancellorship over the conflict. Henry probably would have let this pass, so strong was his regard for his friend. Unfortunately, More sealed his fate when he refused to take the Oath of Supremacy, which would acknowledge Henry as Supreme Head of the Church of England. More was confined to the Bell Tower at the Tower of London in April 1534, tried for high treason at Westminster on July 1, 1535, and subsequently executed on Tower Hill on July 6 of that year. He was canonized St. Thomas More by Pope Pious IX in 1935.

*If you're interested in Sir Thomas More, be sure to rent the classic movies, *A Man for All Seasons* and *Anne of a Thousand Days*.

Two different Chelsea homes are associated with Thomas More. The first, Crosby Place, was the More family home for a brief period of time; oddly, the home was not then located in Chelsea, but rather in Bishopsgate. The lovely Chelsea manor that Thomas More commissioned for his children, 11 grandchildren, a pet monkey and a well-stocked aviary was destroyed many years ago. There is, however, a modern statue of the saint in front of Chelsea Old Church, where he wears the chains of his office not around his neck but across his knees.

Chelsea Old Church

Cheyne Walk, SW3 (020-7352-7978)
Sloane Square Tube, then bus or taxi to King's Road

OPEN

10:00 a.m.–1:00 p.m. and 2:00–5:00 p.m. Monday–Saturday
1:30–5:00 p.m. Sunday
Frequently closed for private functions; phone ahead

WORSHIP

10:00 a.m. and 11:00 a.m. Sunday

Although much of Chelsea Old Church was rebuilt following World War II destruction, the medieval chancel and the glorious collection of Tudor memorials make this a site worth seeing. The private north chapel (c. 1325) was built for the Lord of Chelsea Manor. It was here that Henry VIII and Jane Seymour were secretly wed, prior to their 1536 state wedding at Whitehall. The south chapel was built for Sir Thomas More. On the wall, to the right of the altar, you can spot More's self-scribed epitaph requesting that he be buried with his wife. Despite the plea, Alice Middleton More rests alone in a stark, Gothic tomb; the beautifully carved capitals were a tribute from family friend Hans Holbein. A third Old Church chapel is dedicated to the Elizabethan merchant Thomas Lawrence.

It is commonly believed that Sir Thomas More's remains are buried at the Tower of London, uncomfortably close to Anne Boleyn's (who played no small part in More's losing his head) in the Chapel Royal of St. Peter ad Vincula. However, Old Church parishioners have long favored the story that More's daughter did, in fact, manage to secure her father's head after it was removed from the traitor's spike on London Bridge, and bring it back to Chelsea for burial. This is a mystery that time, perhaps, will tell.

Other Tudor-era luminaries buried in Chelsea Old Church include Lady Jane Guildford, Duchess of Northumberland (d. 1550), Gregory Finnes, Lord Dacre (d. 1594), and Anne Sackville (d. 1595).

While you're in the neighborhood . . .

Visit Roper's Garden. Located just outside the church, it is dedicated to More's daughter, Margaret Roper, and her husband, William, who wrote More's biography.

◊◊

KATHERINE PARR (1512–1548)

Of all of Henry VIII's six wives, Katherine Parr is perhaps the most interesting to modern women and certainly the most intelligent. A brilliant and charming woman, Katherine was a prime example of a Renaissance woman whose court was a hub of intellectual activity for young women.

Her marriage to Henry probably was his most successful. She was about 31 when they were married on July 12, 1543, at Hampton Court and had already been married twice before, so she was better equipped than her predecessor had been to manage a fat, querulous, irritable old man with an ulcerated leg that leaked and sometimes stank. In addition, Katherine was lively and personable with a keen mind. She was very well educated and inclined toward the intellectual. She managed Henry with grace and charm, careful always to stroke his ego and give him no chance at doubting her virtue. She was popular with the people and instrumental in reconciling Henry with his estranged daughters, Mary and Elizabeth. Katherine also kept Henry entertained and engaged by matching wits with him on the subject of religion.

Historians suspect that Katherine had long harbored secret leanings toward Protestantism. She greatly encouraged Henry in his reform of the Church of England and supported his views by writing and publishing two well-received theological books of her own. This was the first time in English history that a queen had made public her own personal views about an issue of state policy.

In fact, Katherine's strong religious viewpoints almost brought about her downfall. Henry—never one to be satisfied with a wife for too long—soon became irritated by his queen's forthright expression of her religious views. The Catholics in his retinue fed the flames of Henry's unstable temper by pouring tales into his ears of Katherine's complicity with Protestants. Henry went so far as to sign a warrant for Katherine's arrest on charges of heresy, but Katherine quickly learned of his action and was able to assuage his anger through flattery, and by adopting the role of the meek and dutiful wife. Henry was appeased and the royal couple continued to live together congenially until Henry's death on January 28, 1547.

Soon after Henry's death, Katherine moved her household to the Old Manor at Chelsea. Almost immediately Thomas Seymour, a former romantic interest, re-entered the picture as a fervent suitor of the Dowager Queen, now 35 years old, as attractive as ever and rich to boot. It didn't take long for Katherine to succumb to the wiles of the very handsome, charming, and unscrupulous Seymour. The two were secretly married, probably at the house in Chelsea, some time before the end of April 1547.

Katherine, who for the first time was married by choice to someone she loved, was very happy and content in her new life. In March 1548, she discovered that after 20 years of marriage with four different husbands she was pregnant for the first time. It didn't take long for scandal to disturb the domestic peace of the Chelsea household.

Early in 1548, the 14-year-old Princess Elizabeth joined the Dowager Queen's household. Katherine had remained on good terms with all of Henry's children and she warmly welcomed Elizabeth to her home. Unfortunately, so did her husband. Not to reiterate all the intimate details of this scandalous affair (which you probably know very well), we'll summarize by saying that Elizabeth and Seymour engaged in a shocking dalliance; Katherine caught them in each other's arms in April 1548 at the Chelsea manor; Elizabeth was banished from the household, and the affair ended. The house at Chelsea now held too many unhappy memories, so Katherine and Seymour retired to Sudeley Manor in Gloucestershire in June to await the birth of their child.

Katherine gave birth to a daughter on September 7 and then developed puerperal (childbed) fever. She died on September 7. She was buried under a magnificent tomb in the chapel at Sudeley Castle. Lady Jane Grey, a ward of Seymour and a member of Katherine's household, was the chief mourner at the funeral.

◊◊

CONTENTS

13

Medieval & Tudor London on Display

Musings on Museums

To overlook the museums of London would be to overlook some of the city's richest cultural resources. London has more than its fair share of extraordinary fine art and artifact collections, and to send you off in search of *only* medieval and Tudor treasures hardly does the London museums justice. But focus your attention we must!

We have tried our best to give you a taste of what each museum offers from our favorite period of history. However, collections travel, rotate and expand. You may discover that something wonderful has been added since our last visit—just as likely, you may bemoan the fact that a particular item is out "on loan." In any event, we are certain that you will enjoy the light that these museums shed on London's ancient history.

Tip!

Do not try to tour too many museums in one day—it's simply too much to take in. We favor the idea of seeing ancient *sites* for half the day and taking in a museum for the other half day. This type of variety, we feel, makes so much medieval and Tudor history easier to assimilate.

Also, due to increased security, most museums will require you to check bulky items (shopping bags, backpacks, umbrellas) in the cloakroom. We have found it is best to carry as little as possible on your museum tours, or risk leaving something important behind—like this book!

The Museum of London

150 London Wall, EC2 (0171-600-3699)
Barbican, St. Paul's or Moorgate Tube

OPEN

10:00 a.m.–5:30 p.m. Tuesday–Saturday and bank holidays
Noon–5:30 p.m. Sunday

ADMISSION

£4.00 Adults and children
£9.50 Family ticket
£2.00 Concessions
Free after 4:30 p.m.

CONVENIENCES

Gift shop with a particularly well stocked section on medieval and Tudor London; restaurant; audio guides; guided tours; lectures; workshops. It is worth thumbing through *Time-Out Magazine* or stopping by the information desk to see if there are any special events taking place of interest to amateur historians—there often are!

The first thing that will thrill you *(at least it thrilled us!)* about this gem of a museum is that the ultra-modern building straddles the site of the old Roman fort. Guides are on hand to accompany you into the fort's excavation site, where you will be briefed on the fort's importance in the layout of London. You'll also be able to view a diorama depicting ancient Londinium.

Unlike the British Museum and the Victoria & Albert, both of which also display treasures from this era, the items on display at the Museum of London are—by and large—directly linked to London per se. Once inside, you'll have a difficult time limiting yourself to the two rooms devoted to artifacts of the medieval and Tudor periods. For instance, the display of Roman wall paintings is beautiful to behold, and the entire museum is a delight for history buffs, Anglophiles, or those simply addicted to London.

If time limits you to our specific quest, here's a sample of what you can expect to find.

MEDIEVAL LONDON, 410–1484

This gallery contains a 6th-century Saxon brooch; 11th-century Norman battle-axes; a model of William the Conqueror's White Tower; a chain-mail hauberk; a carved elm panel depicting scenes from *The Canterbury Tales* (c. 1400); fragments of the original Eleanor Cross; the earliest version of a swinging cradle; household and commercial artifacts from the 13th through 15th centuries; a carved door from St. Ethelburga-within-Bishopsgate and medieval carvings from the Guildhall.

TUDOR LONDON, 1485–1602

Nearly twice as large as the Medieval Room, the Tudor gallery focuses on daily life in London in the late 15th and early 16th centuries. The costumes are incredible!

✝ The Victoria & Albert Museum

Cromwell Road, SW7 (020-7938-8500)
South Kensington Tube

>>

OPEN

10:00 a.m.–5:50 p.m. Tuesday–Sunday
Noon–5:50 p.m. Monday
6:30–9:30 p.m. Wednesday evening

ADMISSION

£6.00 Adults
£3.00 Concessions
Students, free of charge

CONVENIENCES

Restaurant/cafeteria with a very popular Sunday jazz brunch; elaborate gift shop with replicas of jewelry and decorative items from our favorite era; audio guides; guided tours; lectures and special children's programs.

>>

One of the world's largest and most impressive museums dedicated to the decorative arts, the Victoria & Albert (a.k.a. "the V&A") houses a wealth of items from the medieval period and a smaller, though impressive, trove from the Tudor era. Unfortunately, there is no handy way to pre-distinguish those artifacts specific to London—or Britain, for that matter.

The V&A is a beautiful, serene museum with items displayed in a thoughtful, evocative manner. You can immerse yourself in medieval decorative arts (albeit many from Italy, Germany and other European nations) in just under two hours if you limit yourself to Galleries 23, 24 and 43. Vestiges of later eras—post-1500—can be seen in the European collections on Level A, and in the Britain Galleries 52–58 on Level B.

If you are traveling with children, one of the most clever introductions we've seen to our period of history is the V&A's "Gothic Gallery Trail." Set up in treasure-hunt style, the Gothic Trail focuses on Gallery 23's collection, which dates from 1200 to 1450. A well-designed "trail map," available from the front information desk, leads your child from treasure to treasure, offering imaginative insights that even grown-ups will find charming. Among the Gothic Trail's highlights are the effigy of a knight from the de Lucy family, a wooden chest carved with a jousting scene, an elaborate "wild man" tapestry, and familiar household and religious items.

Another V&A highlight you'll want to scout down is the Great Bed of Ware (c. 1590). The nine-foot-high bed, with its elaborate carvings and inlays, was mentioned by Shakespeare in *Twelfth Night.* There are several early Tudor costumes on display in the Costume Court, and the famous Hardwick Hunting Tapestries can be admired in the Medieval Tapestry Court.

The National Portrait Gallery

2 St. Martin's Place, WC2 (020-7306-0055)
Leicester Square or Charing Cross Tube

OPEN
10:00 a.m.–6:00 p.m. Monday–Saturday
Noon–6:00 p.m. Sunday

ADMISSION
Free of charge

If it's the medieval monarchs that *really* excite you, the National Portrait Gallery is certain to be a favorite stop of yours. An entire gallery is dedicated to portraits of the queens and kings of England, their consorts, their offspring and their famous courtiers. While not *every* monarch from 1066 to 1600 is portrayed in the collection, some are featured multiple times—Henry VIII and Elizabeth I, in particular—which *almost* makes up for the incomplete showing. Those not fortunate enough to be royal are at least regally displayed . . . musicians, clergy, philosophers and writers (including what is believed to be the only "from-life" portrait of William Shakespeare) are well represented in this post-14th-century collection.

Once you've seen them all *(and then seen them all again!)*, venture into the NPG's lovely bookshop—you can sate your appetite with postcard reproductions of nearly every portrait in the museum.

The National Portrait Gallery bookshop also is one of the very best sources for books on medieval and Tudor history. We have been able to track down many hard-to-find biographies to enhance our collection . . . one can never have too many "*Lives of* . . ." on a bookshelf!

While you're in the neighborhood . . .

Be certain to allow some time for a visit to the inspiring church St. Martin-in-the-Fields, directly across from the National Portrait Gallery. Although this is not a medieval church, it has a very special medieval brass-rubbing gallery, where you and your children can while away the hours making your very own handmade souvenir. The café is far better than average—a reasonably priced option for a midday meal—and there are frequent lunchtime concerts held at the church, free of charge. All in all, a highly recommended respite!

The National Gallery

Trafalgar Square, WC2 (020-7747-2885)
Charing Cross, Leicester Square or Picadilly Tube

OPEN

10:00 a.m.–6:00 p.m. daily
Open until 8:00 p.m. Wednesday

ADMISSION

Free of charge

CONVENIENCES

Lectures, tours, special events, videos and a gallery-guide CD-ROM

There is very little in the National Gallery that has to do with historical events of the medieval and Tudor eras. However, there are many, many paintings from this period, and we particularly like the fact that they are hung chronologically. Select paintings from 1260–1510 or 1510–1600; the majority are religious in nature (the Church being the primary patron of fine art at the time), but there are the occasional windows on everyday medieval and Renaissance life, which are inspiring.

The British Museum

Great Russell Street, WC1 (020–7636–1555)
Tottenham Court Road, Holborn or Russell Square Tube

OPEN
10:00 a.m.–5:00 p.m. Monday–Saturday
Noon–6:00 p.m. Sunday

ADMISSION
Free of charge; donations welcome

CONVENIENCES
Gift shop, lectures, film presentations, special events

Because this museum can be overwhelming in its wealth of treasures, we are delighted, from a convenience standpoint, to limit ourselves to a small portion of the myriad offerings. Oddly grouped *(in our opinion)*, the Medieval, Renaissance and Modern Objects rooms are located in the far east, or extreme right-hand, wing of the museum. Begin in room 41, where you'll find the amazing Sutton Hoo treasure of elaborate burial jewelry and plate from a 7th-century Saxon king. As you wend your way through the 40s rooms, you'll see intricately carved medieval chessmen, watches, household artifacts and decorative items, many—although not all—of British origin.

The British Library

96 Euston Road, WC1 (020-7412-7332)
St. Pancras or Kings Cross Tube

OPEN

9:30 a.m.–6:00 p.m. Monday–Friday
Open until 8:00 p.m. Tuesday
9:30 a.m.–5:00 p.m. Saturday
11:00 a.m.–5:00 p.m. Sunday

ADMISSION

Free of charge

Depending upon your interest, there are two ways to enjoy the British Library. If you are research bent, apply in advance for a reader's ticket, and immerse yourself in the library's 15 million volumes—virtually every book printed in the English language can be found in this mammoth collection.

Alternatively, there are three exhibition galleries open to the general public. Among the many wonderful items on display are an original draft of Magna Carta, the Lindisfarne Gospels, a Gutenberg Bible and Shakespeare's First Folio of plays. There is a touching array of personal correspondence from the medieval and Tudor eras, including portions of letters personally penned by Elizabeth I.

Note: The British Library bookshop isn't as vast as the library itself—it only feels that way. Believe us when we tell you we spent more time perusing the shelves of this wonderful store than we did in the exhibition galleries! There is a wealth of literature pertaining to the medieval and Tudor periods, some considerably more erudite than we cared to embrace. Still, we managed to fill the entire checkout counter with our purchases, and were delighted to find that the library willingly ships parcels.

The Public Record Office

Ruskin Avenue, Kew
Richmond, Surrey (020-8876-3444)

OPEN

9:00 a.m.–5:00 p.m. Monday, Wednesday, Friday and Saturday
10:00 a.m.–7:00 p.m. Tuesday and Thursday
Closed Sunday

ADMISSION

Free of charge

With over 84 miles of archival records on hand, a wealth of surviving medieval and Tudor documents is housed at the PRO. This includes two original copies of the *Domesday Book* (1086); *The Pipe Roll* (1129); *Magna Carta* (1215); Sir Francis Drake's report on the defeat of the Spanish Armada (1588); a letter from a repentant Cardinal Wolsey begging forgiveness from Henry VIII; the indictment of Sir Thomas More; and Will's will (Shakespeare, that is!). The changing display does an excellent job of highlighting documents that track a millennium of English history . . . fascinating for any amateur historian who delights in the paper trail.

Madame Tussaud's

Marylebone Road, NW1 (020-7935-6861)
Baker Street Tube

OPEN

9:30 a.m.–5:30 p.m. daily, May–October
10:00 a.m.–5:30 p.m. Monday–Friday, October–May
9:30 a.m.–5:30 p.m. Saturday and Sunday, October–May

ADMISSION

£9.00 Adults and children
£6.00–£7.00 Concessions
Combination ticket available for Planetarium admission

CONVENIENCES

Restaurant, gift shop

Just so you can't say we didn't warn you: Madame Tussaud's is absolutely one of the most insanely busy tourist attractions you'll ever visit. No matter what time of day, no matter what time of year, no matter what the weather holds in store, you can be certain that the lines outside the world-famous wax works will be long and that the crowds inside the museum will be dense. You may be able to shorten your wait outside by purchasing a combination ticket to visit the Planetarium, seeing the Planetarium first, and then entering the wax works through the specially designated entrance. Other line-clipping tactics include buying a ticket in advance at the British Travel Authority, the London Transport Office, with your Original London Bus Tour, or by calling ahead and booking a reservation with your credit card. None of these options guarantees that you'll avoid lines altogether, but your wait will certainly be within reason.

Is all the planning, waiting and jostling worth an amateur historian's time and trouble? We definitely think so! After so many Norman crypts and Gothic arches, we're usually ready for something lighthearted, and Madame Tussaud's fits the bill: Plantagenet kings and Tudor queens in a venue no one can take *too* seriously!

Needless to say, our favorite wax works in the museum are of the monarchs and consorts from ages past. We blush to tell you how many snapshots we have of ourselves posed with a very life-like *(well, we assume!)* Richard III. We never tire of trying to "guess" which of the six wives of Henry VIII is Catherine Howard and which is Jane Seymour (no fair peeking at the key), and it's always a pleasure to drop a curtsey before Gloriana herself! If you're in the mood to really challenge your skill at "who's who," take a look at the collection of heads that line the upper reaches of Madame Tussaud's replicated workshop—we have found several Henrys and Edwards; can you?

The museum's Chamber of Horrors is gratuitously gory, and overlooks our period of history entirely. In our opinion, you can skip this treat. However, the Time Taxi takes you on a merry tour of London's history, and is a welcome break after being on your feet for so long. Enjoy!

CONCLUSION

Over the course of writing this book, we traveled in the "*Amateur Historian's*" footsteps through medieval and Tudor London six separate times. Believe us, that is a *lot* of visits to the Tower of London and many miles of "walking the wall." But no matter how many times we've poked into the nooks and crannies of these ancient treasures, we've never failed to find the vestiges of medieval and Tudor London fascinating, entertaining and engaging. We hope that we have helped you to feel the same.

It was on our last visit to the Tower of London that we turned to one another and said, "That's it! We've now *done* London!" And although we will certainly plan to return on numerous occasions for our own edification (and to update this book for you), we are now ready to turn our attention to those tantalizing castles, abbeys, churches and manor homes that lie just outside the City. We are already investigating the medieval and Tudor day trips that can be made within an easy drive of London—leave the capital in the morning, take in a castle or two and be back in time for Shakespeare in the City.

Now that's our idea of heaven! We can't wait to share what we find with you!

GLOSSARY

Avid consumers of medieval and Tudor literature and lore, we have become well acquainted over the years with the "lingo" of those eras and have sprinkled our text with terms that may, or may not, be familiar to other amateur historians. Here are a few of the terms you will run across that may warrant further explanation.

Attainder: An Act of Parliament that sanctioned execution of a noble without trial. The heirs of an attainted noble lost the right to inherit that person's lands or titles.

Bailey: The courtyard of a castle, also known as the *ward.*

Baron: A tenant-in-chief of the monarchy who held land and titles specifically granted by the king or queen.

Bastion: A flanking tower used exclusively for defensive purposes.

Canon: Non-monastic member of the cathedral chapter whose primary responsibility was conducting religious services.

Canon Law: The law of the church.

Castellan: The official in charge of a castle while the owner was away. Also known as a *constable.*

Chamber: Typically, the bedroom. Often also used for the storage of household treasures.

Chancellor: The royal minister whose primary responsibility was as keeper of the monarch's great seal and chancery. Bishops and major nobility also frequently had chancellors.

Chancery: The monarch's writing room, overseen by the chancellor.

Chantry: One or more priests financially endowed to offer Holy Communion on a daily basis for the benefit of a specific soul, as designated by the endower.

Chapter: The governing body of a cathedral. If the cathedral was monastic (run by monks), the chapter consisted of a prior and priory monks. If the cathedral was run by non-monastic clerics, the chapter consisted of a dean and canons. The term evolved from the fact that "chapter meetings" were traditionally "called to order" with the reading of chapters from the Bible.

Charter: The formal written record of a transfer of rights or property.

Crenelation: Parapets of a castle that are divided into distinctive solid chunks of wall (used as shields), interspersed with gaps ("crenels") used for aiming weapons at one's enemy. Also known as *battlements.*

Crypt: See *undercroft.* These are Carole's absolute favorite part of any medieval structure *(ha!).*

Curtain Wall: The wall that surrounded the bailey, distinguished by the crenelated battlement on top.

Danegeld: A land tax used as leverage to "buy off" Danish invaders.

Diocese: A religious territory, also known as a *bisphoric* or *see.*

Exchequer: A royal minister from the palace at Westminster responsible for the Crown's finances. The Exchequer answered to the Lord Treasurer and was, therefore, a second-tier official.

Excommunication: Punishment levied by the pope, which denied the offending party the right to receive Holy Communion, thereby putting the individual's soul in jeopardy of eternal damnation, unless papal absolution (pardon) was received.

Fealty: An oath of fidelity sworn to a lord. Fealty did not necessarily involve reciprocal gifts (as did *homage*). Fealty to the monarch took precedent over all other oaths of fidelity, including homage to a lesser mortal.

Friars: Religious orders committed to poverty and missionary work. The five principal orders of friars were the Augustinians (Austins), Benedictines, Carmelites, Dominicans and Franciscans. Also known as *mendicants.* The orders also were distinguished by the color of the robes they wore; hence the Carmelites were the *Whitefriars,* the Dominicans were the *Blackfriars* and the Franciscans were the *Greyfriars.*

Guild: Also, *gild.* Organizations that oversaw the regulation of trade in a particular town. Many also had religious functions as well. In London, certain guilds were alternatively known as *livery companies* or *liveries.*

Hundred: A subdivision of a shire that would include its own court.

Keep: The primary tower of a castle, also known as a *donjon* or *great tower.* For instance, the White Tower is the "keep" of the Tower of London.

Magnates: "The swells." These were the important members of the nobility with a hefty amount of sway in the politics of the time.

Minster: A large church served by a clerical community, not necessarily monastic.

Parapet: The defensive structure atop a castle wall.

Perpendicular: The swan song of Gothic architecture, this uniquely English style of design is characterized by uniform, parallel lines, as opposed to the flowing tracery of early Gothic work. The Perpendicular style was popular in London from the mid 1300s until the reign of Elizabeth I.

Portcullis: A suspended, spiked grill that could be lowered to block entrance to the inner wards of a castle.

Puritans: Broadly used to include Protestant reformers who sought to "purify" the church.

Ramparts: A castle wall with a walkway on top.

Serf: A legally "unfree" peasant bound to servitude.

Sheriff: From the Anglo-Saxon *shire-reeve.* After 1066, the sheriff was appointed by the monarch to officially administer the Crown's lands and justice in a shire. The sheriff acted as the Crown's primary financial and judicial representative until the 12th century, when the role was surpassed by the *justiciar* (or *justices-in-eyre*). By the end of the 13th century, the Exchequer maintained a hands-on control of royal revenues throughout the land and the role of the sheriff was reduced to the maintenance of law and order.

Shire: The main territorial subdivision of England. Derived from the Anglo-Saxon *scir,* meaning "bit" or "part."

Tiltyard: A field designed specifically to host the "sport" of *jousting,* in which a pair of knights in chain mail and/or armor would start at opposite ends of the field and charge their horses, aiming long wooden poles known as *lances* at each other. The object of the sport was to hit your opponent with the lance with enough force to unseat him from his horse. In reality, jousting was a means of practicing for military campaigns.

Translation: A solemn religious ceremony in which the remains of a dead person are moved from one burial site to another.

Undercroft: The lower level of a medieval structure, typically used for storage. Because many undercrofts were above ground level, they were not necessarily cellars. In religious structures, the undercroft also was known as the *crypt.* These usually have vaulted ceilings.

Usury: The charging of interest on loaned money. Christians were forbidden to charge interest under Canon Law until the late Middle Ages.

Vassal: A person who owed *fealty* to another, higher-ranking individual and had sworn *homage* to that person. For example, all barons were vassals of the king or queen.

Vault: An arched stone roof.

Writ: The written command of the Crown, signed and sealed by the monarch. By the 12th century, these official documents were required in order to initiate any proceedings in the royal courts of justice.

INDEX

Bold type indicates places or touring information. (It does *not* mean that a place is in London or that it still exists.) *Italics* indicate streets or location information. Standard type indicates historical events or people.